国家教育部新世纪网络课程建设工程项目
商务英语系列课程教材

国际市场营销

International Marketing

（修订本）

总主编　肖云南

主　编　胡　凌　胡志雯

清 华 大 学 出 版 社
北京交通大学出版社
·北京·

内 容 简 介

　　本书是《商务英语系列课程教材》之一。本书不仅讲述了国际市场营销的基本知识和操作原理，还通过案例分析加深对所学知识的理解，从而使学生对国际市场营销的过程和基本实践有一个全面的了解，有利于培养既有良好的英语基础又具备专业知识的复合型人才。本书分 6 个部分，共 18 章，按照国际市场营销的基本步骤进行讲述。每章开始都有学习目标，方便学生掌握本章重点；结尾附有本章关键术语和练习，便于学生进一步学习新知识和巩固所学知识。

　　本书以英语介绍专业知识，相对原版教材而言，语言简练，通俗易懂。本书可供国际贸易、经济管理、国际商务、英语等专业三年级以上本科生作为复合型专业英语教材使用，同时也可供具有一定英语和商务知识基础的自学者学习参考。

图书在版编目（CIP）数据

国际市场营销/胡凌，胡志雯主编. —修订本 .—北京：清华大学出版社；北京交通大学出版社，2004. 5（2019. 3 修订）

（商务英语系列课程教材/肖云南总主编）

国家教育部新世纪网络课程建设工程项目

ISBN 978-7-81082-286-2

Ⅰ. 国…　Ⅱ. ① 胡…　② 胡…　Ⅲ. 国际市场-市场营销学-教材-英、汉

Ⅳ. F740. 2

中国版本图书馆 CIP 数据核字（2004）第 017559 号

国际市场营销

GUOJI SHICHANG YINGXIAO

责任编辑：张利军　　特邀编辑：伍　伟

出版发行：清 华 大 学 出 版 社　　邮编：100084　　电话：010-62776969　　http://www.tup.com.cn
　　　　　北京交通大学出版社　　邮编：100044　　电话：010-51686414　　http://www.bjtup.com.cn

印 刷 者：北京鑫海金澳胶印有限公司

经　　销：全国新华书店

开　　本：185 mm×230 mm　　印张：21.75　　字数：488 千字

版　　次：2004 年 5 月第 1 版　　2019 年 3 月第 1 次修订　　2019 年 3 月第 17 次印刷

书　　号：ISBN 978-7-81082-286-2/F·43

印　　数：41 001～43 000 册　　定价：42.00 元

本书如有质量问题，请向北京交通大学出版社质监组反映。对您的意见和批评，我们表示欢迎和感谢。

投诉电话：010-51686043，51686008；传真：010-62225406；E-mail：press@bjtu.edu.cn。

前　言

迈入新世纪和加入 WTO，我国正逐步地参与国际竞争，同世界接轨。随着全球经济的发展和市场化的运作，英语作为国际贸易用语变得越来越重要，社会上也越来越迫切地需要既有专业知识又能熟练运用英语的人才。怎样才能有效地提高学生的实际语言运用能力，培养既有专业知识又能熟练运用英语的人才，使学生所学的知识跟上时代的节奏，符合社会经济生活的实际需求，已成为英语教育工作者的历史责任，也是日益发达的经济和社会发展的需要。

为此，我们根据高等院校经贸专业英语的课程设置，以国际贸易的知识体系为背景，编写了这套《商务英语系列课程教材》。本系列课程教材不仅注重英语听、说、读、写、译等基本技能的训练，而且注重经贸专业知识的培养。本系列课程教材可供国际贸易、经济管理、国际金融、法律、英语专业商务英语方向的学生作为双语教材使用，亦可供具有一定英语基础的其他专业人员培训英语和国际贸易专业知识使用。

《商务英语系列课程教材》是国家教育部新世纪网络课程建设工程项目成果之一，本系列教材包括《商务英语听说》、《商务英语阅读（精读本）》、《商务英语选读（泛读本）》、《商务英语写作》、《国际商务谈判》、《国际贸易实务》、《国际市场营销》、《国际支付与结算》、《国际商法》等九本。随着国际商务的发展和读者的需要，我们还将不断对这一系列教材进行补充和修改，以期形成读者欢迎的动态系列教材。本系列教材具有以下特色。

1. 内容新，专业性、可操作性强。

2. 强调专业基础，重视语言运用，各书均配有大量练习，注重全面提高学生运用商务知识和英语听、说、读、写、译的能力。

3. 设计有配套的课程软件，便于学生自主学习。操作上可灵活掌握，不仅可供在校生课堂学习，还可以面向全国网络课程的学生和在职人员自学，覆盖面广。

4. 编写者都是从事商务英语教学的一线教师，具有多年丰富的教学经验和极强的事业心和敬业精神。在系列教材的基础上，作者根据自身教学经验编写了配套的教师指导书和参考答案，可与同行交流，便于教师授课和辅导学生进行课后实践。如有需要者请与湖南大学商务英语系联系。电子邮件地址：business@ lingchina. org。

《国际市场营销》是《商务英语系列课程教材》之一。全书分 6 个部分，共 18 章，按照国际市场营销的基本步骤进行讲述。本书以英语介绍专业知识，相对原版教材而言，语言简练，通俗易懂。本书不仅讲述了国际市场营销的基本知识和操作原理，还通过案例分析加深对所学知识的理解，从而使学生对国际市场营销的过程和基本实践有一个全面的了解，有利于培养既有良好的英语基础又具备专业知识的复合型人才。本书每章开始设有学习目标，方便学生掌握本章重点；结尾附有本章关键术语和练习，便于学生进一步学习新知识和巩固所学知识。

　　本书作者胡凌负责第 1、4、5、6 部分的编写工作，胡志雯负责第 2、3 部分的编写工作。全书经肖云南教授和 Ian Winchester 博士审稿。由于编著者水平有限，书中不妥之处在所难免，敬请广大读者批评指正。

编　者

于长沙市岳麓山

2008 年 1 月

注：本书课后练习答案可到网站 http：//press. bjtu. edu. cn 下载或发邮件到 cbszlj@ jg. bjtu. edu. cn 索取。

学 习 指 导

　　《国际市场营销》是《商务英语系列课程》之一。本书分为 6 个部分，共 18 章，内容涉及国际市场营销的基本知识和操作原理。本书通过案例加深学生对所学知识的印象，并在增加学生的商务知识的同时扩大其专业英语词汇量与知识面，从而使其对国际市场营销过程和基本实践有一个全面的了解。本书每章的课后附有相关的练习，可供读者进一步学习使用。此外，由于受课程时间的限制，某些内容无法全盘讲解，所以本书最后还附有针对各个章节中出现的不同知识相应的网络站点（web links），可以使学生有机会更多地接触自己感兴趣的内容，激励学生自主学习。本书可供英语、国际商务和经贸等相关专业三年级以上本科生作为复合型专业英语教材使用，亦可供具有一定英语基础和商务基础知识的自学者自学使用。本教材课时可安排为 54 学时。

　　本书各章的基本组成如下。

1. 教材主体

　　每章开始为学习目标（objectives），即本章主要的知识点。学习目标简明扼要，使学生对要学习的新知识一目了然，同时也方便学生掌握本章的重点知识。各章节的具体内容都分别依照营销知识的要点进行讲述。

2. 案例学习

　　结合各章要点，用实际案例（cases）对知识点进行说明。各个章节案例都是世界营销领域的实际事例，从而可以使学生将所学知识和社会实际联系起来，更理性地看待营销中的各种问题。

3. 专业术语

　　对各章相关的关键术语（key terms）进行总结和整理，帮助学生快速回顾知识要点，同时也可以为复习提供帮助，增加专业知识。

4. 难点注释

　　对各章中出现的语言和知识难点在注释部分（notes）进行解释，并对各章的一些难句进行翻译，以降低学习难度，帮助学生更好地理解和掌握专业知识。

5. 练习

练习（exercises）素材广泛，形式活跃，主要包括 3 种题型：多项选择、判断正误和讨论。本部分主要帮助学生复习本章重点内容，巩固已学的知识。

在学习本教材时，建议先掌握每章的要点，然后熟悉关键术语并浏览难点注释，再通读每章主体，最后在理解的基础上仔细阅读并思考各章案例所体现的知识要点和与之相关的社会实践。每章课后所附的练习主要供复习使用，因此最好在掌握每章的知识要点后再做。有兴趣的读者还可以登陆相关的网站更详细地了解相关知识。

编　者
2008 年 1 月

Contents

V

Part I

国际市场营销基础

International Marketing Basics

Chapter One

International Marketing Briefing

国际市场营销简介

📣 Objectives 学习目标

When students finish this chapter, they should be able to accomplish the following:

☑ Definition of marketing

☑ Marketing concepts and functions of marketing

☑ Definition of international marketing

☑ Reasons to do business in international markets

☑ International marketing practice of Chinese companies

1.1 What Is Marketing? 什么是市场营销?

1.1.1 Definition 定义

"Market" is derived from the Latin "mercari" which means "to buy or trade". But marketing is more than just buying and trading.

S. Carter defines marketing as: "The process of building lasting relationships through planning, executing and controlling the conception, pricing, promotion and distribution of ideas, goods and services to create mutual exchange that satisfy individual and organizational needs and objectives".

1.1.2 Marketing and sales 市场营销与销售

Many people think that marketing means the activity of persuading potential customers to buy a particular product or service in preference to any other similar ones. That is to say, marketing is selling and advertising. These two are very important, but they are only the tip of the marketing iceberg. There are many more functions of marketing. Marketing is the process of seeking to uncover consumers' requirements and adopting the information to products' distribution[1] and promotion.

The marketing process can be shown as Figure 1-1.

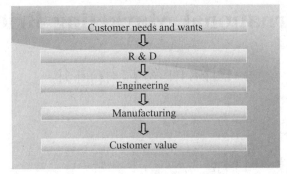

Figure 1-1　Process of Marketing

1.1.3　Basic elements of the marketing concept　市场营销概念的基本点

Today, marketing must be understood not in the old sense of making a sale, but in a new sense of satisfying customer needs. If a marketer does well in understanding consumer needs, develops products that provide superior value, and prices, distributes and promotes them properly, the products will be best sellers.

1. Needs, wants and demands

Needs is a state of deprivation of some basic satisfaction, e. g. the need for food, shelter, clothing and belonging. Wants are devices for specific items that can satisfy those needs, so that an individual may need to eat, but wants to consume a particular brand of food. Needs are a basic feature of all human society, but wants are different as the social forces and the influences are different.

Demands are human wants backed by buying power. It is the ability and willingness to buy a particular product that is backed up by purchasing power either immediately via a one-off payment[2] or over time by phased payments[3].

For a marketer, it is very important to satisfy the wants and needs of a consumer.

Products are anything that can be offered to an individual to satisfy a need or want. This definition implies that products cover both intangible and tangible products. The importance of physical products lies in their use to satisfy a want, so a TV set is an item that convert information and offer entertainment.

2. Consumer value and consumer satisfaction

Why does a consumer prefer one product to another? This issue is a very important part which guarantees the success of any marketer. Generally speaking, consumers make buying decisions based on their perceptions of the value that various products and services deliver. [4]

Consumer value is the difference between the values the consumer gains from owning and using a product and the costs of obtaining the product.

Consumers often do not judge product values and costs accurately or objectively. They act on perceived value. [5]

Consumer satisfaction is the extent to which a product's perceived performance matches a buyer's expectations. If performance matches or exceeds expectations, the buyer is satisfied or delighted. However, the consumer is dissatisfied if the product fails to meet the expectations. Consumer satisfaction is closely linked to quality. Quality has a direct impact on product performance, and hence on customer satisfaction.

3. Markets

The concept of exchange leads to the concept of a market (see figure 1-2). Originally the term of market is the place where buyers and sellers gathered to exchange their goods. Economists refer to a market as a collection of buyers and sellers who transact in a particular product class. As for marketers, a market is the set of all actual and potential buyers of a product or service.

To maintain the market operation efficiency, four flows should be ensured:

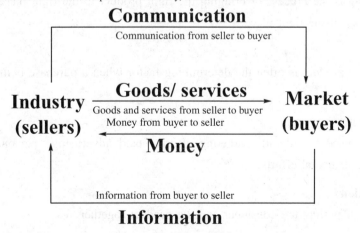

Figure 1-2   A Simple Marketing System

Marketing management is the process of planning and executing the concept, pricing, promotion and distribution of ideas, goods, and services to create exchanges that satisfy individual and organizational goals. Actors and forces in a modern marketing system are shown in Figure 1-3.

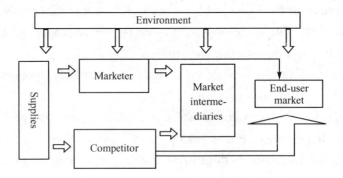

Figure 1-3　Actors and Forces in a Modern Marketing System

1.1.4　Marketing functions　市场营销功能

1. Contact

The seeking out of prospective consumers and it may be based on a variety of determinants. Improper handling of the initial contact can keep a company out of the marketplace indefinitely.

2. Merchandising

Merchandising is the process of bringing the right product to the right place at the right time in the right quantity at the right place.

3. Pricing

The price of a product is often the determining factor when a purchase is made and is always a key to profit.

4. Promotion

Promotion is used to support marketing efforts: paid advertising, personal selling, public relations, and supplemental efforts.

5. Distribution

The process of putting the consumer and the product together.

6. Human resources

Internal marketing that occurs within a company between employers and employees is a reflection in the ability to market externally to the public. It's essential that sellers understand, communicate with, and value buyers.

1.2   What Is International Marketing? 什么是国际市场营销?

1.2.1   Definition 定义

At its simplest level, international marketing involves the firm in making one or more marketing mix decisions across national boundaries. At its most complex, it involves the firm in establishing manufacturing facilities overseas and coordinating marketing strategies across markets. A company may simply sign an agreement with a foreign agent. The agent then takes the responsibility for pricing, qromotion, distribution and market development.

1.2.2   Different levels of international marketing 不同层次的国际市场营销

The different levels of international marketing can be expressed as follows: domestic marketing, the export marketing and international marketing.

Domestic marketing is targeted exclusively on the home country market. A company in domestic marketing may be doing this consciously as a strategic or unconsciously in order to avoid the challenge of managing how to market outside the home country. Fewer and fewer companies practice domestic marketing.

Export marketing is the first stage of addressing market opportunities outside the home country. The export marketer targets markets outside the home country and depends on home country production to supply the product for these markets. In China, the fireworks export, the silk industry and the fishing industry are good examples. In this stage, a sophisticated export marketer will study target markets[6] and adapt products to meet the specific needs of customers in each country.

International marketing (global marketing) refers to the stage when a marketer becomes more involved in the marketing environment in the countries where he is doing marketing. International marketing doesn't mean entering every country in the world, but entering certain countries according to a company's resources and the nature of opportunities and threat.

1.2.3   Differences between domestic marketing and international marketing 国内市场营销与国际市场营销的区别

The principles and process of marketing are universal and can apply for international marketing. However, international marketing is more complex than domestic marketing in a number of ways.

The uniqueness of foreign marketing comes from the range of unfamiliar problems and the variety of strategies necessary to cope with different levels of uncertainty encountered in foreign markets. Competition, legal restraints, government controls, weather, fickle consumers, and any number of other uncontrollable elements can, and frequently do, affect the profitable outcome of good, sound marketing plans. Generally speaking, the marketer cannot control or influence these uncontrollable elements, but instead must adjust or adapt to them in a manner consistent with a successful outcome. What makes marketing interesting is the challenge of molding the controllable elements of marketing decisions (product, price, promotion, and distribution) within the framework of the uncontrollable elements of the marketplace (competition, politics, laws, consumer behavior, level of technology, and so forth) in such a way that marketing objectives are achieved.

1. Environment differences

The environment within which the marketer must implement marketing plans can change dramatically from country to country or region to region. The difficulties created by different environments are the international marketer's primary concern.

In addition to uncontrollable domestic elements, a significant source of uncertainty is the number of factors in the foreign environment that are often uncontrollable (depicted in Figure 1-4 by the outer circles). A business operating in its home country undoubtedly feels comfortable in forecasting the business climate and adjusting business decisions to these elements. The process of evaluating the uncontrollable elements in an international marketing program, however, often involves substantial doses of cultural, political, and economic shock. A business operating in a number of foreign countries might find polar extremes in political stability, class structure, and economic climate — critical elements in business decisions.

Take China as an example, she has moved from a conservative, closed-market system to a market oriented system in which foreign investments are no longer forbidden.

The more significant elements in the uncontrollable international environment, shown in the outer circles of Figure 1-4, include political / legal forces, economic forces, competitive forces, level of technology, structure of distribution, geography and infrastructure, and cultural forces. These constitute the principal elements of uncertainty an international marketer must cope with in designing a marketing program.

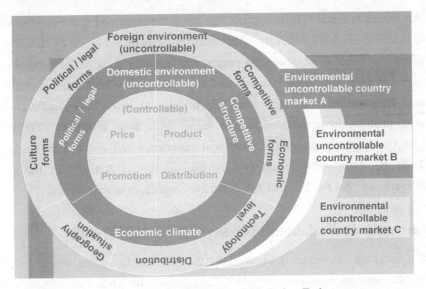

Figure 1-4   The International Marketing Tasks

2. Different applications of marketing principles, concepts and techniques

The existence of global competition has meant that firms now face competitors from all over the globe with their unique competitive advantages and strengths. This means that a China firm will need to cross political boundaries into new markets. This foreign operation will require different applications of marketing principles, concepts and techniques, and the firm will confront unique problems not encountered in the domestic market.

3. The different relations between enterprises and governments

Conflicts may arise because of differences between the business goals of foreign enterprises and the interests of the host government. These conflicts may arise in a number of areas: for example, the transfer of funds out of the country may conflict with the host government's desire to have the funds reinvested in the economy. International marketers are major agents of change in a market — this could cause considerable difficulties with local habits and customs. For example, the introduction of certain products in some markets, such as KFC and Pepsi in China, may cause changes in people's attitudes towards leisure, materialism, etc., which may or may not be deemed desirable by those in authority.

It could be said that competence in domestic marketing is a necessary but not a sufficient condition for success in international markets.

A practical effect of the differences between international and domestic marketing is that managers operating in the international sphere will require a broader competence level. This is reflected in a number of ways. First the future manager of a global firm will need to have cultural empathy. This means being able to recognize cultural differences and understand foreign clients so as to be able to communicate effectively. This empathy can be achieved by developing linguistic skills to a highly competent level where the person will not only think but also experience emotions in that language. In fact, the future international manager must be both internationally experienced and linguistically competent. Managers with this profile are still a rarity today, although some multinational companies do have management teams with these attributes. For example, Carl Hahn, head of Volkswagen, has vast international experience and speaks four languages fluently. In January 1990, E. Artzt was selected as Chairman of Procter & Gamble, the giant American multinational company, on the basis of his extensive international experience.

1.2.4 International marketing process 国际市场营销过程

Generally speaking, as shown in Figure 1-5, the first step for a company to be international is to appraising the international environment. This step will give the company a chance to understand its present situation and its future development. When the company has a better understanding of itself it can decide whether to go abroad.

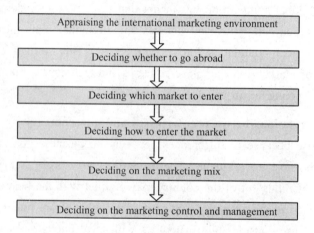

Figure 1-5   The Process of International Marketing

The next step is to decide which market to enter, as different countries or regions may have different advantages and disadvantages; the marketer may also take into consideration of its product and the host government's policy to make his decisions. There are different strategies to enter different markets; a marketer must be very careful to make a sound program so as to be successfully to be accepted by local consumers.

The marketing mix includes product, pricing, promotion and distribution; they are very important because they determine a product's fate in a market. A successful company can never ignore the evaluation and control of its marketing activities. It is necessary for the company to set up a set of measurements and system to control both its long term marketing strategies and its short term plans. The marketing process circles and the company may improve greatly when the marketing activities are properly controlled and managed.

1.3 International Marketing of Chinese Companies
中国公司的国际市场营销

1.3.1 Chinese companies in international markets 国际市场上的中国企业

Compared to many other developed and developing countries, Chinese enterprises have experienced a short period of international marketing activities.

By the end of 1999, the central government approved about 6,142 outward non-financial investment projects with cumulative actual investment of US $10.7 billion (of which the Chinese partners accounted for 67%) in 139 countries and regions, mainly in Hong Kong / Macaw, US, EU, and Japan. These projects were mainly involved in international trade, natural resources exploration, manufacturing industries, transportation, food catering and tourism.

From 1979 to 1985, investing overseas could be undertaken only by state-owned import and export corporations under the umbrella of the Ministry of Foreign Economic Relations and Trade (MOFERT), and provincial and municipal international economic and technological cooperation enterprises regulated by the Commission for Foreign Economic Relations and Trade. Within this seven-year period, Chinese capital went into 185 non-trading enterprises overseas. Chinese investments totaled US $154 million which was roughly 62 percent of total investment amount in the contracts. Most of these investments were in the form of joint ventures and were located in developing countries. Few of the Chinese overseas enterprises were concerned with manufacturing activities. They were mainly in catering, engineering, finance and insurance, and consultancy.

In 1985, a directive that expanded the scope of enterprises eligible for overseas investments was issued by MOFERT. With the new directive, all enterprises, both public and private, can apply for permission to establish subsidiaries in other countries if they possess sufficient capital and technical and operation know-how, and if a suitable foreign partner can be found. The 1985 directive resulted in enhanced Chinese investments overseas so that by the end of 1990, there were a total of 801 Chinese-invested enterprises in the world, involving about US $1.2 billion of Chinese capital, which is more than 3 times the number in 1979 – 1985 and in terms of dollar value, almost 7 times. In this period, Chinese investors started to engage in manufacturing activities. Chinese capital began to flow to metallurgy and minerals, petro-chemicals and chemicals, electronic and light industry, transportation, finance, insurance, medicine, and tourism. The rise of big Chinese transnational corporations such as China National Metals and Minerals Import and Export Corporation and China National Chemical Import and Export Corporation was also in this period.

In the 1990s, the Chinese government encouraged, instead of just allowing, outward directed foreign investments. Top ranking national and local officials publicly expressed the need for Chinese businesses to explore international markets and expand operations overseas to further strengthen themselves and to avoid discriminatory measures imposed by the host government. As a result, Chinese companies continued to expand outwardly with additional 1,184 overseas subsidiaries established between 1991 and 1996. Chinese capital infused in these overseas business undertakings was US $943 million, representing 44 percent of the total investments.

The biggest recipient of Chinese overseas investments in terms of number of enterprises is the United States. Up to 1996, the United States had attracted 238 Chinese investors, representing 12 percent of the total number. Russia hosted 227 Chinese-invested enterprises, just a few firms less than that of the United States. Hong Kong and Macao combined ranked third with a total of 191 Chinese-invested entities by 1996.

In terms of the value of Chinese investments, Canada, though hosting only 77 Chinese enterprises, ranked first with US $371 million of Chinese capital or 17 percent of the total. A close second and third were the United States and Australia accounting for 16 and 15 percent, respectively, of the total value of Chinese overseas investments. Russia, attracts 4 percent though the number ranks second. The Chinese investors in Southeast Asia likewise appeared to be relatively smaller. Thailand, accounted for 3 percent of the total value of Chinese investments while the Philippine share was a measly half of a percent point.

1.3.2   China successfully participating in the WTO brings new challenges and opportunities   中国成功加入 WTO 带来的机遇和挑战

China successfully participating in the WTO offers both challenges and opportunities to Chinese companies.

China officially joined the WTO on 11th December 2001. WTO is one of the most influential international governmental bodies to affect marketing. WTO and the World Court are set up to help to solve international trade disputes, and they also help the member countries to gain fair treatment in international trades. Since China is a member country of the organization, China can also enjoy low trade tariffs and seek equal treatment among association members, which would, of course, give companies more chances to expand their international markets.

Cases

Case 1. Nestlé

In the mid-1860s, Nestlé, a trained pharmacist, began experimenting with various combinations of cow's milk, wheat flour and sugar in an attempt to develop an alternative source of infant nutrition for mothers who were unable to breast feed. In 1905, the company emerged with Anglo-Swiss Condensed Milk Company. The Company formed by the 1905 merger was called the Nestlé and Anglo-Swiss Milk Company. By the early 1900s, the Company was operating factories in the United States, Britain, Germany and Spain. In 1904, Nestlé added chocolate to its range of food products after reaching an agreement with the Swiss General Chocolate Company. After World War II, Nestlé's growth was based on its policy of diversifying within the food sector to meet the needs of consumers. Dozens of new products were added as growth within the Company accelerated and outside companies were acquired. In 1947, Nestlé merged with Alimentana S. A. , the manufacturer of Maggi seasonings and soups, becoming Nestlé Alimentana Company. The acquisition of Crosse & Blackwell, the British manufacturer of preserves and canned foods, followed in 1950, as did the purchase of Findus frozen foods (1963), Libby's fruit juices (1971) and Stouffer's frozen foods (1973). In 1974, the Company became a major shareholder in L'Oréal, one of the world's leading makers of cosmetics. The first half of the 1990s proved to be a favorable time for Nestlé. The opening of Central and Eastern Europe, as well as China, and a general trend towards liberalization of direct foreign investment bode well for a Company with interests as far-flung and diverse as Nestlé.

With a total workforce of approximately 224,541 people in some 479 factories worldwide, Nestlé is not only Switzerland's largest industrial company, but it is also the World's Largest Food Company. Nestlé products are available in nearly every country around the world.

The following link gives you a brief idea about the history of the company.

http://www. nestle. com/all _ about/at _ a _ glance/index. html

Case 2. Haier

Haier is a super-large Chinese enterprise which started out as the Qingdao Refrigerator Factory, founded in 1984 with imported refrigerator production technology from Germany. When it was founded, the company had only one product and 800 staff. Now it is the No. 1 domestic electrical appliance producer in China. More than 20,000 employees are making over 9,000 products in 42 categories.

Starting out with imported technologies, Haier now has the advanced technology and depth of expertise required to set up production facilities in Europe and Southeast Asia.

Haier's development can be divided into three stages — building a brand name (1984 – 1991): seven years to build up a strong brand name in refrigerators through a well-planned TQC (total quality control) system; diversified development (1992 – 1998): seven years diversifying the product catalogue to avoid having all the company's eggs in one basket; going multinational (since 1998): with the aim of building an international brand name, Haier now has 62 distributors and more than 30,000 outlets around the world. The company's target for the beginning of the next century is to enter the top 500 list of Fortune magazine.

Key Terms

multiple environment risks　多重环境风险

international risks　国际风险

consumer value　顾客价值

consumer satisfaction　顾客满意度

market　市场

merchandising　商品销售

pricing　定价

promotion　促销

distribution　分销

human resources　人力资源

domestic marketing　国内营销

export marketing　出口营销

international marketing (global marketing)　国际营销

marketing management　营销管理

marketing　营销

Notes

1. products' distribution　分销
2. one-off payment　一次性支付
3. phased payments　分次付款
4. Generally speaking, consumers make buying decisions based on their perceptions of the value that various products and services deliver.　通常，顾客对各种产品和服务所带来的价值进行判断，并在此基础上做出购买决定。
5. They act on perceived value.　他们依靠自己感觉到的价值判断。

6. target market   目标市场

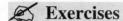 **Exercises**

I. Multiple choices.

1. You are concerned with managing the exchange between the Red Cross and its blood donators. Which of the following costs would you have to be concerned about to create the ideal exchange?

   A. The travel costs incurred by donators visiting the Red Cross blood donation sites.

   B. The personal energy and time expended by the donator.

   C. The opportunity costs lost by not engaging in some other activity.

   D. All of the above are marketing costs that would be of concern to someone managing the exchange situation.

2. Fred Stone, the owner of Neanderthal Products, Inc. is production-oriented. If you were in charge of his marketing operations, which of the following statements might you use as a guiding principle if you wish to meet Mr. Stone's demand?

   A. "I'm a customer and everyone is like me. I buy on price; therefore, everyone does, as well."

   B. "We need to buy the fastest production equipment as possible to raise productivity and keep prices at the lowest possible level."

   C. "We produce the best widgets in the market place."

   D. All of the above would be consistent with Mr. Stone's demands.

3. Peter's company does an excellent and efficient job of churning thousands of Nit-Pickers off the assembly line every day. One problem with this _____ approach to marketing is the failure to consider whether Nit-Pickers also meet the needs of the marketplace.

   A. customer orientation   B. sales orientation

   C. marketing orientation   D. production orientation

4. Jack Chen's company markets golf club polish. Jack knows that buyers may consider the product nonessential, and he assumes that if he hires a team of aggressive, persuasive salespeople, buyers will buy more of the polish. Jack has a _____.

   A. sales orientation   B. production orientation

   C. promotion orientation   D. marketing orientation

   E. customer orientation

5. Beth has noticed the lack of specialty recycling centers in her community, although local neighborhood clubs have repeatedly asked the city to provide such centers. Beth has decided to become certified in waste disposal and hopes to open a battery and motor oil

recycling center next year. She hopes to include the innovative service of home pickup and delivery of recyclables. This business philosophy supports a(n) _____ orientation.

    A. production   B. sales   C. marketing   D. enterprise

6. The Ajax Insurance Company tells its salespeople to try to sell life insurance to everyone they meet or contact. In contrast, the Family Shelter Insurance Company concentrates on special insurance plans designed for single parents. Family Shelter is _____.

    A. missing out by not concentrating on the average customer

    B. a selling-oriented company

    C. recognizing that different customer groups have different needs and wants

    D. aiming at a goal of profit through maximum sales volume

7. Which of the following is NOT a part of the marketing process?

    A. Understanding the organization's mission.

    B. Developing performance appraisals for marketing personnel.

    C. Designing performance measures.

    D. Setting objectives.

    E. Determining target markets.

8. The marketing manager for Oil of Olay, a skin care product, is working with an advertising agency to develop a new TV commercial targeting teen-agers. Which of the following marketing mix variables best describes this activity?

    A. Product.   B. Price.

    C. Target market.   D. Promotion.

9. Tiantang is a mineral water manufacturer that donates 2 cents of each bottle of mineral water it sells to the Hope Project. Which type of orientation the company has?

    A. Production.   B. Sales.

    C. Promotion.   D. Marketing.

    E. Societal marketing.

10. Jackie is a food science major at university and hopes to operate the family restaurant after graduation. Jackie has been advised to take a marketing course in the School of Business as an elective, but she thinks this would be a waste of time. You are her friend and a marketing major. You advise that _____.

    A. Jackie declare a business minor because she needs a backup career

    B. more nutrition and gourmet cooking classes be most useful for Jackie

    C. the main reason to take marketing be to teach Jackie how to advertise the restaurant

    D. marketing knowledge help Jackie to understand how she can satisfy consumers' needs and wants

11. Which of the following is NOT true about marketing?

   A. Marketing is a process.

   B. Marketing can involve any number of parties.

   C. Marketing can be used for ideas, goods, or services.

   D. Marketing involves products, pricing, promotion, and distribution.

II. True or false.

1. A marketing exchange cannot take place unless each party in the exchange has something that the other party values.

2. The owners of the Plane Rubber and Tire Company are pleased with their low unit costs and high production volumes. Salespeople are unnecessary because buyers are always waiting for new tires to come off the assembly line. Plane currently has a production orientation.

3. The president of Hoppity Flea Collars does not find it necessary to conduct much marketing research because the telephone selling campaign has been such a successful marketing strategy. Hoppity has a marketing orientation.

4. Having a sales orientation is the same as having a market orientation since both have the ultimate goal of satisfying customer needs.

5. You are about to start manufacturing and selling ferret food. You have met with your board of directors and you all discussed the benefits and sacrifices regarding the purchase of your food. Knowing the ratio of benefits to sacrifices allows you to specify how much customer value you will achieve.

6. The marketing mix variables are product, place, promotion, and price.

7. Conceptually, international marketing differs from domestic marketing only by virtue of the fact that the marketer must operate in more than one nation.

III. Discussion.

1. What will WTO bring to Chinese firm in international marketing?

2. The differences between domestic marketing and international marketing.

3. What are the functions of marketing?

4. Visit the Bureau of Economic Analysis home page (www.bea.doc.gov). Select the section International Articles and find the most recent information on foreign direct investments in the United States. Which country has the highest dollar amount of investment in the United States? Second highest? Can you explain why?

Chapter Two

Three Basic Theories of International Trade

国际贸易的三个基本理论

◄ Objectives　学习目标

When students finish this chapter, they should be able to accomplish the following:

☑ Briefly explain the theory of comparative advantage

☑ Briefly explain the theory of trade or product cycle

☑ Briefly explain the theory of business orientation

Although international marketing is very different from international trade, the two have very close association. For a keen international marketer, it's necessary to know both the existence and the illustration[1] of some theories which base the international trade so as to have a better understanding of international marketing itself.

2.1　The Theory of Comparative Advantage　比较优势理论

2.1.1　Introduction　简介

The theory of comparative advantage is put forward by Adam Smith and David Ricardo. It can be relatively complex and difficult to understand. But it can be stated simply. The theory believes (under assumptions) that a country can gain from trade even if it has an absolute advantage[2] in the production of all goods. Even though a country has an absolute production advantage it may be better to concentrate on its comparative advantage[3]. To calculate the comparative advantage, one has to compare the production ratios[4], and make the assumption that one country totally specializes in one product. To maximize the well-being of both individuals and countries, countries are better off specializing in their area of competitive advantage and then trading and exchanging with others in the market place.

2.1.2　Simplified model　简化模型

Take the simple two country-two product model of comparative advantage. Country A produces sheep and Country B cows. These are two products, both undifferentiated and produced with production units which are a mixture of land, labor and capital. To use the same production units Country A can produce 100 sheep and no cows, and Country B can produce 70 cows and no sheep. At the other extreme Country A can produce no sheep and 80 cows and Country B no cows and 60 sheep. One extreme of PPF(production possibility frontier)[5] is shown in Table 2-1.

Table 2-1

Product	Country A	Country B	World Total
Sheep	100	0	100
Cows	0	70	70

The other extreme of PPF is shown in Table 2-2.

Table 2-2

Product	Country A	Country B	World Total
Sheep	0	60	60
Cows	80	0	80

Figure 2-1 shows the original PPF of both countries using graphs. For the purpose of this example we will simply make-up a plausible production / consumption point under autarky. Essentially, we assume that consumer demands are such as to generate the chosen production point.

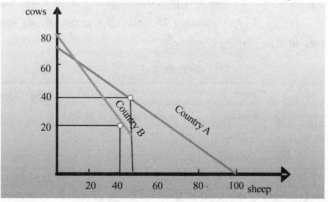

Figure 2-1　The Original PPFs of Country A and Country B

Table 2-3 below shows the autarky production / consumption levels for the two countries. It also shows total world production for each of the goods.

Table 2-3

Autarky Production/Consumption			
Product	Country A	Country B	World Total
Sheep	50	43	93
Cows	40	20	60

Now if the two countries specialize and trade, the position is shown in Table 2-4 as follows:

Table 2-4

Product	Country A	Country B	World Total
Sheep	100	0	100
Cows	0	70	70

Ricardo argued that trade gains could arise if countries first specialize in their comparative advantage good and then trade with the other country. Specialization in the example means that the country A produces only sheep and no cows, while country B produces only cows and no sheep. These quantities are shown in the following Table 2-5.

At this point we can already see a remarkable result. When countries specialize in their comparative advantage good, world output of both sheep and cows rises. Sheep output rises from 93 to 100, while cows output rises from 60 to 70. What's more, the output increases occur without an increase in the quantity of labor used to produce them.

In order for consumption of both goods in both countries trade must occur. In the example, country A is consuming 40 units of cows and producing none, so it must import the 40 unties of cows from country B. Country B is consuming 43 units of sheep with no sheep production, so it must import the 43 units of sheep from country A.

Table 2-5

Product	Country A			Country B		
	Production	Imports	Consumption	Production	Imports	Consumption
Sheep	100	0	50	0	43	43
Cows	0	40	40	70	0	20

Actually, after specialization the total column of both products is higher, both countries can consume more of both goods. Suppose each country split its extra production to the other country, the result would be seen in Table 2-6 as follows:

Table 2-6

Product	Country A			Country B		
	Production	Imports	Consumption	Production	Imports	Consumption
Sheep	100	0	53.5	0	46.5	46.5
Cows	0	45	45	70	0	25

2.1.3 Conclusions 结论

The Ricardian model numerical example assumes that countries differ in their production technologies such that one of the countries is absolutely more productive than the other in the production of each of the two goods. If these two countries specialize in their comparative advantage good then world production rises for both goods. Increased output occurs even though there is no increase in the amount of labor input in the world, thus the example demonstrates that specialization can raise world production efficiency. Because of the increase in output, it is possible to construct a terms of trade between the countries such that each country consumes more of each good with specialization and trade than was possible under autarky. Thus, both countries can gain from trade. The surprising result from this example is that a country, which is technologically inferior to another in the production of all goods, can nevertheless benefit from trade with that country.

2.2 The Theory of Trade or Product Trade Cycle 产品贸易周期理论

2.2.1 Product Life Cycle 产品生命周期

In 1950's, it was somewhat rare for a family to have a record player to give out melodies. And until 1980's, people felt no more strange to see any records but used cassette recorder for music. Then recently in 1990's, except for some cassette recorders were used by students to study English, they were nearly not often playing music because people could afford to have CD players and MP3s to enjoy music. From all this, we can easily see that it is not possible for every kind of products to exist for ever, that's to say, they have their own period of lifetime, which, in a word, means the period of time between the appearance and disappearance of products. The product life cycle concept, typically expressed as an "S" shaped curve in marketing literature, is based on the analogy of the human biological cycle. Products, like living organisms, go through stages of birth, development, growth, maturity, decline and demise[6].

The traditional four-stage life cycle — introduction, growth, maturity, and decline — is a well-documented phenomenon. Attempts are made in the maturity stage to extend the cycle. The market life cycle is very similar and what global marketers have to be wary of is that not all markets are at the same stage globally. It may be appropriate to have tractor mounted ditchers and diggers in Africa or the UK where labor is not too plentiful, but in India, they may be the last things required where labor is plentiful and very cheap. So the appropriate marketing strategy will be different for each market.

2.2.2 The theory of product trade cycle 产品贸易周期理论

The theory of trade / product trade cycle is put forward by Dr. Raymond Vernon. Since Raymond Vernon published his article "*International Investment and International Trade in the Product Cycle*" in 1966, there has been a simultaneous development of literature pertaining to the "product cycle" in marketing. "The model claims that many products go through a trade cycle, during which the United States is initially an exporter, then loses its export markets and may finally become an importer of the product" (Louis T. Wells, Jr.). On the other hand, Warren Keegan refers to the International Product Life Cycle in the following manner: "The International Product Life Cycle model suggests that many products go through a cycle during which high income, mass consumption countries are initially exporters, then lose their export markets, and finally become importers of the product."

The international product life cycle can be defined as market life span stages the product goes through in international markets sequentially, simultaneously or asynchronously. The sequential stages are introduction, growth, maturity, decline and extinction in the international markets. When a product is positioned in different international markets at the same time and is going through similar life cycle stages, the cycle process is simultaneous. The life cycle stages are asynchronous when the product is in different stages in different international markets at the same time. Steel-belted auto radial tires had reached the saturation level in Western Europe when they were being discovered by the US market. Thus it was in the maturity stage in Western Europe and introductory stage in the United States.

From a high income country point of view, phase 1 involves exporting, based on domestic product strength and surplus, to phase 2, when foreign production begins, to phase 3 when production in the foreign country becomes competitive, to phase 4 when import competition begins.

The assumption behind this cycle is that new products are firstly launched in high income markets because a) there is most potential and b) the product can be tested best domestically near its source of production. Thus, new products generally emanate from high-income countries and, over time, orders begin to be solicited from lower income countries and so a thriving export market develops. High-income country entrepreneurs quickly realize that the markets to which they are selling often have lower production costs and so production is initiated abroad for the new products, so starts the second stage.

In the second stage of the cycle, foreign and high-income country production begins to supply the same export market. As foreign producers begin to expand and gain more experience, their competition displaces the high-income export production source. At this point, high-income countries often decide to invest in foreign countries to protect their share. As foreign producers expand, their growing economies of scale make them a competitive source for third country markets where they compete with high-income exporters.

The final phase of the cycle occurs when the foreign producer achieves such a scale and experience that it starts exporting to the original high income producer at a production cost lower than its original high income producer. High-income producers, once enjoying a monopoly in their own market, now face competition at home.

The cycle continues as the production capability in the product extends from other advanced countries to less developed countries at home, then in international trade, and finally, in other advanced countries home markets. The internation product cycle is shown clearly in Figure 2-2.

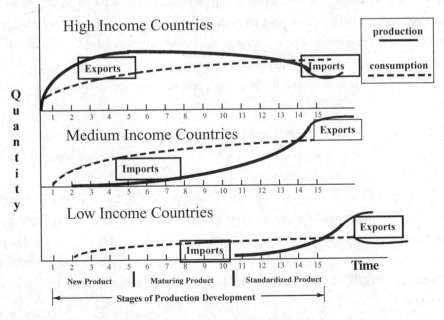

Figure 2-2   International Product Trade Cycle

2.3 The Theory of Business Orientation 商业定位理论

2.3.1 Business orientation 商业定位

Some firms are very involved with international marketing while others show very little interest or motivation. These different attitudes can be called international marketing orientations[7]. Dr. Howard perlmutter put forward the theory of business orientation in 1967. His "EPRG" scheme identified four types of attitudes or orientations associated with successive stages in the evolution of international operations.

According to Perlmutter "a key assumption underlying the EPRG framework is that the degree of internationalization to which management is committed or willing to move towards affects the specific international strategies and decision rules of the firm. "

2.3.2 EPRG scheme EPRG 计划

The EPRG scheme can be expressed as follows:

1. Ethnocentrism — host country superiority — secondary operation

A person who assumes that his home country is superior compared to the rest of the world holds ethnocentrism marketing management orientation. Ethnocentrism is associated with a home country management orientation where overseas operations are secondary. Structure is complex in home country but simple in other countries. The products are not adapted if sold outside the home country. For example, Nissan during its first few years in exporting cars in the US markets sold its car without any change than those sold in Japan.

2. Polycentrism — host country orientation — subsidiary operation

Polycentrism connotes a host country focus where subsidiaries are established in overseas markets. These are varied and independent.

The advantage of the polycentrism approach for any firm is that it is relatively simple, rapid and economical to implement for overseas markets. However, certain facilitating factors are required before this approach can be successfully adopted. The firm would need either technological leadership, high product quality or low production costs, or it would need to focus on those overseas markets where consumer needs and conditions for use are similar to those in the domestic market.

However, there are limits to the long-term success of this approach to international marketing since it does not involve any sort of comparative analysis, (the identification of similarities and differences a two or more markets,) which in turn helps a firm to adapt its marketing strategy for those markets.

3. Regiocentrism — regional orientation — world market strategies

Regiocentrism relates to an integrated regional management approach, increasingly complex and regionally interdependent.

In the long term, the Regiocentrism approach is unlikely to be profitable as duplication of effort and strategies may occur as a result of seeing each market as being different and unique. Clusters of markets may exhibit similar market characteristics and hence duplication can be avoided.

According to Majaro[8], the cluster approach is based on the need to achieve optimum penetration of a group of markets, without the need for the company to spread itself too thinly. These clusters of countries will have highly standardized marketing mixes which can be managed economically. For example, Argentina and Bran are different markets but there are enough common factors between them (i. e. consumption factors) for a company to adopt a cluster approach. A cluster approach then involves channeling a firm's resources into one or more market segments, and by concentrating its resources and efforts on these markets it hopes to capture large market shares.

4. Geocentrism — world orientation — world market strategies

Geocentrism is linked with an integrated world structure of continued physical growth and tied to centralized / decentralized management strategies, highly complex and worldwide interdependent.

This approach is capable of achieving rapid worldwide distribution of a product as well as attaining low production costs partly due to economies of scale.

The difficulty of this approach is that its success depends on careful and continuous global market research which is expensive and time-consuming. Furthermore, there are sharp differences between markets which may necessitate the firm having to drop many markets or, alternatively, abandon its global standardization programs. However, many large firms are trying to develop both global strategies and global products, e. g. Coca Cola, McDonald's, Sony, etc.

Both regiocentrism and geocentrism are based on similarities and differences in markets, capitalizing on similarities to obtain cost benefits, but recognizing differences.

☞ Cases

Case 1.   Kenya and flower exporting

Holland is a worldwide-known nation that produces large quantities of flowers. On the other side, Kenya is less efficient. However, Kenya succeeds in exporting thousands of tones of flowers to Europe every year. Kenya flower growers have achieved legendary reputations in the supply of fresh cut flowers to Europe. Kenya's comparative advantage was based on its low labor costs, the country's location and its diverse agro-ecological conditions. These facilitated the development of a diversified product range, all year round supply and better qualities due to labor intensity at harvest time. Kenya's airfreight costs were kept low due to government intervention, but lower costs of production were not its strength. Their success shows a good example of the theory of comparative advantages.

Case 2.　Textiles industry

A well known case for the international product trade cycle is the textiles industry, specially cotton. In the early and mid twentieth century the UK was a major producer of cotton textile materials, primarily based on its access to cheap raw materials from its Commonwealth countries and its relatively cheap labor. However, some cotton supplier countries such as India, Pakistan and certain African countries realized that they had the labor and materials on their doorstep conducive to domestic production. They began to do so. Such was their success in supplying their own huge markets that their production costs dropped dramatically with growing economies of scale. Soon they were able to support cloth and finished good back to the UK, which by now had experienced growing production costs due to rising labor costs and failing market share. Now the UK has little cotton materials production and it served by many countries over the world, including its former colonies and Commonwealth countries.

Case 3.　Coke Cola in India

In 1977, Coke left India when asked to dilute its equity. It felt that it could not risk losing the Cola formula that made Coke "the real thing". Besides, at that time it had not accepted anywhere in the world the idea of joint ventureship or minority role in a firm. It had hundred per cent subsidiaries in different part of the world and India was no exception. Further, it had not done anything to either develop the soft drink market or industry and most Coke bottlers operated slow speed bottling plants. But in the 1990s, Coke is different. It considers local markets, local government aspirations and competition to decide its market entry and marketing strategy. So in 1993, Coke re-entered India not as a 100 per cent owned subsidiary of its Atlanta parent, but through a strategic alliance with Parle. Same is true for IBM, which re-entered India in 1992 in joint collaboration with Tatas. So, today's firms, some of which are yesterdays multinationals, have the dream of responding to the world Customer through myriad strategies.

Chapter Two　Three Basic Theories of International Trade

Key Terms

the theory of comparative advantage　比较优势理论

the theory of trade or product cycle　贸易产品周期理论

product life cycle　产品生命周期

the theory of business orientation　商业定位理论

EPRG scheme　EPRG 方案

Notes

1. illustration　*n.*　例子，例证

2. absolute advantage　绝对优势

3. comparative advantage　比较优势

4. production ratio　生产比价

5. PPF(production possibility frontier)　生产可能性曲线

6. demise　*n.*　死亡

7. international marketing orientations　国际市场营销定位

8. Majaro　Simon Majaro 是欧洲商业管理学院教授，欧洲管理创造力领域的权威，参与了许多大型跨国公司的创新战略的规划工作，在欧美高层管理者中影响极深。

Exercises

I. Multiple choices.

1. Use the information in Table 2-7 to answer questions 1 & 2.

Table 2-7　Output per Hour

	Cakes	Pies
Jorge	5	10
Rocky	4	6

Which of the following statements is correct?

A. Rocky has the comparative advantage in pies.

B. Jorge has the absolute advantage in pies.

C. Jorge has the absolute and comparative advantage in pies.

D. Jorge has a comparative advantage but not an absolute advantage in pies.

E. Rocky has an absolute advantage but not a comparative advantage in pies.

2. What is the opportunity cost for Rocky to make one cake?

　A. 1.5 Pies　　　　　　　B. 4 cakes　　　　　　　C. the same as Jorge's

　D. 6 pies　　　　　　　　E. 3 cakes

3. Suppose wages in Thailand are 750 baht per worker and they are 1000 won per worker on Korea. The exchange rate is 1.4 baht per won and output per worker is as listed in Table 2-8.

Table 2-8　Output per Hour

	Televisions	Cell phones
Thailand	150	100
Korea	200	200

Which of the following is true?

A. Thailand has a comparative advantage in televisions.

B. Thailand has an absolute advantage in televisions.

C. Thailand has a comparative advantage in cell phone.

D. Thailand has an absolute advantage in cell phone.

4. In the _____ stage of the international product life cycle theory, the high purchasing power and demand of buyers in an industrialized country spur a company to design and introduce a new product concept.

　A. new product　　　　　　　　　　　　B. maturing product

　C. standardized product　　　　　　　　　D. declining product

5. In the _____ stage of the international product life cycle, goods are produced in the home country because of uncertain domestic demand and to keep production close to the research department that developed the product.

　A. new product　　　　　　　　　　　　B. maturing product

　C. standardized product　　　　　　　　　D. declining product

6. In the _____ stage of the international product life cycle, the company directly invests in production facilities in those countries where demand is great enough to warrant its own production facilities.

　A. new product　　　　　　　　　　　　B. maturing product

　C. standardized product　　　　　　　　　D. declining product

7. Increased competition creates pressures to reduce production costs in the _____ stage of the international product life cycle.

　A. new product　　　　　　　　　　　　B. maturing product

C. standardized product　　　　　　　D. declining product

8. All of the following are elements of the EPRG framework for evaluating the degree of internationalism a firm's management is committed to EXCEPT _____.

    A. ethnocentric orientation　　　　　　B. geocentric orientation

    C. raceocentric orientation　　　　　　D. polycentric orientation

9. What is Adam Smith's theory of absolute advantage based on?

    A. The country with more exports than imports has the absolute advantage.

    B. The country with more imports than exports has the absolute advantage.

    C. The country with the most overall trade in exports and imports has the absolute advantage.

    D. The country that exports the goods and services it is most productive in providing and imports those that other countries are more productive in providing has the absolute advantage.

10. The theory of absolute advantage was developed by _____.

    A. Karl Marx　　　　　　　　　　　B. David Ricardo

    C. Adam Smith　　　　　　　　　　　D. Eli Hecksher and Bertil Ohlin

II. True or false.

1. The fact that televisions were originally produced in the US and Japan and now production has moved to low-wage nations proves that the theory of comparative advantage (based on factor abundance) cannot predict the location of production.

2. A country is said to have an absolute advantage when it can produce goods more efficiently than any other nation.

3. According to the theory of comparative advantage, trade is still beneficial even if one country is less efficient in the production of two goods, so long as it is less inefficient in the production of one of the goods.

4. The ability of the international product life cycle theory to accurately depict the trade flows of nations is limited.

5. Much production today in the world resembles what is predicted by the theory of comparative advantage.

6. According to new trade theory, countries export products they were among the first to produce.

7. The Product Life Cycle Theory of Trade focuses on the continuum or cycle of products in general.

8. In the decline stage of the Product Life Cycle Trade Theory the production is moved to the

emerging new markets.

9. The theory of comparative advantage as advocated by David Ricardo maintains that a country gains from trade if it specializes in those products that it can produce more efficiently than other products.

10. If a company in the international market strives to develop standardized marketing mixes for its products that will be generally applicable across national borders, the firm's philosophy would be best described as ethnocentric marketing orientation.

III. Discussion.

Suppose the world consists of just 2 countries, A and B. Each country is capable of producing only 2 products: wheat and cars. Each country has 100 units of resources. A is able to produce 80 units of wheat or 10 cars with each unit of resource. Hence, if it uses all its resources to produce wheat, it can produce 8,000 units of wheat. Alternatively, if it uses all its resources to produce cars, it can produce 1,000 cars. It can also produce some combination of wheat and cars along a (straight-line) production possibility frontier. B is able to produce 40 units of wheat or 8 cars with each unit of resource.

1. Which country has an absolute advantage in producing wheat? cars?

2. What does the theory of comparative advantage say about which country exports what product to the other?

3. Suppose each country initially operates under autarky devoting half its resources to the production of wheat and half to the production of cars. This allocation of resources is what is justified by the local demand. Calculate the world production of wheat and cars. Now, suppose the two countries trade and they each specialize (not necessarily completely) in the production of the product in which they have a comparative advantage. Can you find a solution so that the total world production of both wheat and cars is greater than under autarky? How can both countries do so that each would have more wheat and cars than they would have under autarky?

Part II

国际营销环境

The International Marketing Environment

Chapter Three

The Role of Economy

经济的作用

When students finish this chapter, they should be able to accomplish the following:

☑ To have an overview of world economy

☑ To outline the exchange system in the world

☑ To explain the role of international trade in marketing

3.1 World Economy Overview 世界经济概览

The world economy has undergone revolutionary changes during the past decades. These remarkable changes are contrary to much of the received doctrine of economic theory, and they are of great significance and importance to government and business practitioners[1]. The first change is the increased volume of capital movements. Capital movements rather than trade have become the driving force of the world economy. In the past, when a country ran a deficit on its trade accounts, its currency would depreciate[2] in value. Today, it is capital movements and trade that determine currency value. The second change is that although employment in manufacturing remains steady or has declined, production continues to grow. The third change is the "uncoupling" of the primary products economy from the industrial economy. The fourth major change is the emergence of the world economy as the dominant economic unit. The world economy is in control. The macroeconomics[3] of the nation-state no longer control economic outcomes.

3.1.1   The international economic system   国际经济体系

Several factors have contributed to the growth of the international economy post-World War II. The principal forces have been the development of economic blocs[4] like the European Union and then the "economic pillars" — the World Bank (or International Bank for Reconstruction and Development to give its full name), the International Monetary Fund and the evolution of the World Trade Organization from the original General Agreement on Tariffs and Trade.

Until 1969, the world economy traded on a gold and foreign exchange base. This affected liquidity[5] drastically. After 1969, liquidity was eased by the agreement that member nations to the IMF accept the Special Drawing Rights (SDR) in settling reserve transactions. Now an international reserve facility is available. Recently, the World Bank has taken a very active role in the reconstruction and development of developing country economies.

Until the General Agreement on Tariffs and Trade (GATT) after World War II, the world trading system had been restricted by discriminating trade practices. GATT had the intention of producing a set of rules and principles to liberalize trade. The most favored nation concept, whereby each country agrees to extend to all countries the most favorable terms that it negotiates with any country, helped reduce barriers. The "round" of talks began with Kennedy in the 60s and Tokyo in the 70s. The Uruguay round was concluded in April 1994 and ratified by most countries in early 1995. Despite these trade agreements, non-tariff barriers like exclusion deals, standards and administrative delays are more difficult to deal with. A similar system exists with the European Union, — the Lomè[6] (the capital city of Togo in Africa) convention. Under this deal, African and Caribbean countries enjoy favored status with EU member countries.

Relative global peace has engendered confidence in world trade. Encouraged by this and the availability of finance, global corporations have been able to expand into many markets. This atmosphere of peace has also allowed the steady upward trend of domestic growth and again opened up market opportunities domestically to foreign firms. Peace in Mozambique, the "normalization" of South Africa, as examples, have opened up the way for domestic growth and also, therefore, foreign investment. The liberation of economies under World Bank sponsored structural adjustment programs has also given opportunities. This is very true of countries like Zambia and Zimbabwe, where in the latter, for example, over Z $ 2. 8 billion of foreign investment in the stock exchange and mining projects have occurred in the early 1990s.

Sometimes, market opportunities open up through "Acts of God". The great drought of 1992 in Southern Africa, necessitated a large influx[7] of foreign produce, especially yellow maize from the USA and South America. Not only did this give a market for maize only, but opened up opportunities for transport businesses and services to serve the drought stricken areas.

Speedy communications like air transportation and electronic data transmission and technology have "shrunk" the world. Costs and time have reduced enormously and with the advent[8] of television, people can see what is happening elsewhere and this can cause desire levels to rise dramatically. Only recently has television been introduced into Tanzania, for example, and this has brought the world and its markets, closer to the average Tanzanian.

No doubt a great impetus[9] to global trade was brought about by the development of economic blocs. Blocs like the European Union (EU), ASEAN[10], the North American Free Trade Agreement with the USA, Canada and Mexico has created market opportunities and challenges. New countries are trying to join these blocs all the time, because of the economic, social and other advantages they bring.

In general, there are three types of economic systems: capitalist, socialist, and mixed. The classifications are based on the method of resource allocation in the system, which are market allocation, command allocation or central plan allocation, and mixed allocation. There is no pure market or command allocation systems, all actual systems are mixed allocation.

A market allocation system is one which relies upon the customer or consumer to allocate resources. In a command allocation system, resource allocation decisions are made by government planners. The USA, Western Europe, Japan are examples of market allocation systems, while the former Soviet Union and China were leading examples of countries relying upon command allocation, both countries are shifting to a market allocation system. There are no pure market or command allocation systems. All market systems have a command sector and command systems have a market sector.

3.2   Exchange System   汇率体系

Exchange system is another economic factor a firm would consider in international marketing, especially the stability of currency. Sales and profits could be affected if a foreign country revalues its currency in relation to the company's home currency. As an illusion, assume that one unit of a firm home currency is worth ten units of a foreign currency and its product sells for 100 units at home, that is 1,000 units of the foreign currency in that country. Then the foreign currency is revalued upward: five units are now exchanged for one unit home currency. If the company retains its old home currency price of 100, its new foreign currency price becomes 500 units. The price is cheaper to foreign customers, and unit sales in the foreign country should increase. The opposite situation may also occur. The value of a currency is defined by its strength in world currency markets.

3.2.1 Foreign exchange and international finance 外汇与国际金融

Foreign exchange is the process of converting the currency of one country into the currency of another country. The exchange rate is constantly changing due to supply and demand and the possible financial difficulty a country is experiencing. Balance of payments in a country affects exchange rates. If a country has more money coming in than flowing out, it has a favorable balance of trade. A favorable balance of trade will keep the value of the currency constant or rising due to increased demand for the nation's products and currency. Unfavorable balance of payments will cause the currency to decline in value due to a lower demand for the monetary unit.

Economic conditions affect the value of a country's money. Inflation and changing interest rates certainly affect the buying power of money. As prices increase, buying power of the country's money declines and their currency is less attractive. The value of a country's money is affected by the cost of borrowing; higher interest rates will cause prices of products to rise, lower the demand of consumers, lower the demand for the country's currency, and cause a decline in the currency's value. More borrowing of money equals increased interest rates and inflation means rising prices, higher interest rates, and less buying power of money. A higher risk will mean higher interest rates on a loan.

Political stability also affects the value of money. Uncertainty in a country reduces confidence business people have in its currency. New laws and regulations affect foreign trade; the country will appear to have a friendly versus unfriendly environment.

3.2.2 Foreign exchange activities 外汇行为

Soft currency is not easy to exchange for other currencies because it has limited value in the world marketplace. Hard currency is a monetary unit that is freely convertible into other currencies such as yen, and US dollars. We experience a system of floating exchange rates because currency values are based on supply and demand. As demand for currency increases, the value of that monetary unit increases. Success exporting in Japan and wanting payment in yen, has increased the value of yen.

Foreign exchange market consists of banks and other financial institutions that buy and sell different currencies. These financial institutions come in handy when you are going on vacation to another country or when you intend to conduct international trade. Companies may enter an agreement to buy a monetary unit for a future date at today's prices. Dealing with currency futures involves risk. An importer does not have to exercise the option to buy the currency at the contract price; the currency can be purchased at the going market price instead.

3.2.3   Foreign exchange controls   外汇管制

Government restrictions can be used to regulate the amount and value of a nation's currency. Examples of these controls include fixed exchange rates, limits on the amount and cost of currency, and limits on the amount of local currency a person can take out of a country.

3.2.4   International financial agencies   国际金融机构

The International Bank for Reconstruction and Development (World Bank) was created in 1944 to provide loans for rebuilding after World War II. Today the bank provides economic assistance to less developed countries by building communication systems, transportation networks and energy plains. Over 150 member countries have access the bank's two divisions (International Development Association — IDA and International Finance Corporation — IFC). The International Development Association loans money to developing countries for low interest rates and repayment periods of up to 50 years. The International Finance Corporation provides capital and technical assistance to private businesses in nations with limited resources. It encourages joint venture between foreign and local companies and capital investment within the developing nation.

The International Monetary Fund promotes economic cooperation and maintains an orderly system of world trade and exchange rates. It was established in 1946 when interdependence of nations was escalating. Over 150 member nations make up the international monetary fund; it is a cooperative deposit bank which provides assistance to countries experiencing balance of payment difficulties. Strategies to prevent increased debt and currency decline for a country include analyzing economic situations, suggesting economic policies and providing loans when necessary. The International Monetary Fund and International Finance Corporation both work for a stable system of foreign exchange.

3.3   International Trade   国际贸易

International trade is the exchange of goods and services between countries in their form of exports and imports. It enables countries to specialize in producing those things they are best suited to make with the resources they have. A country benefits more by producing goods it can make most cheaply and buying those goods that other countries can make at lower costs than by producing everything it needs within its own borders. Even the most prosperous countries seek to exchange goods and services with their neighbors or other countries. For example, the climate of the United States is not suitable for growing coffee, so it imports coffee beans from Brazil.

Though California and Arizona grow olives, the USA imports olives from the Mediterranean countries, as these states do not produce a great enough volume and variety to supply the entire country at prices competitive with those of foreign producers. Since the end of World War II, world merchandise trade has grown faster than world production. In 1989, high-income countries were responsible for more than 80 percent of world merchandise trade exports or imports. Through exporting and importing, people in many countries share the benefit of production in other countries. Exporting and importing are two sides of the same coin. Exports supply customers with products manufactured in another country; imports do exactly the same thing. However, there is one important difference between importing and exporting. Importers are buyers / customers, while exporters are sellers / marketers.

In fact, the greater the level of prosperity, the greater link to high performance in the global markets. Once a general awareness of another nation's products is in place, demand can be readily sparked. International marketers have been this spark and have led the drive toward the globalization of business. The choice of which products to market abroad will depend a great deal on how your own nation views its trading partners and how those partners see themselves in relation to your domestic market.

3.3.1 Balance of trade 贸易差额

Another phenomenon that has increased the responsibility of marketing is the increased importance of its role in the delivery of goods and services in the international arena.

Some countries buy more from foreign countries than they sell, some sell more than they buy from abroad and a rare few have roughly equal amounts in each category. The United States regularly runs overall "trade deficits" (buy more) with its partners while its major rival and trading partner, Japan, continually has "trade surpluses" (sells more) when matching exports to imports of goods and services. So understanding the "balance of trade" will not only affect your ability to penetrate a market but determine the long-term viability[11] of your goods or services in the targeted segment. For a long time in the United States, most marketers enjoyed such a vast national market that they did not have to worry about competing in foreign markets. With foreign products flooding US markets, business corporations are facing stiff competition at home and are beginning to realize that their survival depends upon searching for markets. To give you an idea of the seriousness of the situation, the US balance of trade deficit in 1987 was about $180 billion.

Currently the situation is even worse. The US balance of trade deficit is a staggering figure hovering around $400 billion annually. During Senate hearings in January 2001, Alan Greenspan testified that this situation is of concern, but did not commit as to when to push the panic button.

What this means is that $400 billion is put each year in the hands of foreign customers. It is the responsibility of marketing to rectify this situation, at least partially.

3.3.2   The US-China balance of trade   中美贸易平衡

The US trade deficit with China often assumes center stage in discussions of the US-China commercial relationship, but the deficit is neither the most important barometer[12] of US economic health nor the best measure of the benefits the US gains from trade. The size of the imbalance is often overstated. In 2000, the US Department of Commerce (USDOC) put the bilateral deficit at $91.3 billion — but economists have argued that a more accurate figure would be $68.8 billion.

China as an export market is one of the fastest-growing US export markets. Annual US exports to China have more than tripled since 1990, reaching $16.3 billion in 2000. Major US exports to China include power generation equipment, electrical machinery, fertilizer, and medical equipment. Companies in many US sectors face mature markets at home and look to the Chinese market to grow and remain competitive globally. US services exports to China rose 18.1 percent in 2000, to reach $4.6 billion.

US consumers benefit from the ability to purchase low-cost imports from China, including footwear, apparel, and, increasingly, electrical machinery and equipment.

1. Measurements of exports and imports

As do other countries, the United States measures exports and imports on different bases. US exports typically are calculated on a free-alongside-ship (FAS) basis and US imports are measured using a cost, insurance, and freight (CIF) basis. The FAS value does not include loading, insurance, and freight costs. US exports thus should be adjusted up by 1 percent, and US imports adjusted down by 10 percent, according to a 1999 report by California-based economists Lawrence Lau and K. C. Fung, as shown in Table 3-1.

Table 3-1   Adjusted US Trade Flows and Deficit with China

Year	Department of Commerce Figures			Adjusted Figures		
	Exports	Imports	Trade Deficit	Exports	Imports	Trade Deficit
1989	5.8	12.0	6.2	7.0	10.4	3.4
1990	4.8	15.2	10.4	6.0	13.4	7.4
1991	6.3	19.0	12.7	7.8	16.2	8.4
1992	7.5	25.7	18.2	9.6	21.5	11.9
1993	8.8	31.5	22.8	11.7	25.9	12.2

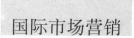

Year	Department of Commerce Figures			Adjusted Figures		
	Exports	Imports	Trade Deficit	Exports	Imports	Trade Deficit
1994	9.3	38.8	29.5	12.8	32.5	19.7
1995	11.7	45.6	33.8	16.5	38.7	22.2
1996	12.0	51.5	39.5	17.5	44.0	26.5
1997	12.8	62.6	49.7	18.4	54.5	36.1
1998	14.3	71.2	56.9	19.1	63.2	44.1
1999	13.1	81.8	68.7	18.1	73.6	55.5
2000	16.3	100.1	83.8	21.9	90.7	68.8

SOURCE: Nicholas Lardy, *China in the World Economy*, @ 1994 Institute for International Economics, with updated information from Nicholas Lardy (Brookings Institution) in 1999 and 2000.

NOTE: Imports are based on US Customs Service general customs value — the actual cost of the goods, excluding import duties, freight, insurance, and other charges.

2. Merchandise trade

The bilateral deficit falls further when trade in services is counted because the United States has enjoyed a small but growing surplus in trade in services with China for much of the past decade. US net services exports surged 52.5 percent in 2000, to reach $1.7 billion, more than triple the trade in services surplus with China in 1992. The US services trade surplus is likely to surge as China's World Trade Organization entry generates unprecedented opportunities for US service providers. Services, which already account for 70 percent of the US economy, will account for much of the future economic growth in the United States.

3. Imports from China are not direct substitutes for US-made goods

According to an Institute for International Economics study, 90 percent of US imports from China are substitutes for US imports from other low-wage economies, largely in East and Southeast Asia. Top US imports from China are low-tech electrical machinery, toys, footwear, and apparel. Only 10 percent of imports from China compete directly with US-made goods.

4. The relocation[13] of Asian production facilities affects the US deficit

PRC trade and investment reforms initiated in the late 1970s made China a more attractive place for foreign investment than neighboring economies such as South Korea. Multinationals thus relocated many of their processing ventures to China, and the bilateral trade deficit with Singapore, and South Korea, declined while the deficit with China climbed. Trends in 2000 – 2001 suggest that a second large-scale shift of production facilities from Japan to China is underway, in fields ranging from appliances to semiconductors. Such developments could further alter the composition of the US trade deficit with countries in the region.

Cases

British Airways — planning for the 21st century

British Airways(BA) have embarked on a major re-evaluation of their requirements for the first twenty years of this century, with a major appraisal of what their customers will require of them. In particular, they have concluded that for long-haul flights, which are increasing in popularity as prices come down and charter provision increases, that their passengers prefer the option of being able to move about the aircraft and have access to leisure and business facilities such as those found on the revamped Channel and North Sea ferries.

A review of mass transportation shows that in addition to major changes in on-board facilities on ferries to meet the challenge of the Channel Tunnel, there are also noticeable changes to rail services throughout Western Europe that aims to offer the same level of provision. BA, therefore, is reviewing these changes, by arguing that this will need a major rethinking of the whole concept of air travel. They have entered into negotiations with the major aircraft manufacturers to come up with a proposal that could incorporate the following features:

- 600 seat capacity aircraft;
- 3 decks — 1 for seats for take off and landing, 1 for a bar and leisure area, 1 for storing of luggage and a business services area;
- quieter and more fuel-efficient aircraft;
- pollution effects to be radically reduced, particularly the ozone effect;
- to provide meals in ways similar to ferries;
- the aircraft to have the ability to use existing airports, i. e. they are to be no longer or their wingspan wider than the existing 747s;
- passenger windows to be replaced by a continuous strip of TV monitors, providing an all round view;
- Each seat to have its own flat screen, providing TV / video games and a stereo system;
- Each jet should have the capacity to reach Singapore, Australia, etc. , without stopovers;
- Total worldwide demand for the new aircraft would be 75, with BA taking up to 15.

These specifications may appear to be asking far too much, but they offer a major challenge to the aircraft manufacturers and also offer a unique insight into the way future aircraft development may take place. Instead of the developments taking place around the product, i. e. the aircraft, they are now based around customer requirements and the needs of the service providers to cater for them.

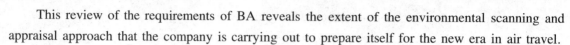

This review of the requirements of BA reveals the extent of the environmental scanning and appraisal approach that the company is carrying out to prepare itself for the new era in air travel.

TASKS

（1）What environmental changes other than those specified would have encouraged BA to come up with its radical proposals?

（2）If the proposals are accepted, what long-term influences would they have on aircraft manufacturers?

Key Terms

the international marketing environment　国际营销环境

the international economic system　国际经济体系

trade practice　贸易惯例

non-tariff barrier　非关税壁垒

exclusion deal　专营

the World Bank　世界银行

the World Trade Organization　世贸组织

exchange system　汇率体系

foreign exchange　外汇

international finance　国际金融

soft currency　软通货

hard currency　硬通货

foreign exchange market　外汇市场

the International Development Association　国际开发协会

the International Finance Corporation　国际金融组织

the International Monetary Fund　国际货币基金会

international trade　国际贸易

balance of trade　贸易差额，国际贸易平衡

trade deficit　贸易赤字

trade surpluse　贸易过剩

free-alongside-ship（FAS）　船边交货

cost, insurance, and freight（CIF）　到岸价格

Notes

1. practitioner　*n.*　从业者，开业者

2. depreciate   *v.*   使贬值，降低

3. macroeconomics   *n.*   宏观经济学

4. bloc   *n.*   组织，集团

5. liquidity   *n.*   流动性，流畅

6. Lomè   the capital city of Togo in Africa

7. influx   *n.*   流入

8. advent   *n.*   到来

9. impetus   *n.*   推动力，促进

10. ASEAN   东南亚国家联盟（简称东盟）

11. viability   *n.*   生存能力

12. barometer   *n.*   气压计，晴雨表

13. relocation   *n.*   再布置，变换布置

✍ Exercises

I. Multiple choices.

1. Which of the following organizations works for a system of foreign exchange?

   A. International Development Association.

   B. World Trade Organization.

   C. International Monetary Fund.

   D. Asian Pacific Economic Cooperation.

   E. European Union.

2. Which of the following is NOT one the largest industry in the United States?

   A. Dentistry.   B. Manufacturing.   C. Import-export trade.

   D. Tourism.   E. Agriculture.

3. If a company is getting started for the first time in exporting, the questions should be answered except _____.

   A. who buys our product?

   B. what need of function does our product serve?

   C. how to improve the volume of our product selling?

   D. when is our product purchased?

   E. why is our product purchased?

4. Changes in exchange rates _____.

   A. occur very infrequently, if at all

   B. routinely reinforce the strength of the US dollar

C. have little impact on international marketing efforts

    D. encourage travel abroad

    E. complicate the exchange of one nation's currency for another's

5. The reason for the difficulty in forecasting foreign exchange rates is _____.

    A. there are a multitude of factors and forces to determine rates, which are not quantifiable

    B. exchange system is complicated

    C. foreign exchange rates are mainly affected by inflation

    D. we don't know how to adjust to offset price level difference

    E. economic analysis is hard to make

6. There are economic factors influencing currency value in foreign exchange markets except _____.

    A. balance of payments

    B. expectations and opinions of analysts, traders, bankers, economists, and businesspeople

    C. foreign exchange reserves

    D. importance of currency in world finance and trade

    E. domestic inflation

7. This agreement among the United States, Canada, and Mexico removes trade restrictions among them over a period of 14 years. It is called _____.

    A. GATT   B. MERCOSUR   C. The EU   D. NAFTA

    E. SOMEPAN

8. Exporting occurs when a firm _____.

    A. makes a continuous effort to market its products to customers abroad

    B. permits a foreign company to produce and distribute its products

    C. shares the risks, costs, and management of its foreign operation with partners who are nationals of the foreign country

    D. maintains a separate marketing or selling operation in a foreign country

    E. acquires an existing firm in a foreign country

9. A company that buys products from domestic producers and resells them abroad, representing one of several alternative means of accessing foreign customers, is an _____.

    A. export management company   B. export trading company

    C. export assistance corporation   D. export facilitation organization

    E. export title company

10. Manufacturing or marketing facilities owned by a domestic firm but located in a foreign country are called _____.

A. foreign ventures

B. international direct investments

C. regular investments

D. joint investments

E. global ventures

II. True or false.

1. Soft currencies can readily be exchanged for other currencies, while hard currencies are not so easily exchanged.

2. Foreign licensing grants foreign marketers the right to use a domestic company's trademark, patent, or process in a specified geographic area.

3. A multinational corporation is a firm that has entered the international marketplace by exporting its products to a foreign market.

4. Though the first multinational corporations were US based, today it is as likely for a multinational to be Japanese, German, or British as to be American.

5. If it is believed that tastes are sufficiently homogeneous in different parts of the world to allow a standard marketing strategy everywhere, then a global marketing strategy is appropriate.

6. Use of a straight extension marketing strategy usually results in economies of scale in production and marketing.

7. In a countertrade, goods and services from one country are exchanged for goods and services from another instead of for cash.

8. Some marketing exchanges are still characterized by transaction-based marketing, such as residential real estate sales.

9. Traditionally, manufacturers have focused their energies on making products and then promoting those products to customers in hopes of selling enough of those products to cover costs and earn a profit.

10. Often, the desirability of partnering in the business market is based upon the fact that each firm brings to the partnership something that the other needs but cannot provide.

III. Discussion.

In what way has the global economy changed in the last 50 years? Why?

Chapter Four

The Role of Governments

政府的作用

◁ Objectives 学习目标

When students finish this chapter, they should be able to accomplish the following:

☑ To outline trade barriers in researching a new foreign market

☑ To explain how governments influence marketing

☑ To list some key trade organizations in the world

☑ To describe the trade risks existing in marketing

4.1 Trade Barriers 贸易壁垒

Yesterday's competitive market battles were fought in Western Europe, Japan, and the United States; tomorrow's competitive battles will extend to Latin America, Eastern Europe, Russia, India, Asia, and Africa as these emerging markets open to trade. More of the world's people, from the richest to the poorest, will participate in the world's wealth through global trade. The emerging global economy in which we live brings us into worldwide competition, with significant advantages for both marketers and consumers. Marketers benefit from new markets' opening and smaller markets' growing large enough to become viable business opportunities. Consumers benefit by being able to select from the widest range of goods produced anywhere in the world at the lowest prices.

Bound together by satellite communications and global companies, consumers in every corner of the world are demanding an ever-expanding variety of goods. World trade is an important economic activity. Because of this importance, the inclination is for countries to control international trade to their own advantage. As competition intensifies, the tendency toward protectionism gains momentum. [1] If the benefits of the social, political, and economic changes now taking place are to be fully realized, free trade must prevail throughout the global marketplace. The creation of the World Trade Organization is one of the biggest victories for free trade in decades. This chapter includes a discussion of the major impediment to trade followed by a review of the General Agreement on Tariffs and Trade and its successor, the World Trade Organization — two multinational agreements designed to advance free trade together with other trade organizations.

4.1.1   Trade barriers: an international marketer's minefield
贸易壁垒: 国际市场营销者的布雷区

The host government of your target market can throw up a vast number of roadblocks to your success. Here listed are some obstructions formulated by government that a marketer should look out for when researching a new foreign market.

1. Tariffs

Import tariffs are the means by which a government controls the in-flow of foreign goods across its borders.

2. Inspections

As for the case with foodstuffs, medical equipment, farm animals, etc., some inspections are performed by certain governmental organizations. It is the government's right and duty to protect its citizens' health and welfare in the form of inspections.

3. Import licensing

Like inspections, import licensing is a legitimate function of government, whereby the product must be formally licensed by the importer's government and a fee paid by the importer. Where inspections control the product quality, licensing is used to control both involved sides of the transaction.

4. Environmental controls

Governments are protecting the environment within their borders. Restrictions on packaging (amount, size, recyclability), product content labeling (chemical proportions), and pollution controls can be placed on foreign exporters before licensing will be granted.

5. Technology transfers

Most developing markets insist on technology transfers if a product is to be sold within their national boundaries. It's a way to catch up with competitors without expensive research or investment. That is why a target company insists that joint venture, product importation or manufacture under license with a foreign marketer must ultimately involve a transfer of technology (physical, process design, managerial, etc.).

6. Customs delays

Even once a product is licensed, it can be held at customs without a stated cause for extended periods. Things such as software, music CDs, and videos are usually a target of this practice. They are delayed by customs for various purposes to protect local markets.

7. Quotas

An import quota is a non-tariff barrier imposed by a government to restrict the quantity of imports; it will take from certain national markets or exporters. This process can also be used to protect local producers from foreign trading practice or as a punishment for political problems between rival powers. The strictest form of trade quota is an embargo, which disallows entry of specified products into a country.

8. Anti-dumping laws

These laws were instituted to prevent foreigners from selling products at extremely low prices into a market (this is called dumping) to drive out competition. Only countries with sophisticated[2] commercial law can use this type of legislation[3].

4.1.2　Trade intervention　贸易干涉

In recent years, Indonesia has liberalized its trade regime[4] and taken a number of important steps to reduce protection. Since 1996, the Indonesian government has issued deregulation packages that have reduced overall tariff levels, simplified the tariff structure, removed restrictions, replaced non-tariff barriers with more transparent tariffs, and encouraged foreign and domestic private investment. The government of Indonesia issued a deregulation package in July 1997, which introduced additional tariff reductions. In conjunction with its stabilization program agreement with the International Monetary Fund, the government has issued a steady stream of reform measures which reduced taxes, tariffs, and quantitative restrictions[5] on exports and imports.

1. Arguments — intervention possibilities of agricultural policy

What can be done to keep China's agricultural policy on its current path of economic and political reform? In particular, what can be done to promote policies that will increase China's future food security?

In politics, it always makes sense to clearly identify the interests involved. China obviously has a vital interest in continued economic development and social stability. Large-scale food crises would threaten these objectives. Therefore, food security has top priority on the political agenda of China's leaders. On the other hand, the developed worlds, especially the large agricultural producers, have an interest in getting more open access to the Chinese market for their products. For example, the USA would probably like to increase agricultural exports to China to reduce its huge trade deficit.

In the food sector, in particular, these interests are compatible. If China were to open its grain market to the outside world, both sides could win. It is certainly more efficient for China to use its limited resources of arable land and water for the production of high-value agricultural products such as vegetables or fruits, which are labor intensive but require less land. On the other hand, China should consider importing a larger share of land-extensive agricultural products such as grain, oilseed and feed crops from foreign suppliers. For example, the USA, Australia, and Thailand have abundant land for cost-efficient production of grain, which could be shipped to China's southern coastal provinces at low prices. Currently, the Chinese government's insistence on self-sufficiency in grain stands in the way of such a rational economic choice. However, in the long run the policy might change if China's leaders calculate the costs of continuously pressing the farmers to step up domestic grain production. Within the next 20 years, China will need to increase annual grain supply by between 130 and 220 million tons, depending on the scenario considered. With grain imports in the range of 40 – 60 million tons, which could be easily provided by the world grain market, this task could be achieved much more easily and at considerably lower costs than by domestic production alone.

From the perspective of the developed countries, it also makes sense to promote China's integration into the global economy and the World Trade Organization. This would not only intensify China's economic, cultural, and social relationships with the outside world (which is good in itself) and open up its potentially huge undeveloped market (which is good for business), but it would also positively affect the formulation of internal economic policies in China. China's further integration into the world market would strengthen its market orientation in all sectors of the domestic economy, including agriculture.

4.1.3   Intervention by the government   官方干预

1. Embargo

Embargoes have a disastrous effect on exporters, although we are still doubtful whether embargoes accomplish their political goals. Marketers must be aware of the political environment they work in and be prepared to calculate, as well as manage risk.

2. National security issues

Some goods such as nuclear materials, strategic minerals, chemicals, computer chips, technical manuals, or military surplus, are considered too strategic militarily and economically to be freely marketed to other nations, regardless of the profit potential. Countries have restrictions to delineate[6] them quite clearly.

3. Export tariffs

Governments tax exports primarily as a source of revenue and use the process as a means of promoting or punishing particular industries. Export tariffs can be used to control flow and businesses.

4. Export licensing

Export licensing is a flow control just like export tariffs. It is often used as a means of denying a rival economy access to both raw and finished products without instituting a full embargo.

4.1.4 Unofficial intervention   非官方干预

1. Public relations

Public relations play an important role in marketing. From poor translated brand names to the lack of locally hired management personnel, bad public relations can sidetrack[7] the best of products.

2. Nationalism

This barrier once was used to restrict Australian wines in France, British movies in Argentina, and major Japanese products in the US during the 1980s. Competitors, host government officials and political activists cry out that the marketing efforts are bad for the nation. It is a very powerful force, it will threaten the product's continued survival or strength, and what's more, it is difficult to control.

3. Religion

Religion plays a greater factor in business every year, with much of it centering around Islamic beliefs regarding profit taking and interest rates. Because religion carries such an emotional impact, pure reasoning and factual presentation will do little to get the product back on track.

4. Ethnic problems

Ethnic conflicts that are centuries old still burn hot. Belief that the product is ethnically dangerous or inferior can stymie[8] your marketing efforts whether the accusations are true or not. Overcoming ethnic stereotypes[9] takes years of work and enormous amounts of money.

5. Society

Since some societies have a structure not to accept certain products, marketers must often approach a market several times before they are permitted to entry. Some industries are bound by edict[10] not to promote foreign products.

6. Education

The educational level of large sectors of the target market's population sometimes is the greatest informal barrier. Training must be part of the marketing plan when educational levels are key to a product's acceptance.

7. Environment

If the product has any potential ill effect on the environment, marketers can expect major market resistance, even without restrictive legislation, once such effects are brought to light. Environmental action groups enlist anyone they can in their effort and are unabashed[11] when it comes to emotionalizing an issue.

8. Science

Product lines that are radically innovative may have a difficult time overcoming the skepticism[12] of the target market. When entering foreign markets, medicines, business software, securities and so on will suffer intense scrutiny[13]. It's best to assemble the proof beforehand and tailor its delivery to the target market.

4.2 Trade Organizations 贸易组织

4.2.1 The regional trade organizations 地区贸易组织

1. GATT (The General Agreement on Tariffs & Trade)

GATT is a binding contract between membership-governments whose objective is to promote trade among members. GATT members include developing nations, all of the Organization for Economic Cooperation and Development (abbr. OECD), central and eastern European countries, plus 29 observer countries. The GATT preamble (1947) states that "trade and economic endeavor should be conducted with a view to raising standards of living, ensuring full employment and a large and steadily growing volume of real income." These basic objectives were reinforced in the Marrakesh Agreement, which established the WTO. Historically, GATT enforced phased-in tariff reductions worldwide. Until the Uruguay Round, which ended in 1994, the trade negotiations focused on nonagricultural goods, mainly because the US wanted to protect its farm sector. Over the years, as the corporate interests if the developed countries have expanded, these countries have also lobbied for more issues to be incorporated into the GATT / WTO. Its agenda now includes agriculture, services(financial, telecommunications, information technology, etc.), intellectual property rights, electronic commerce, and, possibly in the next round, investment, government procurement, and competition policy.

The main operating principle of GATT was the concept of most favored nations (MFN) / extend tariff reduction to all member states. GATT was successful in lowering trade barriers (developed countries' average tariff on manufactured goods dropped from 40% in 1948 to 4% in 1994).

2. APEC (Asian-Pacific Economic Cooperation)

APEC is the primary international organization for promoting open trade and economic cooperation among member "economies" around the Pacific Rim. In 1989 APEC forum was established and currently it has 21 members: Australia; Brunei Darussalam; Canada; Chile; People's Republic of China; Hong Kong, China; Indonesia; Japan; Republic of Korea; Malaysia; Mexico; New Zealand; Papua New Guinea; Peru; Republic of the Philippines; Russia; Singapore; Chinese Taipei; Thailand; USA; Vietnam.

APEC has become the single most important institution in the Asia Pacific region. APEC meeting every year brings top-level attention to APEC's vision of free trade and investment as well as providing a forum for Leaders to meet on a regular basis both as a group and bilaterally to discuss current issues and resolve disputes.

APEC remained a powerful trading group accounting for about half of the world exports and imports. APEC has played an important role in promoting trade and investment liberalization in the region. As a result of these efforts, APEC markets are considerably more open today than they were ten years ago.

APEC has also played a complementary role to the International Monetary Fund and other international financial institutions in fostering a rapid Asian economic recovery. APEC encourages its members to pursue appropriate macroeconomic policies that stimulate domestic demand, and microeconomic polices to promote financial and corporate restructuring and attract investment.

APEC is promoting increased transparency, openness and predictability based on the rule of law. APEC seeks to eliminate impediments to trade and investment by encouraging member economies to reduce barriers, adopt transparent, market-oriented policies and address such issues as unequal labor productivity, restricted mobility of business persons and outdated telecommunications regulatory practices.

APEC can serve a crucial role in advancing long-term projects and initiatives that will assist its members to reform their economies and implement the policy changes that will sustain the economic recovery. It also can help foster development of the physical and human capital necessary to sustain growth in the 21st century.

3. ASEAN (Association of South East Asian Nations)

ASEAN is an organization for economic, political, social, and cultural cooperation among its six member countries: Brunei, Indonesia, Malaysia, the Philippines, Singapore, and Thailand. ASEAN was established in 1967 with the signing of the Bangkok Declaration.

4. NAFTA (North American Free Trade Area)

In 1988 the United States signed a free trade agreement with Canada (US-Canada Free Trade Agreement or CFTA), which was enlarged in 1993 to include Mexico in a North American Free Trade Area (NAFTA). NAFTA created a free trade area and all three governments will promote economic growth through expanded trade and investment. The benefits of continental free trade will enable all three countries to meet the economic challenges of the decades to come.

5. OPEC (Organization of Petroleum Exporting Countries)

OPEC is an international Organization of eleven developing countries which are heavily reliant on oil revenues as their main source of income. The First Conference was held in Sep. 1960 to establish OPEC as a permanent intergovernmental organization. Membership is open to any country which is a substantial net exporter of oil and which shares the ideals of the Organization. The current Members are Algeria, Indonesia, Iran, Iraq, Kuwait, Libya, Nigeria, Qatar, Saudi Arabia, the United Arab Emirates and Venezuela.

Since oil revenues are so vital for the economic development of these nations, they aim to bring stability and harmony to the oil market by adjusting their oil output to help ensure a balance between supply and demand. Twice a year, or more frequently if required, the Oil and Energy Ministers of the OPEC Members meet to decide on the Organization's output level, and consider whether any action to adjust output is necessary in the light of recent and anticipated oil market developments.

OPEC's eleven members collectively supply about 40 per cent of the world's oil output, and possess more than three-quarters of the world's total proven crude oil reserves. More details can be found in the FAQ on OPEC, and in the sections on the individual Member Countries, which feature tables with selected oil, gas and economic data.

6. EU (The European Union)

EU (formerly known as the European Community) was established by the Treaty of Rome in January 1958. The six original members were Belgium, France, Holland, Italy, Luxembourg, and West Germany. Since the end of 1992, people have been able to move freely across national borders inside the EC. The EC has agreed to create a single European currency and bank. This is known as economic and monetary union (EMU). The member governments have also agreed in principle to a European political union.

On January, 2002, the euro coins and notes enter into circulation in the twelve participating Member States: Austria, Belgium, Finland, France, Germany, Greece, Ireland, Italy, Luxembourg, the Netherlands, Portugal and Spain. In February, The euro becomes the sole currency within the twelve participating Member States, as the period of dual circulation comes to an end. In October, the European Commission recommends the conclusion of accession negotiations by the end of the 2002 with the following 10 countries: Cyprus, the Czech Republic, Estonia, Hungary, Latvia, Lithuania, Malta, Poland, the Slovak Republic and Slovenia. The Commission considers that these countries will be ready for EU membership from the beginning of 2004.

On April, 2003, the Treaty of Accession between the EU and the Czech Republic, Estonia, Cyprus, Latvia, Lithuania, Hungary, Malta, Poland, Slovenia, and Slovakia is signed in Athens, Greece.

7. MERCOSUR (Southern Cone Common Market)

Argentina, Brazil, Paraguay, and Uruguay with a combined population of 198 million and a gross domestic product of \$513 billion agreed in March 1991 to form the Southern Cone Common Market(MERCOSUR) for goods, services, capital, and labor by 1995. The four nations plan to dismantle non-tariff barriers and implement a common external tariff. Their accord also commits them to pursue common trade, agriculture, transport, and communications policies.

In order to have a better understanding of the above organizations, please see Table 4-1.

Table 4-1   The Regional Trade Organizations

Names	Time	Aims	Members
GATT/WTO	1947/1995	Trade and economic endeavor should be conducted with a view to raising standards of living, ensuring full employment and a large and steadily growing volume of real income.	146 on 4th April, 2003
APEC	1989	To promote open trade and economic cooperation among member "economies" around the Pacific Rim.	21
ASEAN	1967	For economic, political, social, and cultural cooperation among its six member countries.	6
NAFTA	1988	To create a free trade area and promote economic growth through expanded trade and investment	3
OPEC	1960	To bring stability and harmony to the oil market by adjusting their oil output to help ensure a balance between supply and demand.	11

续表

Names	Time	Aims	Members
EU	1958	To create a single European currency and bank, and to form a European political union.	22 till 2004
MERCOSUR	1991	To dismantle non-tariff barriers and implement a common external tariff and pursue common trade, agriculture, transport, and communications policies.	4

4.2.2   The WTO（World Trade Organization） 世贸组织

The WTO replaced the GATT in 1995. On January 1, 1995, the WTO established on the basis of the document signed before the conclusion or the Uruguay Round by the ministers of 97 countries formally started its operation and began its administrative work, taking over all the unfinished work left by GATT and continuing to carry out the agreements reached during the Uruguay Round. Till Feb. 1999, WTO has 134 members. It is the organization's objective to work towards the realization of full employment, expansion or production and trade as well as the optimal use of the resources of the world so as to raise the income level and standard of living of its member countries. The new organization engaged for the first time in negotiation and supervision of the service trade. It has an important role to play in settlement of trade disputes and supervision of the implementation of trade policies and measures. The WTO aims at facilitating the creation of an optimal environment for international trade amongst nations to flourish and further strengthen the multilateral trading system.

Compared to GATT, the WTO is much more powerful because of its institutional foundation and its dispute settlement system. Countries that do not abide by its trade rules are taken to court and can eventually face retaliation. Being a new, improved replacement of GATT, the WTO is a permanent international organization to which all the members of GATT have automatically become members.

China officially joined the WTO on 11th December, 2001. This entitled China to enjoy low trade tariffs and seek equal treatment among association members, and would give Chinese companies more chances to expand their international markets.

4.2.3   Types of regional economic arrangements 地区贸易分类

1. Free trade areas

Formal agreement among two or more countries to reduce or eliminate customs duties and non-tariff barriers / no common external tariff.

2. Customs union

Addition of common external tariffs to the provisions of free trade agreements.

3. Common market

Elimination of all tariffs and other barriers, adopts a common set of external tariffs on nonmembers, and removal of all restrictions on the flow of capital and labor among member nations.

4. Monetary union

Represents the fourth level of integration with a single currency among politically independent countries.

5. Political union

Highest level of integration resulting into a political union. Sometimes, countries come together in a loose political union for historical reasons, as in the case of British Commonwealth which exists as a forum for discussion and common historical ties.

Examples：

Free trade area — North American Free Trade Agreement；

Customs union — ASEAN (Association of Southeast Asian Nations)；

Common market — MERCOSUR (Southern Cone Free Trade Area) by 2005；

Monetary union — European Union.

4.2.4 The trade risks 贸易风险

Marketing abroad can be a very risky pursuit as the legal landscape in some countries is extremely fluid. Laws are sometimes unmodified and even when they are, interpretation can be arbitrary. The trade risks exist as follows：

1. Taxation

Governments of all size and economic standings view business as a source of tax revenue. Taxation allows the government to receive a portion of a foreign company's operation directly. Some authorities lure foreign business with initially low tax rates, with the full intention that once the company has been committed and is operating successfully, tax rates will soar almost to the point of being confiscator. There are no universal international laws governing the levy of taxes on companies that do business across national boundaries. However, the taxation polices of the home and host nations can have both negative and positive effects on a company.

2. Expropriation

Expropriation refers to governmental action to dispossess a company or investor of property, for which compensation is provided. Governments will take over a foreign company outright during periods of extreme political stress or due to inordinate levels of greed. Expropriation occurs quite regularly in war-torn countries under extreme political stress, the cause of inordinate levels of greed has rarely been seen since the early 1980s and has been usurped by the somewhat more subtle domestication. The total expropriation loss to companies during last century is trivial compared with the total amount of foreign direct investment and is concentrated entirely outside of the high-income countries.

3. Sponsored competition

Sponsored competition puts a favored local company or person under a government protection. These sponsorships are further aided by technology transfers that were mandated by the government as part of allowing the foreign company to operate within its borders.

4. Bribery

Government officials seeking bribes from foreign firms are a worldwide problem. It can take various forms. Bribery in some economies becomes the grease that makes the wheels of commerce turn more easily. The fact of bribery in world markets will not change; anyone engaged in international marketing must be prepared to deal with different briberies. What should you do if you are unwilling to offer a bribe and your competitors are willing? Two approaches may be employed. One is to ignore bribery and act as if it does not exist. The other is to recognize the existence of bribery and evaluate its effect on the purchase decision as if it were just another element of the marketing mix.

Cases

Case 1.   Indonesia's tariff

Indonesia's tariff regime is in rapid flux, with accelerated tariff reductions included in many of the reform measures put into place. Indonesia's applied tariff rates range from 5 to 30 percent. Major exceptions to this range are the 170 percent duty applied to all imported distilled spirits and the 125 percent duty assessed to build up passenger vehicles (subject also to a 75 percent import surcharge). In May 1995, the Indonesian government unveiled a comprehensive tariff reduction package covering roughly two thirds of all traded goods, designed to reduce most tariffs to under 5 percent by 2003. All tariff items with a rate of 20 percent or less are to be reduced to no greater than 5 percent by 2000 while items with rates of more than 20 percent are to be brought to no more than 10 percent by 2003. Tariffs on all food items were cut to a maximum of 5 percent in February, 1998.

Services trade barriers to entry continue to exist in many sectors, although the Government of Indonesia has loosened restrictions significantly in the financial sector. Foreign law firms, accounting firms, and consulting engineers must operate through technical assistance or joint venture arrangements with local firms.

Indonesia is liberalizing its distribution system, a trend which is likely to accelerate as it implements the IMF package which includes an end to restrictions on trade in the domestic market. For example, restrictive marketing arrangements for cement, paper, cloves, other spices, and plywood were eliminated in February, 1998. Indonesia opened wholesale and retail trade to foreign investment, lifting most restrictions in March, 1998.

Case 2. China subject to most restriction by US trade barriers

Media reported that the EU stopped importing China's honey in excuse of excessive antibiotic in it. Currently Japan, Canada and the United States also have intensified checks on China's honey.

China's agricultural and animal products have been plagued by "green trade barriers" since the country entered into the WTO. In January, 2002 Zhejiang Zhoushan's frozen shrimp meat was returned by the European countries; that February the export of bulk agricultural products, like frozen chicken, peanut and vegetable in Shandong province, dropped sharply; in the first five months of that year, China's animal and sea food products were not allowed to export to Europe. The negative effects exerted by the green trade barriers are as follows. First, more kinds of agriculture products are restricted by the barriers, which range from honey to frozen chicken and extend to the whole livestock and sea food products. Second, the countries which set up the barriers to China are expanding from developed countries such as the EU, the US and Japan to some developing ones like the ROK and Singapore. Third, China becomes the country subjected to the most restriction by the US barriers. From this January to May, the United States had detained 12,025 batches of products, of which 1,140 belong to China, accounting for 9.47 percent of the total. Fourth, the items for check on China's agricultural and livestock products are increasing. The check items of China's tea by the EU have been up to 62 from the previous 6. Fifth, the green trade barriers have adversely effected the exports from the country's well-developed provinces and cities. China's 896 batches of products were detained by America from this January to March, 78.6 percent of China's total products detained. Sixth, the incessant barriers imposed on the above-mentioned Chinese products will probably give rise to proliferation and chain effects.

By PD Online Staff Yang Ruoqian

People's Daily Online — http://english.peopledaily.com.cn/

Case 3.   The trade disputes between US and Japan

We all know the story about the trade disputes between US and Japan. Japan has so many trade barriers and high tariffs that US manufacturers are unable to sell in Japan as much as Japanese companies sell in the United States. For example, the Japanese claim that "unique" Japanese snow requires skis made in Japan, and that US baseballs are not good enough for Japanese baseball. Even when Japan opened their rice market, the popular California rice had to be mixed and sold with inferior grades of Japanese rice. However, the Japanese are not alone; it seems every country takes advantage of the open US market while putting barriers in the way of US exports. The French, for example, protect their film and broadcast industry from foreign competition by limiting the number of American shows that can appear on television, the percentage of American songs broadcast on radio, and the proportion of US movies that can be shown in French theaters. The French also protect small retailers by disallowing any retailers (Amazon or Carretown) to advertise on TV. Not only do these barriers and high tariffs limit how much US companies can sell, but they also raise prices for imported products much higher than they sell for in the United States.

Consider the fiscal hazards[14] facing international marketing managers at a company like Neutrogena that is contemplating exporting its products to Russia. Upon arrival there, the firm's products might be classified by Russian customs officers into any one of three separate categories for the purposes of assigning tariffs: pharmaceuticals[15] at a 5 percent duty, soap at 15 percent, or cosmetics at 20 percent. Of course, Neutrogena managers would argue for the lowest tariff by pointing out that their hypoallergenic[16] soaps are recommended by dermatologists[17]. And, as long as shipments remain relatively small, the customs officers might not argue. However, as exports to Russia grow from cartons to container loads, the product classification receives more scrutiny. Simple statements on packaging, such as "Pure Neutrogena skin and hair care products are available at drug stores and cosmetic counters.", would give the Russians reason to claim the highest duty of 20 percent. Barriers to trade, both tariff and non-tariff, are one of the major issues confronting international marketers. Fortunately, tariffs generally have been reduced to record lows, and substantial progress has been made on eliminating non-tariff barriers. However, nations continue to use trade barriers for a variety of reasons, some rational and some not so rational.

📖 Key Terms

trade barrier   贸易壁垒
import tariff   进口税
import licensing   进口许可证

technology transfer　技术转让

quota　配额

anti-dumping　反倾销

trade intervention　贸易干预

embargo　禁运

military surplus　军事转让

unofficial intervention　非官方干预

public relations　公共关系

nationalism　民族主义

ethnic conflict　种族冲突

regional trade organization　地区贸易组织

the Organization for Economic Cooperation and Development（OECD）经济合作与发展组织

Asian-Pacific Economic Cooperation（APEC）　亚太经济合作组织

Association of South East Asian Nations（ASEAN）　东南亚国家联盟（简称东盟）

North American Free Trade Area（NAFTA）　北美自由贸易区

Organization of Petroleum Exporting Countries（OPEC）　欧佩克，石油输出国家组织

the European Union（EU）　欧盟

World Trade Organization（WTO）　世贸组织

free trade area　自由贸易区

customs union　关税联盟

common market　共同市场

monetary union　货币联盟

trade risk　贸易风险

taxation　征税

expropriation　征收

bribery　贿赂

Notes

1. As competition intensifies, the tendency toward protectionism gains momentum.　随着竞争的强化，保护主义倾向获得前进的动力。
2. sophisticated　*a.*　老练的，久经世故的
3. type of legislation　立法形式
4. regime　*n.*　政体，政权，政权制度
5. quantitative restriction　定量限制

6. delineate   *v.*   描绘

7. sidetrack   *vt.*   导入；使受牵制

8. stymie   *v.*   从中作梗，完全妨碍

9. stereotype   *n.*   陈腔滥调，老套

10. edict   *n.*   布告，法令

11. unabashed   *a.*   不害羞的

12. skepticism   *n.*   怀疑论

13. intense scrutiny   详细调查

14. fiscal hazard   财政危机

15. pharmaceutical   *n.*   药物

16. hypoallergenic   *a.*   ［医］低变应原的

17. dermatologist   *n.*   皮肤学者，皮肤科医生

✍ Exercises

I. Multiple choices.

1. If IBM was concerned about the interest rate it must pay in the next quarter to acquire needed financial resources, this concern would involve _____ .

   A. a marketing environment input   B. its marketing mix

   C. its marketing approach   D. a marketing environment output

2. Many marketers view political forces as _____ .

   A. easily ignored   B. easily influenced

   C. simple to recognize   D. beyond their control

3. Which one of the following statements about self-regulatory programs is FALSE?

   A. They are usually less expensive than governmental ones.

   B. Their guidelines are generally more realistic and operational.

   C. Non-governmental ones have neither the tools nor the authority to enforce guidelines.

   D. The guidelines are generally stricter than governmental ones.

4. If the Kellogg Company decides to build a new cereal plant because that it anticipates the next five years will bring low unemployment and increases in buying power, it is forecasting a period of _____ .

   A. depression   B. prosperity   C. recovery   D. austerity

   E. recession

5. Why are marketers interested in the level of disposable income?

   A. It accurately represents future buying power.

  B. It increases current buying power.

  C. It is what is left after taxes to buy luxuries with.

  D. It is a ready source of buying power.

  E. It is essential for forecasting future business trends.

6. What type of competitive structure exists when a firm produces a product that has no close substitutes?

  A. Monopoly.   B. Oligopoly.   C. Monopolistic competition.

  D. Perfect competition.   E. Mixed competition.

7. Protective tariffs are used by countries to _____.

  A. raise the retail price of imported products to match or exceed that of similar domestic products

  B. raise revenue for the country of origin of foreign products

  C. counter the effects of revenue tariffs on the domestic market

  D. stabilize the prices of imported goods

  E. ban sales of certain types of imported products

8. A trade restriction that limits the number of units of certain goods that can enter a country is known as _____.

  A. an embargo   B. a trade limit   C. an import quota

  D. an exchange limit   E. a trade ligature

9. Compaq Computers collects information about political, legal, regulatory, societal, economic, competitive and technological forces that may affect its marketing activities. This process is called _____.

  A. environmental scanning   B. survey of environment

  C. marketing information analysis   D. environmental analysis

10. The period in the business cycle in which there is extremely high unemployment, low wages, minimum total disposable income, and a lack of confidence in the economy by consumers is _____.

  A. recovery   B. prosperity   C. depression   D. recession

  E. growth

II. True or false.

1. US firms operating in the international marketplace are clearly affected by a legal environment including US laws, international laws, and laws of the host country.

2. Government regulations that tax or otherwise set limits on the number of goods and

services by foreign producers are known as trade barriers.

3. A free trade area extends a customs union by seeking to reconcile all government regulations affecting trade.

4. Trade officials are in full agreement as to the direction the WTO should follow in pursuing its major policy initiatives.

5. Foreign licensing can build revenues without the capital outlay required for establishment of manufacturing facilities in a foreign country.

6. The trend toward increased foreign ownership of assets in the United States will probably decline because of the increased hostility toward and government regulation of foreign-owned businesses operating in the United States.

7. Income left over after an individual pays taxes and purchases the basic necessities of food, clothing and shelter is called disposable income.

8. A comprehensive spending pattern shows the percentages of annual family expenditures allotted to general classes of goods and services.

9. Import tariffs are the means by which a government controls the in-flow of foreign goods across its borders.

10. Although WTO is a global institutional proponent of free trade, it is not without critics.

III. Discussion.

1. Describe the major tariff / duties and non tariff barriers which can be used in international trade as barriers to entry. Give examples.

2. List some different forms of govermental intervention and unofficial intervention, and try to get examples to illustrate.

Chapter Five

The Role of Culture

文化的作用

📢 Objectives 学习目标

When students finish this chapter, they should be able to accomplish the following:

☑ To list the important factors of culture in marketing

☑ To explain how religions affect marketing

☑ To list ways in which education affects marketers

☑ To identify the roles of social institutions and political life

☑ To describe the effect of weather condition in marketing

5.1 Language and Local Customs 语言与当地风俗

Culture is a system of learned, shared, unifying, and interrelated beliefs, values, and assumptions. Successful international trade is dependent upon learning about and appreciating other cultures.

Low-context cultures communicate very directly. They value words and interpret them literally. Germany and the United States are countries which have low-context cultures. High-context cultures communicate indirectly and place little value to the literal meanings of words. Japan and Iraq are two examples of countries with high-context cultures. Low-context cultures have people who are not concerned about embarrassment; whereas, high-context cultures believe embarrassment must be avoided at all costs or jeopardize[1] your business relationship. Intention is much more important than what is actually done in Iraq.

Cultural differences necessitate adjustments to other cultures. Ethnocentrism[2] believes that one's culture is better than other cultures. This becomes a major obstacle to conducting international business. Cross-cultural experiences are very important. Culture shock (happiness, frustration, adaptation, and acceptance) is common when people experience different cultures. Reverse culture shock happens when a person comes back to their original culture after living in a foreign culture. Success in business depends upon cultural sensitivity and a willingness to make the appropriate accommodations[3].

Characteristics of culture: 1) It is not innate, but learned; 2) The various facets of culture are interrelated — touch a culture in one place and everything else is affected; 3) It is shared by the members of a group and defines the boundaries between different groups.

Main elements of culture are language, social norms, religion, ethics, socio economics, mores, traditions, societal regulations, nationalism, aesthetics, material culture, attitudes, values, social organization.

5.1.1   Language   语言

Language is a central element in culture and communication. It may pose a barrier if its use obscures meaning and distorts intent.

English is the language of international business; however, Mandarin (Chinese) is the language spoken by the most people in the world. English is precise and concise and it has a large number of business-related words. Language represents the highest form of a group's culture. People prefer to transact business in their native language. There are many useful business languages to learn; the language you choose to learn depends on where you plan to conduct the most international business.

The ability to communicate in one's language is not an easy task. Whenever languages change, there is an additional communications challenge. This is especially so when the language and the culture are different. For example, "yes" and "no" are used in an entirely different way in some Asian languages than in western languages. This has caused much confusion and misunderstanding. In English, if the answer to a question is affirmative, you say "yes"; if the answer is negative, you say "no". In Japanese or Chinese, this is not so. For example, in Chinese if you were asked, "Don't you like Hamburg?" you would answer "yes"; if your answer is negative, you might say, "Yes, I don't like Hamburg."

A country's language is the part of its culture. If a person is to work extensively with another culture, it is imperative to learn the language. As representatives or agents of companies, they must understand the language when they want to communicate with political leaders, employees, and customers. In a real sense, a language defines a culture; thus, if a country has several spoken languages, it has several cultures.

Language reflects the nature and values of society as well. There may be many sub-cultural languages like dialects which may have to be accounted for. Some countries have two or three languages. Belgium has two national languages, French in the South and Flemish in the North. There are political and social differences between the two language groups. Canada is also a country with two formal languages — English and French. In Hungary, it is common for citizens to learn two or three languages — Hungarian, French and German. Singapore has two official languages — Chinese and English. In Zimbabwe[4] there are three languages — English, Shona and Ndebele with numerous dialects. Many African and Asian nations have a far larger number of languages and cultural groups. Language can cause communication problems — especially in the use of media or written material. It is best to learn the language or engage someone who understands it well. So, marketing explorers must understand the importance of language in developing markets internationally.

5.1.2 Local customs and religions   当地风俗和宗教

1. Local customs

Local customs are both interesting to learn from and important to respect for a marketer. They mostly pertain to preparation of food or codes of dress. Many places of worship will require that people should not wear shorts or off the shoulder tops; in some cases head coverings may be expected or the removal of shoes before entry. Some restaurants will not serve certain meats or combinations of food. The consumption of alcohol may also be forbidden or restricted. Law in general may be less lenient so care to avoid antisocial behavior is well advised. Particularly in Islamic countries some matters considered to be of a personal nature in Britain, especially in regard of sexual morality, are legislated against and the rulings enforced on visitors as well as citizens.

1) Appointment in Hong Kong

Appointments are mandatory, therefore arrange prior to arrival. Confirm and reconfirm appointment times. The fast pace of Hong Kong may result in a last minute change; this is usually delivered via fax or phone. Do have your cards translated on one side into Chinese (gold ink is considered most prestigious for Chinese characters). "Accepting" compliments is an acquired skill. To say "thank you" is often considered immodest. The best response if you are complimented is to politely deny or dismiss the compliment, and move onto another subject. Do not change negotiation team members during the negotiations — despite how long it may take, keep the same team. This will help build the relationship and move closer towards the deal. Be prepared to "reserve" some position as you may find that near the end of negotiations the Chinese negotiating team may suggest a compromise which translates to a large discount.

2) Tipping in USA

Tipping is mandatory in all cities of the United States. For restaurants, a 15% tip is sufficient although 20% may be needed for fine dining restaurants. No tipping is required in fast food outlets. Hotel porters will appreciate a $1 gratuity per piece of luggage and housekeeping likewise. Taxi drivers expect a tip of 10% – 15% of the fare.

3) Gift giving (Malaysia)

(1) General guidelines

Gifts may be perceived as a bribe, if you have not already established a relationship with the recipient. There are strong laws against bribery in Malaysia. Be cautious not to be too generous with gifts, and to only give gifts to people you have established relationships with. There is a cultural belief that the giver and recipient may be embarrassed if the gift turns out to be a poor choice; therefore, gifts should be put aside and opened when alone. This allows both the giver and recipient to "save face." A gift should be received in both hands, palms facing upwards. However, you give gifts with your right hand. When invited to someone's home, present a small practical gift shortly before departing, not when arriving.

(2) Acceptable gifts to give

Quality pens , desk accessories, items representative of your country or city. Gifts of food are acceptable, but not at dinner parties or other occasions where appetizers and meals will be served. Lollies, sweets, candy and fruit baskets are appreciated as thank-you gifts sent after these events.

(3) Gifts to avoid

Do not give Muslim gifts of alcohol, pork, personal items such as lingerie, anything that has pictures of dogs, anything that has images of nude women (even if depicted with artistic merit).

Do not give Chinese gifts of clocks, handkerchiefs, towels, or anything that predominantly has the colors white, black or blue. These symbols and color are representative of death, mourning and endings. Be sensitive that observant Hindus do not eat beef or use cattle products. Therefore, leather products of any kind (including belts and purses) should not be considered as a gift.

4) Doing deals (Singapore)

Confrontations are avoided in Singapore; for example, you will not get a direct answer of "no". A "yes" that sounds hesitant or weak usually means "no". Yes does not mean yes, maybe probably means no. An avoidance of answering your question may indicate a no. Schedule smaller meetings afterwards to confirm that agreement has been reached. Smiling is often used to mask real feelings, e. g. embarrassment, anger, loss of face. If someone laughs or smiles at what seems like an inappropriate moment, don't be surprised or angry. The group, rather than the individual, prevails in Singaporean business culture. It will probably take a few months for negotiations to be scheduled. Relationships need to be built prior to any "real business" discussion and scheduling of negotiations. You will need to make a few trips. The very strong work ethic in Singapore means that professional competence, merit, and the ability to work within a team are heavily emphasized.

2. Religions

Religion provides the best insight into a society's behavior and helps answer the question why people behave rather than how they behave.

A survey in the early 1980s revealed the following religious groupings (see Table 5-1).

Table 5-1　Religious Groupings

Groups	Animism	Hinduism	Buddhism	Islam	Shinto	Christianity
Million	300	600	280	800	120	1500

1) Animism

This religion is found in all parts of the world and, in some situations, preceded other historical religions. It is often defined as spirit worship, distinguishing it from worship of God or gods. Magic is the key element and attempts to achieve results through the manipulation of the spirit world. Other aspects of animism include spells[5], ancestor worship, taboos[6], and fatalism[7]. These beliefs tend to promote a traditionalist, status quos[8] in society that is extremely interested in protecting their traditions.

2) Hinduism

Most Hindus live in India and practice this ethnic, non-creedal religion with origins back to about 1, 500 B. C. One of the major beliefs is that a Hindu is born of Indian descent. Although non-Indians cannot become Hindus in the general sense, they may study and become part of the Order of Hinduism. Modern Hinduism is a combination of ancient philosophies and customs, animistic beliefs, legends, and even Western influences such as Christianity. One important Hindu practice is the caste system[9]. Each member of a particular caste in Hindu society has a specific occupation and social role. This role is hereditary[10] and cannot be changed. Discrimination based on caste is forbidden in India, but such deep-rooted customs do not disappear easily. The caste system is aimed at preserving the status quo in society. Another strength of Hinduism is the notion of the joint family. After marriage, the bride becomes part of the groom's home. After a series of marriages, there is a large joint family where the father or grandfather is the chief authority. The elders advise and consent in family council. Perhaps the best-known Hindu custom is the respect and near worship of the cow. However, Hindu worship of the cow not only involves protection of the cow but also includes the belief that eating the products of the cow is a means of purification. Women are greatly restricted, because many believe that to be born a woman is a sign of sin in a former life. Nirvana[11] is the ultimate goal of both the Hindu and Buddhist. It represents the extinction of all cravings and the final release from suffering.

3) Buddhism

Buddhism comes from Hinduism and dates from around 600 B. C. Buddhism in many forms is a reformation of Hinduism that did not abolish caste but released Buddhists from caste system. While Buddhism accepted the philosophical insights of Hinduism, it tried to avoid its dogma[12] and ceremony, while stressing tolerance and spiritual equality. Four Noble Truths exist at the heart of Buddhism.

- Noble Truth of Suffering. Suffering is omnipresent[13] and part of the very nature of life.
- Noble Truth of the Cause of Suffering. The cause of suffering is desire, for possession and selfish enjoyment of any kind.
- Noble Truth of the Cessation of Suffering. Suffering ceases when desire ceases.
- Noble Truth of the Eight-fold Path. This leads to the Cessation of Suffering by showing how to achieve cessation of desire. The steps include: (1) the right views; (2) the right desires; (3) the right speech; (4) the right conduct; (5) the right occupation; (6) the right effort; (7) the right awareness; (8) the right contemplation.

4) Islam

Islam dates from the seventh century A. D. and is found primarily in portions of Africa and Asia. Muslim theology defines all a man should believe, while the law prescribes everything he should do. The Koran[14] is the ultimate guide. Anything not mentioned in the Koran is often rejected by Islam faithful. The major belief is that everything that happens, good or evil, comes directly from Divine Will[15] and is already irrevocably recorded on the Preserved Tablet. This restricts any changes; they may be seen as a rejection of what Allah[16] ordered. Allah is the deity worshiped. The Five Pillars of Islam are the duties of a Muslim and include (1) the recital of the creed, (2) prayer, (3) fasting[17], (4) almsgiving[18], and (5) the pilgrimage[19]. The creed is "There is no God but God, and Mohammed is the Prophet of God." Muslims must pray five times daily. Ramadan[20] is the holy month during which Muslims are required to fast completely from dawn to sunset. This means no food, drink, or smoking. Muslims are required by law to share alms with the poor, and all Muslims must make at least one pilgrimage to Mecca[21], the Holy City. Muslims are not allowed to consume alcohol or pork.

5）Japanese religion（Buddhism and Confucianism[22]）

Japan is a homogeneous culture with a composite religious tradition. Shinto is the original national religion and "the way of the gods". Buddhism and Confucianism combined thousands of years ago when Japan was under the influence of China. The most important aspects of the modern Shinto religion are reverence for the special or divine origin of the Japanese people and reverence for the Japanese nation and the imperial family as the head of that nation. This aggressive sense of patriotism was exhibited especially during World War II and more recently during the tremendous economic growth by Japan during the 1980s.

6）Christianity

Both Roman Catholics and Protestant[23] Christians agree on the same basic Christian elements but differ on other beliefs. Roman Catholics traditionally emphasize the Roman Catholic Church and the sacraments[24] as the principal elements of religion and the way to God. The church and its priests are the intermediaries between God and man, and there is no salvation without the church. Protestants stress that the church, its sacraments, and its clergy are not essential to salvation. It is important to remember the various roles Christianity plays in different countries. Countries that are predominantly Roman Catholic, such as Italy, Spain, and Brazil, would differ in their beliefs and ethics than countries with a varying mixture of Catholics and Protestants, such as the United States.

7）Judaism[25]

Five main forms of Judaism exist in the world today: conservative, humanistic, orthodox, re-constructist, and reform. Orthodox Jews observe the oldest and most conservative form of Judaism and attempt to observe their religion as close to its original forms as possible. About 70% of the Jews in the world are considered Reform Jews. Some Jews believe a Jew is any person whose mother was Jewish or who underwent formal conversion to Judaism. However, others argue that a person who was raised as a Jew by a Jewish father could also be Jewish.

Judaism has traditional beliefs that are followed. These include the beliefs about God's existence. He is the only God, the creator of everything, all knowing, present in all places at all times, all powerful, just and merciful, holy and perfect, and eternal. Jews believe the Messiah[26] will come and gather the Jews again into the land of Israel. Christianity emerged from Judaism when those who believed that Jesus Christ was the Messiah divided from those who did not.

Judaism directly affects the sale of agricultural products because of the strict food laws called "Kosher[27]". Kosher describes foods that are permissible to eat under Jewish dietary laws. Foods prepared under strict religious supervision complying with these dietary laws are accepted as being "Kosher" and stamped with a "K" on their packaging.

Religious holidays vary greatly among countries. This not only applies to Christian and Muslim countries but even from one Christian country to another. Sundays are a religious holiday in Christian countries, but in Islam, the entire month of Ramadan is a religious holiday.

Consumption patterns of food or drink may be affected by religious requirements. The classic example has been fish on Friday for Catholics. Other examples include no beef for Hindus and no pork for Muslims or Jews. Muslims also prohibit the consumption of alcohol.

The role of women varies greatly, primarily due to religious beliefs. Women may be restricted in their capacity as consumers or decision-makers. However, in some African nations, women are considered heads of the household. The caste system restricts participation in the economy. The Hindu joint family has economic effects, including nepotism[28] and pooled income.

The church or any organized religious group can block the introduction of new products or techniques or may even aid their introduction. For example, the Ayatollah[29] Khomeini and the Islamic leaders had a strong impact on consumption of consumer goods in Iran. Religious divisions in a country can cause management problems. Northern Ireland has had numerous clashes between its Catholic and Protestant populations. India formed the separate Muslim state of Pakistan due to its fierce Muslim-Hindu fighting. Lebanon[30] has constant fights between its Christians and Muslims, while the Netherlands has major differences between its Catholic and Protestant groups.

Religion can affect marketing in a number of ways, so marketing researchers should keep in mind the above features in different religions to avoid marketing failure.

5.2   Social Organization, Education and Political Structures
社会组织、教育和政治结构

Social institutions include social organization, education, and political structures. These concern the ways in which people relate to one another, organize their activities to live in harmony with one another, teach acceptable behavior to succeeding generations, and govern themselves. The positions of men and women in society, the family, social classes, group behavior, and age groups are interpreted differently within every culture.

5.2.1   Social organization   社会组织

Social organization refers to the way people relate to other people. In many cultures the key unit is the family, which has many definitions depending upon cultural heritage. Some cultures have large family units. Examples include the Hindu joint family and the extended families of many less developed cultures. Social organization could include special interest groupings (religious, occupational, recreational, or political), caste (class) groupings (detailed and rigid or loose and flexible), age groupings (senior citizens), and gender groupings (females or males).

5.2.2　Education　教育

Education refers to the transmission of skills, ideas and attitudes as well as training in particular disciplines. Education can transmit cultural ideas or be used for change. Education usually means formal training in school.

However, even people living in indigenous[31] cultures are, at a minimum, educated through the transmission of the existing culture and traditions to the new generation. Education can be used for cultural change. Prime examples include the education systems from the former Soviet Union and the People's Republic of China. Most education information about foreign countries is limited primarily to information about formal education. This can provide insight into the knowledge of consumers in these different countries.

According to the education information gathered by the UN agency UNESCO(United Nations Educational, Scientific, and Cultural Organization), for example, it shows in Ethiopia[32] only 12% of the viable age group enrolls at secondary school, but the figure is 97% in the USA.

Education levels, or lack of it, affect marketers in a number of ways:
— Advertising programs and labeling;
— Girls and women excluded from formal education (literacy rates);
— Conducting market research;
— Complex products with instructions;
— Relations with distributors and;
— Support sources — finance, advancing agencies, etc.

5.2.3　Political structures　政治结构

The stability or instability of the prevailing government policies is one of the most important concerns with conducting international business. Governments might change and new political parties might be elected, but the continuity of the laws, rules, and customs of conducting business is important. In Italy, more than 50 different governments have been formed since the end of World War II, but it has not affected business. Conversely, in Mexico, the same political party has been in control for over 40 years, but it has been risky to conduct business in Mexico because of the changing policies.

Nationalism is an intense feeling of national pride and unity. These feelings of nationalism can be manifested in a variety of ways, including "buy our country's products only", restrictions on imports, restrictive tariffs, price controls, exchange control, and expropriation (official seizure of foreign property). Generally speaking, the more a country feels threatened by some outside force, the more nationalistic it becomes in protecting itself against the intrusion. It is important to remember that no nation, however secure, will tolerate penetration by a foreign company into its market and economy if it perceives a social, cultural, or economic threat to its well being.

5.3   Weather Conditions and Geography   气候条件及地理

It's no secret that climate influences the tone of a nation's culture. Hot, humid climates tend to produce gregarious[33], outgoing people; cold, pristine climes result in introspective[34], self-sufficient people; temperate zones are conducive to year-round labor and less subsistence-type people.

Marketers often follow these same geographic patterns as they attempt to have a nation adopt their products. Finding a place that can afford a product is just as important as finding a group that has a use for it. Sometimes it is a matter of introducing a product to one portion of a population with the knowledge that it will spread throughout a culture in due course.

Large urban populations have a tendency to consider and adopt goods or services far more readily than their less urban, and less urbane, countrymen. Such cities have become major centers usually due to their geographic location, and they have attracted risk-takers in droves over decades and centuries. Because cities are viewed as centers of culture as well as commerce, suburban and country folk tend to adopt the lifestyles of their urban counterparts. But nowadays, television and telecommunication in the form of Internet have shortened this urban-to-rural flow from months to days and extended it far beyond national borders.

One British authority admonishes foreign marketers to study the world until the mere mention of a town, country, or river enables it to be picked out immediately on the map. Although it may not be necessary for the student of foreign marketing to memorize the world map to that extent, a prospective international marketer should be reasonably familiar with the world, its climate, and topographic differences[35]. Otherwise, the important marketing characteristics of geography could be completely overlooked when marketing in another country.

The need for geographical and historical knowledge goes deeper than being able to locate continents and their countries. Geographic hurdles must be recognized as having a direct effect on marketing and the related activities of communications and distribution. For someone who has never been in a tropical rain forest with an annual rainfall of at least 60 inches (and sometimes more than 200 inches), it is difficult to anticipate the need for protection against high humidity. Likewise, it is hard to comprehend the difficult problems caused by dehydration[36] in constant 100-

degrees-plus heat in the Sahara region. Indirect effects from the geographical ramifications[37] of a society and culture may be ultimately reflected in marketing activities. Many of the peculiarities of a country (i. e. , peculiar to the foreigner) would be better understood and anticipated if its geography were studied more closely. Further, without a historical understanding of a culture, the attitudes within the marketplace may not be fully understood.

Aside from the simpler and more obvious ramifications of climate and topography[38], there are complex geographical and historical influences on the development of the general economy and society of a country. In this case, the need for studying geography and history is to provide the marketer with an understanding of why a country has developed as it has, rather than as a guide for adapting marketing plans. Geography and history are two of the environments of foreign marketing that should be understood and that must be included in foreign marketing plans to a degree commensurate[39] with their influence on marketing effort.

Appendix: Main approaches to culture

1) Anthropological approach

Culture can be deep seated and, to the untrained can appear bizarre. The Moslem culture of covering the female form may be alien, to those cultures which openly flaunt the female form. The anthropologist, though a time consuming process, considers behavior in the light of experiencing it at first hand. In order to understand beliefs, motives and values, the anthropologist studies the country in question anthropology and unearths the reasons for what, apparently, appears bizarre.

2) Maslow approach

In searching for culture universals, Maslow's (1964)[1] hierarchy of needs gives a useful analytical framework. Maslow hypothesized that people's desires can be arranged into a hierarchy of needs of relative potency. As soon as the "lower" needs are filled, other and higher needs emerge immediately to dominate the individual. When these higher needs are fulfilled, other new and still higher needs emerge.

3) The self-reference criterion (SRC)

Perception of market needs can be blocked by one's own cultural experience. Lee (1965)[II] suggested a way, whereby one could systematically reduce this perception. He suggested a four-point approach.

(1) Define the problem or goal in terms of home country traits, habits and norms.

(2) Define the problem or goal in terms of the foreign culture traits, habits and norms.

(3) Isolate the SRC influence in the problem and examine it carefully to see how it complicates the pattern.

(4) Redefine the problem without the SRC influence and solve for the foreign market situation.

4) Diffusion theory

Concepts and patterns are extremely useful to international marketers because they are involved in introducing innovations in the form of their products into markets. In international marketing, companies are in the position of marketing products that may be simultaneously new-product innovations in some markets and mature, postmature, or declining products in other markets. So, the findings from studies of the diffusion of innovations have great relevance to the various circumstances in which international marketers finds themselves.

5) High and low context cultures

The concept of high and low context cultures serves as a way of understanding different cultural orientations (Hall, 1977[III]). In low-context cultures messages have to be explicit; in high-context cultures less information is required in the verbal message. In low-context cultures, for example like Northern Europe, a person's word is not to be relied on, things that must be written. On the other hand, in high-context cultures, like Japan and the Middle East, a person's word is their bond. It is primarily a question of trust.

6) Perception

Perception is the ability to see what is in culture. The SRC can be a very powerful negative force. High perceptual skills need to be developed so that no one misperceive a situation, which could lead to negative consequences.

Many of these theories and approaches have been " borrowed " from other contexts themselves, but they do give a useful insight into how one might avoid a number of pitfalls of culture in doing business overseas.

Culture has both a pervasive and changing influence on each national market environment. Marketers must either respond or change to it. Whilst internationalism in itself may go some way to changing cultural values, it will not change values to such a degree that true international standardization can exist. The world would be a poorer place if it ever happened.

Notes:

I. Maslow A H. A theory of human motivation. In: Leavitt H J, Pondy L R. ed. Readings in managerial psychology. Chicago: University of Chicago Press, 1964:6 ~ 24

II. Lee J A. Cultural analysis in overseas operations. Harvard Business Review, 1966; Mar ~ Apr: 106 ~ 114

III. Hall E T. Beyond culture. New York: Anchor Press/Doubleday, 1976

Cases

A few years ago, one of the top ten manufacturing companies in the world was a failure in Australia. What had gone wrong with their first foreign plant in Australia? They had done everything according to the book from an engineering perspective. They had a sound business development plan which began with low technology, screw driver operations, and slowly moved to higher value-added operations. They had built the plant in Nagoya and made sure it worked well. Then, they broke it down, shipped it to Australia, and assembled it on site. No problems thus far. They hired local production and human resource managers and trained them in their company philosophy and procedures. The relationships between these two key local managers and the expatriate with their Japanese colleagues, however, failed to mature into cross-cultural partnerships but something kept the two cultures apart. The Japanese plant manager complained that he would have long talks with his Australian managers and they would find agreement on all the major project. However, the next day the Australian manager would do things that indicated that they did not really understand. These Japanese and Australian managers never became partners. The Australian managers never developed an interest in the success of the transplant. The Japanese and the Australian partners never developed a third culture together. The consequence of this failure to achieve cross-cultural partnership between Japanese and Australian was a major embarrassment for one of the top manufacturing companies in the world. This plant failed to perform and was plagued by wildcat strikes, grievances, and low quality. This last point was a severe blow to a company that had earned the Emperor's prize for quality in Japan. This would not be allowed to happen again as it was a major embarrassment. Later, with the help of professional consulting team, this organization carefully selected their managers for compatibility, ethnocentricity (i. e. low level of), and empathy, trained them in cross-cultural partnership knowledge and skills, and facilitated third culture partnerships between Japanese and American managers, and developed third culture networks in depth — not only first line managers, but also second and third line managers to develop cross-cultural partnerships which allowed them to share "insider" hopes, fears and solutions. They achieved real understanding and developed third culture decision-making procedures. The third culture is an important concept in cross-cultural marketing management nowadays.

Key Terms

sub-cultural language 亚文化语言

local custom 当地风俗

Animism 万物有灵论

Hinduism 印度教

Buddhism 佛教

Islam 伊斯兰教

Shinto 日本之神道教

Confucianism 儒教

Christianity 基督教

Judaism 犹太教

social organization 社会机构

political structure 政治构成

UNESCO(United Nations Educational, Scientific, and Cultural Organization) 联合国教科文组织

weather conditions 气候条件

Notes

1. jeopardize *v.* 危害

2. ethnocentrism *n.* 民族优越感，民族中心主义

3. accommodation *n.* 迁就融合

4. Zimbabwe 津巴布韦

5. spell *n.* 符咒

6. taboo *n.* 宗教禁忌，避讳

7. fatalism *n.* 宿命论

8. status quo 现状

9. caste system 印度的世袭阶级，社会等级制度

10. hereditary *a.* 世袭的

11. Nirvana *n.* 涅槃，天堂

12. dogma *n.* 教条

13. omnipresent *a.* 无所不在的

14. the Koran 《可兰经》

15. Divine Will 神的意志

16. Allah *n.* 阿拉，真主

17. fasting *n.* 禁食

18. almsgiving　*n.*　施舍

19. pilgrimage　*n.*　朝圣

20. Ramadan　*n.*　斋月

21. Mecca　*n.*　麦加圣地

22. Confucianism　*n.*　儒教

23. Protestant　*n.*　新教

24. sacrament　*n.*　基督教圣礼，圣餐

25. Judaism　*n.*　犹太教

26. the Messiah　弥赛亚，犹太人盼望的复国救主

27. Kosher　犹太教所规定允许的食品

28. nepotism　*n.*　裙带关系

29. Ayatollah　〈伊斯兰〉阿亚图拉

30. Lebanon　黎巴嫩

31. indigenous　*a.*　本土的

32. Ethiopia　埃塞俄比亚（非洲东部国家）

33. gregarious　*a.*　社交的，群居的

34. introspective　*a.*　（好）内省的，（好）自省的，（好）反省的

35. topographic differences　地形、地质差异

36. dehydration　*n.*　脱水

37. ramification　*n.*　分枝，分叉

38. topography　*n.*　地形学

39. commensurate　*a.*　相称的，相当的

✍ Exercises

I. Multiple choices.

1. Firms that truly adopt the marketing concept develop a distinct organizational culture based on a shared set of beliefs that make _____ the pivotal point of the firm's decisions about strategy and operations.

    A. beating competitors   B. increasing market share

    C. customers' needs   D. marketing implementation

    E. marketing control

2. Which of the following is NOT a factor in the attractiveness of the US to foreign investors?

    A. High levels of discretionary income.   B. Political stability.

    C. Well-controlled economic problems.

D. A positive attitude toward foreign investment.

E. Good weather.

3. Moral philosophies _____.

   A. are concerned with maximizing the greatest good for the greatest number of people

   B. are principles or rules that individuals use to determine what is right or wrong

   C. focus on the intentions associated with a particular behavior and on the rights of the individual

   D. remain consistent in both work and family situations

4. Ethical formalism philosophies focus on _____.

   A. the rights of consumers and the greatest good for society

   B. situational ethics and increasing profits

   C. maximizing the greatest good for the greatest number of people

   D. the intentions associated with a particular behavior and the rights of the individual

5. _____ refers to the specific development, pricing, promotion, and distribution of products that do not harm the environment.

   A. Marketing ethics   B. Social responsibility

   C. Environmental marketing   D. Green marketing

6. Product-related ethical issues can arise when marketers _____.

   A. do not provide consumers with enough information about how a product is priced

   B. force intermediaries to behave in a specific manner

   C. bribe salespeople to push one product over another

   D. fail to disclose information to consumers about the risks associated with using a product

   E. manufacture a product that is very similar to a competing product

7. Which of the following is NOT one of the factors that interact to determine the ethical decision-making process in marketing?

   A. Relationships with superiors.   B. Laws and regulations.

   C. Opportunity.   D. Individual factors.

   E. Relationships with coworkers.

8. As a new employee, John is most likely to look to which one of the following to learn the ethical culture of his new organization?

   A. Coworkers.   B. Customer contact employees.

   C. Other new employees.   D. The legal department.

   E. Top management.

9. Joan recently changed employers within the same industry. At her old company, employees routinely took home company pens, pencils, and note pads, and they frequently made

personal long-distance calls on company phones. Joan observes that employees do not engage in such practices at her new company. What Joan sees could best be described as a difference in _____.

    A. significant others　　　B. profit objectives　　　C. corporate culture

    D. legal climate　　　　　E. corporate goals

10. The reason cultural factors are a challenge to global marketers is _____.

    A. different cultures usually mean different behaviors

    B. cultural factors are various

    C. cultural factors are hidden from view, difficult to learn

    D. marketers fail to grasp all cultures

II. True or false.

1. Culture is learned behavior passed on from generation to generation, but it is not difficult for the inexperienced or untrained outsider to fathom.

2. Equality, disadvantaged members of society, safety and health, education and general welfare, pollution are social responsibility issues related to community relations.

3. All marketing employees are responsible for setting the ethical tone for the entire marketing organization.

4. Green marketing refers to the development, pricing, promotion and distribution of products that do not harm the environment.

5. Water pollution, air pollution, land pollution, safety and health are social responsibility issues related to the environment, or green marketing.

6. The vital, critical skill of the global marketer is perception, or the ability to see what is so in a culture.

7. Gestures, carriage, proximity of speakers, eye contact, and smiling all play key roles in a culture's use of language.

8. Every country and culture has a history that will greatly affect both the market and the marketer.

9. Being enthusiastic about a product and having a personal attachment to it are two similar things.

10. Although the hospitality and tourism industries are slightly affected by religious holidays, marketers with products related to those industries need to be highly sensitive to this issue.

III. Discussion.

1. Describe the main elements of culture.
2. List the major approaches to the study of culture and show their relevance in international marketing citing examples.

Part **III**

国际市场营销目标

Targeting International Markets

Chapter Six

International Marketing Information System and Research

国际市场营销信息系统和研究

📣 Objectives 学习目标

When students finish this chapter, they should be able to accomplish the following：

☑ To describe a marketing information system and distinguish it from marketing research

☑ To list the steps in the marketing research process

☑ To identify the sources of developing information

☑ To identify the methods of distributing information

6.1 The Marketing Information System 营销信息体系

A marketing information system（MIS）consists of people, equipment, and procedures to gather, sort, analyze, evaluate and distribute needed, timely, and accurate information to marketing decision makers. [1] The main components of MIS are shown in Figure 6-1.

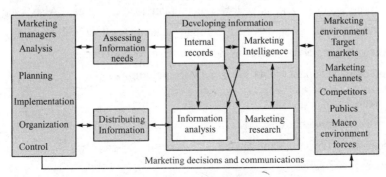

Figure 6-1   The Marketing Information System

6.1.1 Assessing information needs 评估信息需求

A good marketing information system balances the information managers would like to have against what they really need and what is feasible to offer. The company needs:

— to interview managers to find out what information they would like;

— to watch the marketing environment in order to provide decision makers with information they should have to make key marketing decisions;

— to decide whether the benefits of having an item of information are worth the costs of providing it.

Sometimes the MIS cannot supply all the information needed because of the MIS' limitations. Sometimes because the information is unavailable, the needed information cannot be provided as required. Marketers must notice that too much information can be as harmful as too little. Information has no worth; its value comes from its use. Since the costs of obtaining, processing, storing, and delivering information can mount quickly, it is quite necessary to assess information needs. In many cases, additional information will do little to change or improve a manager's decision, or the costs of the information may exceed the returns from the improved decision. Marketers should not assume that additional information will always be worth obtaining; they should weigh carefully the costs of additional information against the benefits resulting from it.

6.1.2 Developing information 信息形成

Information can be broken into two types: primary or secondary.

Both serve as an extremely important source of information for marketing researchers.

Secondary data consist of information that already exists somewhere, having been collected for another purpose. Researchers usually start by gathering secondary data. Secondary data usually can be obtained more quickly and at a lower cost than primary data. Also, secondary sources sometimes can provide data an individual company cannot collect on its own-information that either is not directly available or would be too expensive to collect.

Various sources of secondary data are available including:

1) Governments
- Central office of information (UK);
- Central Statistical Office (Zimbabwe);
- EU documentation centers;
- Boards of trade, or Ministry of Commerce.

2) International bodies

- The UN Statistical Yearbook[2];
- World Bank — general statistics;
- OECD — general statistics;
- ITC — Geneva (information service).

3) Business, trade, professional

- Chambers of Commerce;
- Institute of Marketing;
- American Management Association;
- The Market Research Society.

4) Foreign embassies, trade missions

- Commercial newspapers;
- Financial agencies — Price Waterhouse;
- Kompass Register of companies;
- Economist Intelligence Unit (UK).

5) Other

- Libraries, universities, colleges.

Secondary data from such sources are relatively cheap to obtain and readily available. However, the disadvantages of secondary data are legion[3].

(1) The data may have been collected and manipulated for a specific use, therefore it may be incomplete, ambiguous or out of context.

(2) Data may be compiled in different ways in different countries making comparability difficult. For example, in Germany consumer expenditures are estimated largely on the basis of turnover tax receipts; in the UK they are measured on tax receipts plus household surveys and production sources. Similarly with GNP measures, it only reflects average health per head of population and not how it is dispersed. As seen earlier, bi-modalities[4] are normal, thus introducing bias. GNP may be understated for political reasons and may not reflect education (i. e. wealth based on minerals). Also infrastructure[5] may reflect channeled funds, say for tourism, rather than society as a whole — typical of many African countries.

(3) Data may be corrupted by methodological and interpretive problems. For example, definitional error, sampling error, section error, non-response error, language, social organizations, trained workers, etc.

(4) Data may be nonexistent, unreliable or incomplete thus making inter-country comparisons very difficult.

（5）Data may be inflated or deflated for political purposes.

Therefore, secondary data must be treated with care and caution.

Primary data refers to data that is collected for the first time during a marketing research study. Primary data consist of information collected for the specific purpose at hand. A study to collect primary information might take weeks or months and cost a lot. Although secondary data provide a good starting point for research, and often help to define problems and research objectives, in most cases, however, the company must also collect primary data. While collecting primary data, researchers must take great care to assure that it will be relevant, accurate, current, and unbiased information.

Primary data can be collected by observation, focus-group research, surveys and experiments, as shown in Table 6-1.

Table 6-1　Planning Primary Data Collection

RESEARCH APPROACHES	CONTACT METHODS	SAMPLING PLAN	RESEARCH INSTRUMENTS
Observation	Mail	Sampling unit	Questionnaire
Focus group	Meeting	—	Topics, issues
Survey	Telephone	Sample size	Mechanical instruments
Experiment	Personal	Sampling procedure	—

The information needed by marketing managers can be obtained from internal records, marketing intelligence, and marketing research.

1）Internal records

The most basic information is internal records; it refers to information gathered from sources within the company to evaluate marketing performance and to detect marketing problems and opportunities, such as financial statements and detailed records of sales, costs and cash flows from the accounting department; reports on reseller reactions and competitor activities; reports on production schedules, shipments, and inventories; data bases of customer demographics, psychographics, and buying behavior from the marketing department; information on customer satisfaction or service problems from the customer service department, etc.

Internal records usually can be accessed more quickly and cheaply than other information sources; but on the other hand, it may be incomplete or in the wrong form for making marketing decisions. In addition, a large company produces great amounts of information, and keeping track of it all is difficult. So, information gathering, organizing, processing and indexing is the key task that the marketing information system must do so that the managers can find it easily and

quickly.

2) Marketing intelligence

Marketing intelligence refers to everyday information about pertinent developments in the marketing environment that helps managers prepare and adjust marketing plans. Marketing intelligence can be gathered from many sources. A well-run company takes 4 steps to improve the quality and quantity of marketing intelligence.

The company trains and motivates the sales force to spot and report new developments. But they are very busy and often fail to pass on significant information; the company must "sell" its sales force on their importance as intelligence gatherers.

(1) The competitive company motivates distributors, retailers, and other intermediaries to pass along important intelligence. Specialists even will be appointed to gather marketing intelligence by some companies.

(2) The company purchases information from outside suppliers such as some famous research firms who gather data at a much lower cost than the company could do on its own.

(3) It is necessary to establish an internal marketing information center to collect and circulate marketing intelligence. It collects and files relevant information and assists managers in evaluating new information.

3) Marketing research

Managers cannot always wait for information to arrive in bits and pieces from the marketing intelligence system. They often require formal studies of specific situations, that is marketing research. Marketing research is the function that links the marketer to consumers and the public through information. It is used to identify and define marketing opportunities and problems; to generate, refine, and evaluate marketing actions; to monitor marketing performance; and to improve understanding of the marketing process. Marketing researchers engage in market potential and market share studies, assessments of customer satisfaction and purchase behavior, studies of pricing, product, distribution, and promotion activities. The starting point of a marketing research project, of course, is the need for information with which to make a marketing decision. An information need can relate to a specific marketing decision or an ongoing set of decisions. When an information need is perceived, the marketing research process can be used to produce the relevant marketing knowledge and this by definition would require continuous marketing research.

6.1.3   Distributing information   分发信息

The information gathered through different sources must be distributed to the right marketing managers at the right time, otherwise marketing information has no value until managers use it to make better marketing decisions.

With recent advances in computers, software, and telecommunication, most companies are decentralizing their marketing information systems although they have centralized marketing information systems already. Marketing managers have direct access to the information network through personal computers and other means. They can obtain information from internal records or outside information services, analyze the information using statistical packages and models, prepare reports on a word processor or desk-top publishing system from any location, and communicate with others in the network through electronic communications.

Decentralized marketing information systems enable the managers to get the information they need directly and quickly. Improvements in the technology make them more economical; they will be widely adopted by marketers.

6.2　The Marketing Research Process　营销研究过程

The marketing research process involves 6 steps: defining the problem, exploratory research, formulating a hypothesis, research design, collecting data, interpretation and presentation, as shown in Figure 6-2.

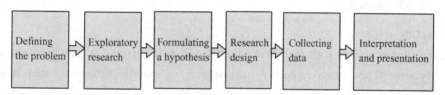

Figure 6-2　The Marketing Research Process

6.2.1　Problem definition　问题定义

Problems are barriers that prevent the attainment of organizational goals, so a clearly defined problem permits researchers to focus the research process on securing the data necessary for solving the problem.

In most cases, however, defining a problem is far more difficult. Researchers must not confuse symptoms with the problem itself. A symptom merely alerts marketers that a problem exists. Symptoms are often obvious; for example, falling market share is a symptom of a problem and the firm needs to know what action to take. To define its problem, the firm must look for underlying causes of market share loss. A logical starting point would be the firm's marketing mix elements and target market. Suppose that the firm has made no recent changes in its products, pricing or distribution strategies but has adopted a new promotional strategy, so a close look at the

promotional strategy may reveal the problem. Alternatively the problem could stem from the external environment in the form of new competitors entering the market with superior products and lower prices. The possible causes of the problem are then further explored in the next step of the marketing research process — exploratory research.

6.2.2   Exploratory research   探测性研究

Searching for the cause of a problem allows the researcher to learn about the problem area and to focus on specific areas for study in seeking solutions. This search, often called exploratory research, consists of discussing the problem with informed sources within the firm and with wholesalers, retailers, customers and others outside the firm, and examining secondary sources of information. Marketing researchers often refer to internal data collection as the situation analysis and to exploratory interviews with informed persons outside the firm as the informal investigation. Exploratory research also involves evaluating the company's own records, as in sales and profit analysis, and the sales and profits of competitors. Using internal data in this stage plays a very important part in the whole research process. An organization's sales records contain valuable sources of information. Analysis of these records should provide a basis for obtaining an overall view of company efficiency and a clue to the problem under investigation. The basis for analyzing internal data is the traditional accounting information provided by the relevant department which is usually summarized on the firm's financial statements.

6.2.3   Formulating hypotheses   叙述假设

After the problem has been defined and an exploratory investigation conducted, the marketer should be able to formulate a hypothesis — a tentative explanation for some specific event. A hypothesis is a statement about the relationship among variables and carries clear implications for testing this relationship.

A marketer of industrial products might formulate the following hypothesis: failure to provide a 72-hour delivery service will reduce our sales by 20 percent. Such a statement may prove correct or incorrect. Its formulation, however, provides a basis for investigation and an eventual determination of its accuracy. Also, it allows the researcher to move to the next step: development of the research design.

6.2.4   Research design   研究方案

The research design represents a comprehensive plan for testing the hypothesis formulated about the problem. Research design refers to a series of decisions that, taken together, comprise a master plan or model for the conduct of the investigation. A company marketing alcoholic beverages is concerned about the environmental factors that might affect its market, so it may set up an environmental monitoring system that is able to scan published data to pick up environmental trends and the like.

Sometimes published data are not enough. In such cases, the research design must call for the direct test of a hypothesis. Published data, for example, indicate that people drink diet sodas because they want to control their weight. Would this information be of direct use to the company in question in its raw form, or, as seems more likely, would it require further investigation?

6.2.5 Information collecting and analyzing 信息收集与分析

The researcher next puts the marketing research plan into action. This involves collecting, processing, and analyzing the information. The data collection phase is generally the most expensive and the most prone to error, it can be carried out by the company's marketing research staff or by outside firms. Thanks to modern computers and telecommunications, data collection methods are rapidly improving. Researchers must process and analyze the collected data to isolate important information and findings. They need to check data from questionnaires for accuracy and completeness and code it for computer analysis. The researchers then tabulate the results and compute averages and other statistical measures, such as advanced statistical techniques and decision models in the hope of discovering additional findings.

6.2.6 Interpretation and reporting 解释和陈述

The researcher now must interpret the findings, draw conclusions, and report them to management. Interpretation should not be left only to the researchers. Although they are expert in research design and statistics, the marketing manager knows more about the problem and the decisions that must by made. So, discussions between researchers and managers will help point to the best interpretations. Data should be reviewed after being collected so that data coding and tabulating can be more easier to conduct. Then the manager should check that the research project was carried out properly and that all the necessary analysis was completed. Finally, the manager is the one who ultimately must decide what action the research suggests. The researchers may even make the data directly available to marketing managers so that they can perform new analyses and test new relationships on their own.

Presenting the results of a marketing research study to management generally involves a formal written report as well as an oral presentation. The report and presentation are extremely important. Preparing a research report involves three steps: understanding, organizing and writing. The general guidelines that researchers should be encouraged to follow for any report are as follows:

(1) Think of the audience: The information resulting from the study is ultimately of importance to marketing managers, who will use the results to make decisions. Thus, the report has to be understood by them; the report should not be too technical and jargon avoided wherever possible.

(2) Be concise yet complete: On the one hand, a written report should be complete in the sense that it stands by itself and that no additional clarification is needed. On the other hand, the report must be concise and must focus on the critical elements of the project and must exclude issues that are not material to the decisions that the managers wishes to be in a position to make.

(3) Understand the results and draw conclusions: The managers who read the report are expecting to see interpretive conclusions in the report. The researcher must therefore understand the results and be able to interpret these.

The summary of findings is usually put right after the title page, or is bound separately and presented together with the report. The introduction should describe the background of the study and the details of the research problem. Following that, automatically the broad aim of the research can be specified, which is then translated into a number of specific objectives. Furthermore, the hypotheses that are to be tested in the research are stated in this section. In the methodology[6] chapter the sampling methods and procedures are described, as well as the different statistical methods that are used for data analysis. Finally, the sample is described, giving the overall statistics, usually consisting of frequency counts for the various sample characteristics.

Figure 6-3 contains a suggested outline format for writing the research report.

Once the sample has been described, the main findings are to be presented in such a way that all objectives of the study are achieved and the hypotheses are tested. As mentioned before, it is essential that the main findings are well interpreted and conclusions are drawn wherever possible.

Marketing research findings and conclusions must be effectively communicated to management. Written reports need to be both clear and concise. A sensitivity towards the needs of the reader is of prime importance. The report should not be too technical and jargon[7] avoided wherever possible, must exclude issues that are not material to the decisions that the

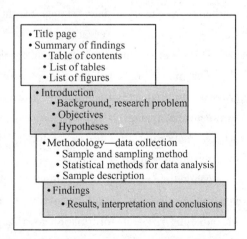

Figure 6-3 Research Report Writing Format

managers wishes to be in a position to make and should be rich in interpretive conclusions.

Appendix：In what aspect of marketing system is marketing research of limited applicability?

Marketing research can supply information regarding many aspects of the marketing system. This domain ranges from monitoring and describing situational factors to evaluating marketing programs and measuring the performance of these programs.

In summary, marketing research plays a role in supplying all kinds of regarding marketing information for marketing system. Marketing research is a systematic and objective approach to development and provision of information for the marketing management decision-making process. We can also say that marketing research serves for the decision-making process in marketing management, and each step of decision-making needs the information coming from marketing research. So it's not difficult to find out in what aspect of marketing system marketing research is of limited applicability via analyzing what information each step needs.

The first step of decision-making is the recognition that a unique marketing problem exits or that an opportunity is present. Marketing problems and opportunities result from the dynamic nature of the situational factors and/or the implementation of the marketing program. Performance measures often signal the presence of problems, while the monitoring of the situational factors can signal the presence of both problems and opportunities. Consequently, one could find out that marketing research do monitoring the situational factors for the recognition-step of decision-making.

By involving the research function, the marketing manager can benefit from more effective formulation of problems and opportunities, while at the same time assuring more effective use of marketing research in later stages of the decision process. Then, by the further information supplied by marketing research, the marketing manager could implement the second step a little easier, the definition of the decision problem of the decision-making process.

The marketing manager and researcher have to search for new ideas, which come from creative thinking and imagination. Various marketing research approaches are available that can stimulate the manager's creative process and broaden the domain of alternatives identified. In this aspect, marketing research serves for the third step — identification of alternative courses of active in decision-making process.

Marketing research is a valuable tool in evaluation of alternative courses of action. Often, non-routine decision situations involve substantial uncertainty and risk. The manager is interested in marketing research information as a way to reduce the uncertainty inherent in the selection of a course of action. In this aspect, marketing research supplies information to the fourth and fifth steps in decision process. They are evaluation of alternatives and the selection of a course of action.

The final step in the decision-making process is the implementation of selected course of action. Again, marketing research supplies the means for monitoring the effectiveness of the action selected and the situational variables that influence the program's performance.

 Cases

Tanzanian Sisal

The once world leading Tanzanian Sisal Industry is a classic example of failure due to its inability to monitor market trends, through lack of an adequate intelligence system, as well as many, in-country problems. Basically, it failed to take account of the shrink in demand for sisal fiber in Western Europe. Many sisal mills were being closed because of the fact that they were old and labor intensive (hence uneconomic), and the disintegration of markets for sisal fiber in Eastern Europe due to that region's political crises. Sisal was brought into Tanzania by a German Agronomist, Dr. Richard Hingdorf in 1892 and the first estates were established in Tanga and Morogoro regions. After World War I, most estates were sold to Greeks, Swiss, Dutch, British and Asians, although a number of Germans re-acquired their estates from 1926 onwards. From that time, up to and after World War I, Tanzania remained the world's leader in both production and exports.

In the early 60's sisal was Tanzania's largest export, accounting for over a quarter of foreign exchange. Production was around 200,000 – 230,000 tons per annum. However, during the 70's and 80's production dropped dramatically. In 1970's production was at 202,000 tones; in 1979 it was 81,000 tones; by 1985 production was at 32,000 tones, a drop of 87% from the peak of 230,000 tones in 1964. Since then production has stagnated at around 30,000 – 33,000 tones per annum. Needless to say Tanzania has long since ceased to be the number one world producer and its export earnings fallen well behind that of coffee, cotton tea, tobacco and cashew nuts. Since 1985 Tanzania has been producing 7% – 9% of the world's sisal fiber exports and is in fourth place behind Brazil, Morocco and Kenya.

The decline in sisal production came in two stages, an initial stage up to 1987 and then 1990 onwards. Both internal and external factors account for the decline. In the initial stage, the internal factors included the nationalization of some of the sisal estates in the late 1960's, an overvalued exchange rate, high export taxes and a controlled single channel marketing system. In the second stage, liquidity problems affected production. However, the external factors in the two periods had the most significant effect and show clearly the consequences of an ill prepared intelligence system. In the initial stage up to 1987, Tanzania experienced declining world prices of sisal fiber and the introduction of a substitute, cheap synthetic fiber-polypropylene twines. These factors led to low investment in replanting, leaf transport facilities and factory machines at the estate level. In the second stage of the 1990's onwards, the collapse of the former USSR, one of the major markets for Tanzania sisal fiber and changing world demand were the major factors. An inability to pick up these changes in demand by the intelligence system was a major player in the industry collapse. However, there is a ray of hope with a new swing worldwide to more "greener" and more environmentally friendly products. Tanzania sisal could make a comeback.

🗋 Key Terms

marketing information system（MIS）　营销信息体系

assessing information need　评估信息需求

primary data　一手数据

secondary data　二手数据

ITC　国际贸易中心

Chambers of Commerce　商会

internal record　内部档案

marketing intelligence　营销情报

marketing research　市场调研

distributing information　分发信息

statistical package　统计包

marketing research process　营销研究过程

exploratory research　探测性研究

formulating hypothesis　叙述假设

research design　研究方案

information collecting and analyzing　信息收集与分析

interpretation and reporting　解释和陈述

📄 Notes

1. A marketing information system（MIS）consists of people, equipment, and procedures to gather, sort, analyze, evaluate and distribute needed, timely, and accurate information to marketing decision makers.　营销信息体系是由人员、设备及收集、分类、分析、评估、并向营销决策者分发所需的、及时的、准确的信息的过程所构成。

2. yearbook　*n.*　年鉴

3. legion　*n./a.*　很多（的），大批（的）

4. bi-modality   双重特征

5. infrastructure   *n.*   下部构造，基础组织

6. methodology   *n.*   方法学，方法论

7. jargon   *n.*   行话

✍ Exercises

I. Multiple choices.

1. A company's structure must facilitate the provision of quality products by _____.

   A. using efficient systems and processes

   B. the physical appearance of its facilities

   C. maintaining a high level of cleanliness in its plants

   D. developing a steep organizational hierarchy

   E. using special sales promotions

2. A firm packs a product registration card with each item it ships even though the warranty requires only that the customer retain the sales slip. The purpose of the registration card is to help the firm _____.

   A. decrease its product's price sensitivity   B. encourage product trial by customers

   C. promote increased product usage   D. build a marketing database

   E. encourage increased buying

3. Electronic data interchange (EDI) involves _____.

   A. computer-to-computer exchanges of invoices, orders, and other business documents

   B. extensive use of a large staff of buyers to call on manufacturers

   C. the use of the telephone or mail to communicate with suppliers

   D. lots of face-to-face contact between buyers and sellers

   E. a loss of ability to gather marketing information

4. The first step in evaluating the desirability of investing in database systems is to _____.

   A. implement such a system and see how it works out

   B. change the firm's organizational philosophy to reflect the use of database marketing

   C. identify and compare their costs and the benefits they create

   D. examine what competitors are doing

   E. wait a while and see if prices come down

5. The starting point for marketing planning is the organization's _____.

   A. product or service mix   B. major competitor

   C. marketing objectives   D. resource base

E. technological capacity

6. One of the reasons marketers conduct research is: they can better _____.

　A. create new procedures for statistical quality control

　B. excuse their mistakes when new products fail

　C. understand the technology used in their industry

　D. understand why employees are late for work

　E. develop effective marketing strategies

7. One thing researchers must carefully avoid is _____.

　A. purchasing computer equipment that is more powerful than is needed

　B. using software that carries too low a price tag

　C. confusing symptoms of a problem with the problem itself

　D. using random processes to pick a group of people to interview

　E. using statistical tools that are too sophisticated

8. An MIS gathers information from _____.

　A. only sources within the company's industry　　B. only inside the organization

　C. inside and outside the organization　　D. only outside the organization

　E. non-financial sources only

9. External marketing research data include _____.

　A. sales force activity reports　　B. company sales and expense records

　C. trade association data　　D. product performance reviews

　E. past company research projects

10. Secondary data _____.

　A. are more expensive per unit sampled than primary data

　B. are usually on magnetic tape which requires significant conversion

　C. are the results of personal interviews and intercepts

　D. come from questionnaires given to people who were missed by primary research

　E. require relatively little time and expense to locate and use

II. True or false.

1. Early marketing research was fairly sophisticated because statistical techniques were sufficiently refined to produce high levels of accuracy in research findings.

2. In the event that a new competitor were to enter a market in which you were involved, one question marketing research might help answer for you would be "What must we do to differentiate our company from our competitor?"

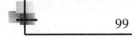
3. A hypothesis is a statement about the relationship among variables that carries clear implications for testing the relationship. It sets the stage for more in-depth research by clarifying what researchers need to test.

4. Trade associations represent an excellent source of private data for particular industries.

5. Sampling is the process of selecting survey respondents or other research participants.

6. Information related to global markets is not readily available to American firms seeking to enter foreign markets. The Department of Commerce has only recently begun to collect data to assist firms in this area.

7. Telephone interviews are a suitable method of collecting primary marketing research data all over the world because the telephone is now the universal appliance found in every home.

8. An MIS is a planned, computer-based system designed to provide managers with a continual flow of information relevant to specific decision areas.

9. An MIS gathers data only from inside the organization and processes it to produce relevant marketing information.

10. Computers have automated the buying process at large retailers, opening new channels for gathering marketing information.

III. Discussion.

1. Distinguish between primary and secondary data. When should each type be used?

2. Distinguish among marketing information systems, marketing decision-support systems, and data mining. What contributions can each make to the marketing research function?

Chapter Seven

Segmentation, Targeting and Positioning

市场细分、目标营销和市场定位

◀ Objectives   学习目标

When students finish this chapter, they should be able to accomplish the following:

☑ To identify levels and patterns of market segmentation

☑ To identify the steps in the market segmentation process

☑ To explain the criteria for effective segmentation

☑ To describe the definition and process of market targeting

☑ To explain how to position products and brands

Target marketing requires marketers to take three major steps: market segmentation, market targeting and market positioning, as shown in Figure 7-1.

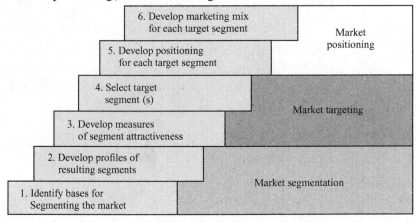

Figure 7-1   Steps in Segmentation, Targeting and Positioning

7.1   Market Segmentation   市场细分

1. Definition

Market segmentation: dividing a market into distinct groups of buyers with different needs, characteristics, or behavior who might require separate products or marketing mixes.

2. Benefits of market segmentation

The overall objective of using a market segmentation strategy is to improve a company's strategy competitive position and better serve the needs of its customers. There are four major benefits of market segmentation analysis and strategy.

(1) Design or provide responsive products to meet the needs of the market place. Proper segment enable a company to employ a more interactive, personalized approach which goes a long way in building relationship and customer loyalty which leads to a closer movement towards the marketing concept — customer satisfaction as a profit on the base of great customer satisfaction.

(2) Determine effective and cost efficient promotional strategies. As a planning tool, appropriate promotional campaigns can be designed and targeted to the right media vehicles. This marketing investment can be supplemented by public relations initiatives and sales promotion methods. In addition, the personal sales process can be improved by providing sales representatives with useful background customer research, recommended sales appeals, and on going support.

(3) Evaluate market competition, in particular a company's market position. If the information collected was thorough, the marketer would be able to explore the company's market position — how it is perceived by its customers and potential customers relative to the competition.

(4) Provide insight on present marketing strategies. It is important to periodically reevaluate a company's present marketing strategies to try to capitalize on new opportunities and circumvent potential threats. Segmentation research is useful in exploring new markets — perhaps secondary smaller or fringe markets which might have otherwise been neglected by concentrating on primary markets. With all those information, the marketer has the necessary research base upon which all other marketing strategies can be successfully formulated and implemented.

3. Trends in Market Segmentation

— Becoming increasingly sophisticated.

— Computer programs and databases assisting with more thorough segmentation analysis.

— Switching from "traditional" segmentation bases to more sophisticated bases such as behavioral and psycho-graphic.

7.1.1 Bases of market segmentation 市场细分的基本原则

Variables can be used to segment markets. Segmentation variables should be related to consumer needs for, and uses of or behavior toward the product.

There are four variables (bases) for segmenting consumer markets, as shown in Figure 7-2.

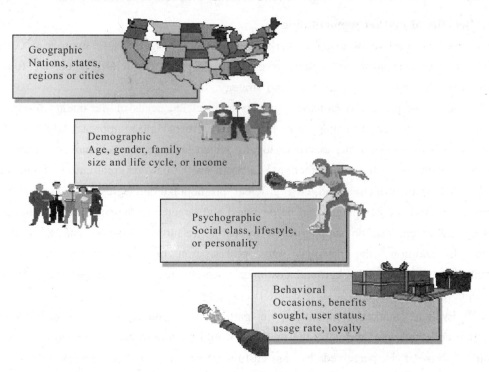

Figure 7-2   Bases for Segmenting Consumer Markets

1. Geographic segmentation

A logical starting point in market segmentation is the examination of population characteristics. Geographic segmentation — the dividing of an overall market into homogeneous[1] groups on the basis of population location — has been used for hundreds of years.

Consumers in different geographic locations are subject to varying conditions in terms of climate, terrain[2], natural resources and population density. Markets can be divided into regions because one or more of the geographical variables cause differences to appear from one region to another. A company that sells products throughout the European Community will, for example, need to reflect the different languages spoken in the labeling of its goods.

City size can be an important segmentation variable. Some marketers want to focus their efforts on cities of a certain size.

Geographic segmentation is useful only when differences in preference and purchase patterns for a product emerge along regional lines. Moreover, geographic subdivisions of the overall market tend to be rather large and often too heterogeneous[3] for effective segmentation without careful consideration of additional factors. In such cases, several segmentation variables may need to be utilized.

2. Demographic segmentation

The most common approach to market segmentation is demographic segmentation, the dividing of consumer groups according to demographic variables. These characteristics — age, sex, income, occupation, education, household size, lifestyle, and stage in the family lifecycle, among others — typically are used to identify market segments and develop appropriate marketing mixes. Demographic variables are used in market segmentation for three reasons:

— They are easy to identify and measure.

— They are associated with the sale of many products and services.

— They are typically referred to in describing the audiences of advertising media so that media buyers and others can easily pinpoint[4] the desired target market.

3. Psycho-graphic segmentation

Psychographic segmentation generally means the psychological profiles[5] of different consumers developed from the responses of consumers asked to agree or disagree with AIO (activities, interests and opinions) statements.

Some market research bureaus are designed to supply advertisers with detailed and specific information on specific target groups of consumers, in particular focusing on who makes the decision to purchase appliances and consumer durables. In addition, the advertisers will get to learn more about the habits and lifestyles of the consumer, finding out what the person reads, watches and listens to. Obviously this adds greatly to the psychographic profile many marketers now require.

The marketing implications of psychographic segmentation are considerable. Psychographic profiles produce a much richer description of a potential target market and can assist in promotional decisions in attempting to match the company's image and product offerings with the type of consumer who uses the products.

When combined with demographic/geographic characteristics, psychographics is an important tool for understanding the behavior of present and potential target markets.

4. Behavioral segmentation

Behavioral segmentation divides buyers into groups based on their knowledge, attitudes, uses, or responses to a product. Many marketers believe that behavior variables are the best starting point for building market segments.

1) Occasions

Occasion segmentation divides the market into groups according to occasions when buyers get the idea to buy, actually make their purchase, or use the purchased item. It can help firms build up product usage.

2) Product benefits

Benefit segmentation divides the market into groups according to the different benefits that consumers seek from the product. It focuses on such attributes as product usage rates and benefits derived from a product. In other words, it is the division of a market according to the benefits the consumer wants from the product. These factors may reveal important bases for pinpointing prospective target markets. When differences among competing brands are slight, a firm may introduce a brand with a new benefit that appeals to a certain market segment.

3) User status

Markets can be segmented into groups of nonusers, ex-users, potential users, first-time users, and regular users of a product. Potential users and regular users may require different kinds of marketing appeals. Market share leaders will focus on attracting potential users, whereas smaller firms will focus on attracting current users away from the market leader.

4) Loyalty status

A market can also be segmented by consumer loyalty. Consumers can by loyal to brands, stores, and companies. According to their degree of loyalty, the buyers can be divided into several groups: completely loyal, somewhat loyal, or showing no loyalty to any brand. Companies should be careful when using brand loyalty in their segmentation strategies. Marketers must examine the motivations behind observed purchase patterns.

Hardly can any enterprise achieves its marketing goal by using only one variable to segment (single variable). More than one variables are adapted to divide market which provides more information about segment and enable the marketer to satisfy customers more precisely. More variables create more segments reducing the sales potential in each segment. So in general, there is no single way to segment a market. A marketer has to try different segmentation variables, alone and in combination, to find the best way to view the market structure.

7.1.2　Market segmentation procedure　市场细分的过程

Is there a formal procedure to identify the major segments in a market? Here is one common three-step approach used by marketing research firms.

1. Survey stage

The researcher conducts exploratory interviews and focus groups to gain insight into consumer motivations, attitudes, and behavior.

2. Analysis stage

The researcher applies factor analysis (a statistical technique used to determine the few underlying dimensions of a larger set of inter-correlated variables. *Example*: A broadcast network can reduce a large set of TV programs down to a small set of basic program types.) to the data to remove highly correlated variables, then applies cluster analysis (a statistical technique for separating objects into a specified number of mutually exclusive groups such that the groups are relatively homogeneous. *Example*: A marketing researcher might want to classify a miscellaneous set of cities into four groups of similar cities.) to create a specified number of maximally different segments.

3. Profiling stage

Each cluster is profiled in terms of its distinguishing attitudes, behavior, demographics, psychographics, and media patterns. Each segment can be given a name based on a dominant distinguishing characteristic.

7.1.3 Criteria for effective segmentation 有效细分的准则

To be successful, market segments must have the following characteristics: measurability, market potential, accessibility and responsiveness, as shown in Figure 7-3.

Measurability — be able to measure its size and characteristics	Market Potential — total purchases in a segment in a specified period given a specific level of marketing activity
Accessibility — be able to reach members of target segment with customized marketing mixes	Responsiveness — respond differently to some aspect of the 4P than other segments

Figure 7-3   Criteria for Effective Segmentation

Measurability is a reference to the degree to which the size and purchasing power of segments can be assessed.

Accessibility is a reference to the degree to which a firm can reach intended target segments efficiently.

Market Potential refers to the total potential sales for a product in a designated market for a specified period of time. Market potential relates to the total capacity of that market to absorb everything that the entire industry can produce.

Responsiveness is a reference to the degree to which identified target segments are large enough or have sufficient sales and profit potential to warrant unique or separate marketing programs.

7.2　Market Targeting　目标市场选择

Definition

Market targeting is the process of evaluating each market segment's attractiveness and selecting one or more segments to enter. There are 2 phases in developing a target market strategy：

— analyzing consumer demand；

— targeting the market(s)：undifferentiated, concentrated, and multi-segmented.

7.2.1　Analyzing consumer demand　分析消费者需求

Analyzing Demand needs to aggregate consumers with similar needs. Potential customers are not necessary to have similar needs or desires. A marketer must analyze its customers according to their characteristics. Generally, there are 3 types of demand patterns.

1）Homogeneous Demand is uniform demand, that is, everyone demands the product for the same reason(s).

2）Clustered Demand means consumer demand classified in 2 or more identifiable clusters. For instance, automobiles buyers according to their taste and income level, etc., are interested in luxury, cheap, sporty, spacious automobiles separately.

3）Diffused Demand refers to more costly product differentiation and more difficult to communicate. For example, cosmetic market need to offer hundreds of shades of lipstick. Firms try to modify consumer's demand to develop clusters of at least a moderate size.

7.2.2　Targeting the market segments　细分市场的目标营销

After evaluating different demands of different segments, the company must now decide which and how many segments to serve.

1.　Three factors to be considered

To targeting market segments, a company should：segment size and growth, segment structural attractiveness, and company objectives and resources.

1）Segment size and growth

The company must first collect and analyze data on current segment sales, growth rates, and expected profitability[6] for various segments. To have the right size and growth characteristics will attract interest in segments. But it is difficult to decide what "right size and growth" is. The requirements for current sales, growth rate and profit margin in targeting segments vary from big companies to small companies.

2) Segment structural attractiveness

A segment might have desirable size and growth and still not offer attractive profits. The company must examine several major structural factors that affect long-run segment attractiveness. Segment attractiveness will be affected by competitors, buyers, and suppliers.

3) Company objectives and resources

If a segment fits the company's objectives, the company must decide whether it possesses the skills and resources needed to succeed in that segment. On the contrary, it should not enter the segment. Even if the company possesses the required strengths, it needs to employ skills and resources superior to those of the competition in order to really win in a market segment.

2. Strategies to target the market segments

Three market-coverage strategies can be adopted to achieve consumer satisfaction: undifferentiated marketing, differentiated marketing and concentrated marketing. See Figure 7-4.

1) Undifferentiated marketing

Although marketing managers using an undifferentiated marketing strategy recognize the existence of numerous segments in the total market, they generally ignore minor differences and focus on the broad market. To reach the general market, they use mass advertising, mass distribution and broad themes.

One advantage of undifferentiated marketing is production efficiency. But there exist dangers in the strategy of it. Firms using undifferentiated marketing develop an offer aimed at the largest segments in the market. When several firms do this, heavy competition develops in the largest segments, and less satisfaction results in the smaller ones. The final result is that the larger segments may be less profitable because they attract heavy competition. Recognition of this problem has led firms to be more interested in smaller market segments.

2) Differentiated marketing

This strategy is aimed at satisfying a large part of the total market, but instead of marketing one product with a single marketing program, the organization markets a number of products designed to appeal to individual parts of the total market.

By providing increased satisfaction for each of numerous target markets, the company with a differentiated marketing strategy can produce more sales than would be possible with undifferentiated marketing.

In general, the costs of a differentiated marketing strategy are greater than those of an undifferentiated one. Production costs, inventory costs, and promotional costs increase. Under a differentiated marketing strategy, consumers are usually better served because products offered are specifically designed to meet the needs of smaller segments. A firm that wants to employ a single marketing strategy for an entire market may be forced to choose a strategy of differentiated marketing.

3) Concentrated marketing

Concentrated marketing is particularly appealing to new, small firms that lack the financial resources of their competitors. Rather than attempting to market its product offerings to the entire market, a firm may choose to focus its efforts on profitably satisfying a smaller target market.

Concentration on a segment of the total market often allows some firms to maintain profitable operations. But it also poses dangers. The particular market segment can turn sour, or larger competitors may decide to enter the same segment. For these reasons, many companies prefer to diversify in several market segments.

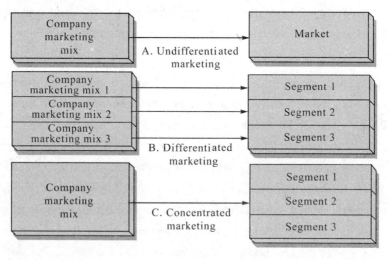

Figure 7-4   Three Market-coverage Strategies

7.3   Positioning   市场定位

1. Definition

The final market selection decision is positioning. Positioning is the development of a service and a marketing mix to occupy a specific place in the minds of customers within target markets. After the target market has been chosen, marketers want to position their products or fix them in the minds of the target markets. For example, a minor league baseball team may wish to position itself as an inexpensive, family entertainment alternative. In order to understand how a product is positioned relative to its competition, perceptual maps are developed through marketing research techniques. Perceptual maps are a way of revealing how customers see markets. They show which products customers see as alike and those that are not. They can also show segments and the dimensions customers use to split up the market. By looking at perceptual maps, marketers can identify whether or not they have achieved their desired image or whether they need to reposition their products in the minds of the target market. There is a sample positioning map of automobiles, as shown in Figure 7-5.

```
                        Luxurious
              ·Mercedes          ·Lexus
       Cadillac·
         Lincoln·          ·BMW        ·Porsche
              ·Chrysler
       Oldsmobile·  ·Buick   ·Pontiac
  Traditional ─────────────────────────── Sporty
       Mercury·    Ford·   ·Chevrolet
                              ·Nissan
              Dodge·       ·Toyota
         Plymouth·                ·Saturn
                           ·VW
                        Functional
```

Figure 7-5   Sample Positioning Map: Automobiles

2. Positioning across markets

Firms often have to make a tradeoff between adapting their products to the unique demands of a country market or gaining benefits of standardization such as cost savings and the maintenance of a consistent global brand image. There are no easy answers here. On the one hand, McDonald's has spent a great deal of resources to promote its global image; on the other hand, significant accommodations are made to local tastes and preferences — for example, while serving alcohol in US restaurants would go against the family image of the restaurant carefully nurtured over several decades, McDonald's has accommodated this demand of European patrons.

There are several positioning strategies for shifting and holding customers' perceptions. Positioning works by associating products with product attributes or other stimuli. Successful firms usually maintain a clear differential advantage and do not make violent changes to their market position.

Cases

Segmentation and targeting research for a leading energy company

1. Business problem

This leading consumer energy corporation was looking to develop a company-wide understanding of how they might reposition and redefine their offering in order to acquire new customers and maximize their current customers through more effective communications. They also wanted to expand their product image, which was most often identified with fuel to the wider convenience store market.

2. Solution

Segmentation research was conducted in the company marketing regions, collecting information on consumer attitudes, behaviors, and characteristics. The segmentation was designed to identify consumers who were both currently valuable to the company and that offer future opportunity. Five segments were identified based on their activity levels and their attitudes toward the category. Segment motivations and needs were uncovered to guide and optimize marketing communications.

3. Implementation

Marketing messages were developed to resonate with the unique attitudes and needs of the most lucrative segments. These messages were distributed through specific media channels appropriate to the target segments, saving the company hundreds of thousands of dollars in mass advertising. The segmentation was disseminated company-wide to insure a unified view of the company's key consumers, and new product offerings are underway to meet the needs of the future customer with the greatest revenue potential.

Key Terms

market segmentation 市场细分
marketing mix 市场营销组合
geographic segmentation 地理细分化
demographic segmentation 人口统计细分化
psycho-graphic segmentation 心理图解细分化
behavioral segmentation 行为的细分化
benefit segmentation 利益细分
user status 使用者状况

loyalty status 忠诚地位

factor analysis 因子分析法

cluster analysis 集群分析

market targeting 选定目标市场

homogeneous demand 同质需求

clustered demand 集群需求

diffused demand 扩散需求

undifferentiated marketing 无差异性营销策略

differentiated marketing 差异性营销策略

concentrated marketing 集中性营销策略

inventory cost 存货成本

positioning 定位

product difference 产品差异

the enterprise image 企业形象

📄 Notes

1. homogeneous *a.* 同类的，相似的，均一的，均匀的

2. terrain *n.* 地形

3. heterogeneous *a.* 不同种类的，异类的

4. pinpoint *v.* 查明

5. profile *n.* 图表，侧面，外形

6. profitability *n.* 收益性，利益率

✍ Exercises

I. Multiple choices.

1. The group of consumers most likely to purchase a particular product are called a _____.

   A. consumer market B. pre-purchase market C. seller's market

   D. buyer's market E. target market

2. The process of dividing the total market into several smaller, homogeneous groups is called _____.

   A. market penetration B. market segmentation C. market mixing

   D. market division E. sorting out the market

3. Red Ryder Industries markets rodeo and equitation (horse riding) supplies specifically to

women. This is an example of _____.

A. market segmentation

B. market stratification

C. market concentration

D. multi-gender marketing

E. non-traditional marketing

4. Which of the following is an example of a marketer targeting a segment that matches its marketing capabilities?

A. A hamburger stand marketing to a fifty-mile radius around itself.

B. Louisiana Rural Electric Power Company marketing to the entire Mississippi Valley.

C. Savannah Harbor Tug Service marketing to all major seaports in the United States.

D. Procter & Gamble marketing to fewer but more specialized market segments.

E. Ferrari Motors offering a minivan in the US market.

5. Demographic segmentation includes _____.

A. an individual's stage in the family life cycle

B. location of a person's residence

C. rate at which a person uses a product

D. the individual's lifestyle preferences

E. benefits sought by people in their purchases

6. Product-related segmentation involves segmenting a consumer population based on characteristics of their relationships to the product. One of these segmenting characteristics is _____.

A. brand loyalty toward the product

B. design and color of the product

C. price and mark-up policy of resellers

D. number of years the product has been on the market

E. shelf life of the product

7. The task in the second stage of the market segmentation process is to develop a profile of the typical customer in each segment. This profile may include information about _____.

A. the process of forecasting our own market share of the segments

B. estimating the costs versus the benefits of accessing each segment

C. typical customers' geographic locations and demographic characteristics

D. selection of specific market segments based on this analysis

E. analysis of competitive forces in each segment and their effect on consumer behavior

8. A useful tool to help marketers evaluate potential market segments on the basis of their relevant characteristics and their potential for satisfying business objectives is _____.

A. the forecast of probable market share technique

   B. the identification of segmentable markets process

   C. target market decision analysis

   D. typology

   E. psychographic patterns for global markets

9. The strategy sometimes referred to as mass marketing is also known as _____ .

   A. differentiated marketing   B. concentrated marketing

   C. micromarketing   D. macromarketing

   E. undifferentiated marketing

10. Costs of production, inventory, and promotion generally increase when a firm practices the concept of _____ .

   A. strategic marketing   B. concentrated marketing

   C. psychographic marketing   D. differentiated marketing

   E. tactical marketing

II. True or false.

1. The target market for a product is the specific segment of consumers most likely to purchase a particular product.

2. The division of the total market into smaller, relatively homogeneous groups is called market selectivity.

3. The number and size of the market segments chosen by a firm must not exceed its marketing capabilities.

4. Marketers must identify segments sufficiently small enough to capture in their entirety and effectively promote to as an exclusive source of some needed product.

5. Marketers are often able to identify totally homogeneous markets segments; there are seldom major differences among the members of a target market group.

6. The information, analysis, and forecasts accumulated through the entire market segmentation decision process allow management to assess the potential for achieving company goals and to justify committing resources to develop one or more segments.

7. Using differentiated marketing, Culture's Edge can market a wide range of trips exploring ethnic, cultural, and lifestyle-based issues that together appeal to the majority of vacation travelers, yet sell them in such a way as to appeal to individual parts of that market.

8. Colorado River White Water Raft Tours may take your breath away, but they don't take American Express! This represents an attempt by Visa Card to position itself with respect

to one of its competitors.

9. The firm's segmentation strategy may change as its product progresses through the stages of the life cycle. During the early stages, undifferentiated marketing might effectively support the firm's attempt to develop initial demand for the product.

10. Marketers can create a competitive positioning map from information solicited from competitors or from public databases that track consumer attitudes, opinions, and interests.

III. Discussion.

1. List and discuss the requirements for effective segmentation.

2. Please comment on the following statement: "It is usually better for a company to have several small market segments very well satisfied, than one large market segment only satisfied to a certain extent."

3. McDonald's has about 22,000 restaurants in 109 countries. Go to its web site: http://www.mcdonalds.com, and determine what country is its largest market outside the US. Do you think it offers more or less opportunity for future growth than the US?

Chapter Eight

Strategies for Entering International Markets

进入国际市场的策略

◀ Objectives 学习目标

When students finish this chapter, they should be able to accomplish the following：

☑ To identify and classify different market entry modes

☑ To explore different approaches to the choice of entry mode

☑ To identify the factors to consider when choosing a market entry strategy

☑ To discuss the advantages and disadvantages of the main intermediate entry modes

8.1 Market Entry Modes 市场进入模式

With rare exceptions, products just don't emerge in foreign markets overnight — a firm has to build up a market over time. Several strategies, which differ in aggressiveness, risk, and the amount of control that the firm is able to maintain, are available. Seen from the perspective of the international marketer, market entry modes can be classified into three groups.

1. Export modes（low control, low risk, high flexibility）

Exporting is a relatively low risk strategy in which few investments are made in the new country. A drawback is that, because the company makes few if any marketing investments in the new country, market share may be below potential. Further, the company, by not operating in the country, learns less about the market（What do consumers really want? Which kinds of advertising campaigns are most successful? What are the most effective methods of distribution?）If an importer is willing to do a good job of marketing, this arrangement may represent a "win-win"

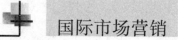

situation, but it may be more difficult for the company to enter on its own later if it decides that larger profits can be made within the country.

2. Intermediate modes (contractual modes) (shared control and risk, split ownership)

Licensing and franchising are also low exposure methods of entry — the company allows someone else to use its trademarks and accumulated expertise. Its partner puts up the money and assumes the risk. Problems here involve the fact that the company is training a potential competitor and that it has little control over how the business is operated. For example, American fast food restaurants have found that foreign franchisers often fail to maintain American standards of cleanliness. Similarly, a foreign manufacturer may use lower quality ingredients in manufacturing a brand based on premium contents in the home country.

Contract manufacturing involves having someone else manufacture products while the marketer takes on some of the marketing efforts himself. This saves investment, but again the marketer may be training a competitor.

3. Hierarchical modes (investment modes) (high control, high risk, low flexibility)

Direct entry strategies, where the company either acquires a firm or builds operations "from scratch" involve the highest exposure, but also the greatest opportunities for profits. The company gains more knowledge about the local market and maintains greater control, but now has a huge investment. In some countries, the government may expropriate assets without compensation, so direct investment entails an additional risk. A variation involves a joint venture, where a local firm puts up some of the money and knowledge about the local market.

8.2　Rules for the Selection of Different Entry Modes
选择不同进入模式的规则

1. Naive[1] rule

The decision-maker uses the same entry mode for all foreign markets. This rule ignores the heterogeneity[2] of the individual foreign markets.

2. Pragmatic[3] rule

The decision-maker uses a workable entry mode for each foreign market. In the early stages of exporting, the company typically starts doing business with a low-risk entry mode. Only if the particular initial mode is not feasible or profitable will the firm look for another workable entry mode. In this case not all potential alternatives are investigated, and the workable entry may not be the best entry mode.

3. Strategy rule

This approach requires that all alternative entry modes are systematically compared and evaluated before any choice is made. An application of this decision rule would be to choose the entry mode that maximizes the profit contribution over the strategic planning period subject to 1) the availability of company resources; 2) risk and 3) non-profit objectives.

8.3　Factors Influencing the Choice of Entry Modes
　　　影响选择进入模式的因素

As shown in Figure 8-1, four groups of factors are believed to influence the entry mode decision.

1. Internal factors

Internal factors are those that can be controlled by company. These include: firm size, international experience, and product complexity and product differentiation advantages.

2. External factors

The marketing environment involves factors that, for the most part, are beyond the control of the company, hence the name external factors.

These factors include: social trends (e. g. Gerber, a manufacturer of baby products, faces a serious challenge with declining US birth rates), technology (e. g. VCR makers are threatened by DVD players), new or potential competitors (e. g. Internet service providers are being threatened by increasing marketing efforts from MSN), or political situation, changing laws and changing interpretations by the courts, market size and growth, demand uncertainty, small number of relevant export intermediaries available, etc. Thus, the company must adapt to these factors. It is important to observe how the environment changes so that a firm can adapt its strategies appropriately.

3. Desired mode characteristics

The company may choose different entry mode according to its marketing subject and firm size which would enable the company to control its foreign market at a proper level.

4. Transaction-specific behavior

Different products and services require different marketing strategy. There is no definite answer to the specific entry model a company should adapt. The opportunity, transaction frequency, asset specificity and the environment's uncertainty may vary the choice of a marketer. Besides, transaction cost is also a very important factor to be considered.

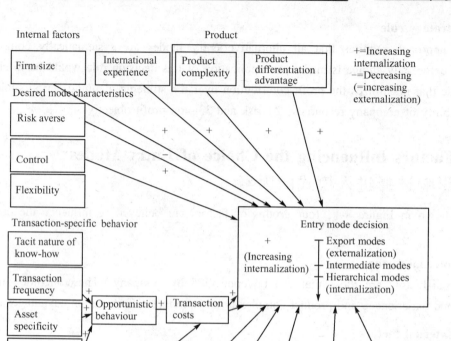

Figure 8-1   Factors Affecting the Foreign Market Entry Mode Decision

8.4   Export Modes   出口模式

While export channels may take many different forms, for the purposes of simplicity three major types may be identified: indirect, direct and cooperative export marketing groups.

8.4.1   Indirect exporting   间接出口

Indirect exporting means that a firm may export only occasionally to sell surplus or obsolete inventory or that part of its production is used in another firm's products and then sold abroad. A firm selling its merchandise abroad but making no special effort on its own behalf is called an indirect exporter. Indirect exporting may entail foreign sales through domestic operations or export management companies. Usually indirect exporting occurs in the following forms.

(1) Domestic-based export merchant: buys the manufacturer's products and then sells them abroad.

(2) Domestic-based export agent: seeks and negotiates foreign purchases and is paid a commission. Included in this group are trading companies.

(3) Export management company (EMC) / export house (EH): agrees to manage a company's export activities for a fee.

(4) Cooperative organization: carries on exporting activities on behalf of several producers and is partly under their administrative control. Often used by producers of primary products — fruits, nuts, and so on.

8.4.2   Direct exporting   直接出口

Direct exporting occurs when a firm makes a commitment to seek export business. Direct representation does not mean that the exporter is selling directly to the consumer or customer. Under direct exporting, the manufacturer rather than the indirect exporter performs all the necessary export functions, including contacting local distributors, conducting the required marketing research, preparing export documentation, and setting prices. Direct exporting typically results in increased sales for the exporter. It often occurs in the following forms.

(1) Domestic-based export department or division: an export sales manager carries on the actual selling and draws on market assistance as needed.

(2) Overseas sales branch or subsidiary: an overseas sales branch allows the manufacturer to achieve greater presence and program control in the foreign market.

(3) Traveling export sales representatives: the company can send home-based sales representatives abroad to find business.

(4) Foreign-based distributors or agents: the company can hire foreign-based distributors or agents to sell the company's goods. They might be given exclusive rights to represent the manufacturer in that country or only limited rights.

8.4.3   Cooperative export marketing groups   合作出口营销群体

Export marketing groups are frequently found among small and medium-sized enterprises attempting to enter export markets for the first time. Many such firms do not achieve sufficient scale economies in manufacturing and marketing because of the size of the local market or the inadequacy of the management and marketing resources available. These companies include some traditional, mature, highly fragmented industries such as furniture and clothing and also recently established high-tech firms.

8.4.4　Advantages and disadvantages of export modes　出口模式的利与弊

Exporting is used as a mode of entry for consumer goods or as a distribution strategy to international markets. It bears a minimal risk and capital required is not very high. It also provides a pedestal[4] for learning from the foreign markets and the barrier to exit the market in case of unsatisfactory results is not either very high.

However there are numerous disadvantages to be identified. First, agency contracts often prove to be unsatisfactory, containing vague and difficult to enforce performance criteria. Attempts to support these criteria by attempting to specify quantitative budgets for traveling, advertising, engineering and support, as well as certain inventory levels in the agent's premises, often prove unsatisfactory. (Bradley, 2001, p. 23) Second, the initial stages of a firm's internationalization can threaten the firm's future market entry and expansion activities. Since it is common for firms to have their initial mode choice institutionalized over time, as new products are sold through the same established channels and new markets are entered using the same entry method, a problematic initial entry mode choice can survive through institutionalization of this mode. The inertia[5] shift process of entry modes delays the transition to a new entry mode. (Hollensen, 2001, p. 229)

8.5　Intermediate Entry Modes　中间商进入模式

8.5.1　Main intermediate entry modes　主要的中间商进入模式

1. Licensing

It is a contractual agreement in which a seller (or licensor) allows its technology, patents, trademarks (brand names), company name, designs, processes, or intellectual property to be used by a buyer (or licensee) in exchange for fees (or royalties[6]). Foreign licensing is an agreement in which a firm permits a foreign company to produce and distribute its merchandise or use its trademark, patent, or processes in a specified geographical area.

The agreement specifies the rights to be granted, the payment, and other issues. Among other things, a licensing contract should contain the following.

(1) Limitations on the rights being granted to the licensee such as geography (permitted use in what country or countries), the duration of the license, its degree of exclusivity for a given area, protection of the trade secrets / designs, etc., the obligations that the licensee has to the

licensor, and rights (for each party) to improvements in whatever is licensed.

(2) The bases for royalty payments (time, production level, sales level, which can be fixed or variable), the currency of payment, schedule of payments, minimum payment, and fees for additional services. One arbitrary rule is the 25% rule of thumb which suggests the licensor seek a 25% share of the licensee's related profits.

(3) Other provisions include: how to end the agreement, type of dispute resolution mechanism to use in case of disagreement, what countries' laws apply, penalties for lack of performance, and compliance mechanisms such as inspection schedules.

In some countries, licensing is not an attractive alternative because of government interference. Governments can require prior approval (Ireland and Spain, for example), institute regulations that disallow exclusive rights, use foreign exchange controls to limit royalty payments, and impose fee limits.

2. Franchising

Franchising involves a comprehensive licensing agreement. A franchisor grants to a franchisee the use of its trademark, operating procedures, products, and various support services in exchange for fees and often, a percentage of the profits. Examples include Holiday Inn, McDonald's, Seven Eleven, KFC, and Pepsi Co.

A type of agreement referred to as contract manufacturing involves a franchise of sorts since a local, foreign firm uses the technology of an international firm and its specifications to make products for the local market (a production agreement). The international firm controls the marketing and may prefer this means of production to sell in small foreign markets not warranting foreign direct investment.

3. Joint ventures

Joint ventures intend to share the risk, cost, and management with a partner in a foreign country. One important reason for joint venture formation is based on the concepts of products and markets. A firm can hope to strengthen its existing business which means improving how it serves its existing markets with its existing products, take its existing products to new foreign markets, bring foreign products to existing markets, or diversify its business by taking new products to new markets. Within a foreign joint venture a domestic firm enters into a partnership with a firm in the target nation. Joint ventures usually require a direct investment and result in a loss of control.

4. Strategic alliances

Non-equity based alliances can be formed to share costs, to gain market knowledge, to serve an international market, to develop industry standards together, or to combine skills. Hence they may achieve goals unattainable by each firm alone and have advantages and disadvantages similar to equity based ventures. However, the partners may feel freer to experiment and maintain flexibility if their creation is not a separate firm.

Typically such alliances use no formal contract, no equity terms, but are a loose, evolving arrangement with guidelines and expectations of shared gains.

Regardless of whether an alliance is equity based or not, finding the right partner and developing the right relationship can be time consuming and expensive. Premature dissolution of the agreement can harm a partner.

5. Management contracting

International management contracts refer to contracts to provide specific services, management expertise or technical assistance to a foreign firm either for a flat fee or a percentage of sales or profits. Notice that management contracting involves providing only management skills; the production facilities are owned by others. For example, Argentinean oil producer uses a few Chevron executives to help run its ongoing operations. Hughes Tool had helped them modernize their plant and cut their oil production costs in half.

8.5.2　Advantages and disadvantages of intermediate modes
中间商进入模式的利与弊

The advantages and disadvantages of the intermediate modes of market entry are quite similar to each other. They require all less capital than foreign direct investment, they have a quick access to markets and they all involve exploiting partner's information about the markets and resources in the international markets. Sometimes intermediary modes are even the only choice of entering the market because of the target country's legislation, high tariffs or taxes. What the intermediate entry modes also have in common is the lack of control over the activities abroad. There is also always a possibility of creating a potential competitor for the firm.

8.6　Hierarchical Modes　全资模式

8.6.1　Main hierarchical modes　主要的全资模式

Successful firms with very narrow product lines are generally committed to maintaining their lead in a limited, well-defined market. Confined to that market they have a high stake in maintaining their quality standards, in protecting and preventing disclosure of their technological skills and in maintaining tight control over market strategy to be applied to their products. Strategic decisions may be relatively few but each is highly important and each affects the firm as a whole. Such firms show a strong preference for wholly owned subsidiaries. They usually enter and stay in foreign markets through foreign direct investment. In the hierarchical modes the company must take care of activities by themselves. A sales subsidiary however is only one example. The other possibilities are domestic-based sales representatives, sales and production subsidiary, region centers / transnational organization, acquisition and greenfield investment.

The control of the foreign activities and the degree of integration rises gradually from an entry mode to another; the domestic-based sales representatives / manufacturer's own sales force has the least control over the market actions and smallest degree of integration to the foreign market when acquisition and greenfield investment have the strongest control over activities.

The higher the control the more the firm is able to affect the business activities in the foreign market place, and, of course, the bigger the risk the greater the revenue. However, the risk also increases going downwards because the capital investment is larger. (Hollensen, 2001, p. 305)

8.6.2   Advantages and disadvantages of hierarchical entry modes
全资进入模式的利与弊

The foreign direct investment process is stimulated more than just economic incentives. The presence of a sales office also assists information collection and better understanding of market opportunities, thereby significantly lowering perceptions of uncertainty and raising the probability that the firm will engage in foreign direct investment if the underlying cost conditions permit. Companies might also find that they have to protect their competitive advantage and source of revenues from potential competitors. (Bradley, 2001, p. 23) However, a foreign direct investment requires much more capital than the intermediate ways of doing international business. The local know-how from distribution channels and culture, etc., might not be as effectively exploited as in intermediate modes. Access to the market might also be slower or in some cases even impossible without a local partner, because of the legislation, taxation or tariffs, etc.

☞ Cases

GB Ltd is a small UK enterprise based in Reading. Its main business is computer graphics and it possesses advanced technology in this field with important applications for engineering. With the advent of the Single European Market in 1992 and the increasing internationalization of the world economy, it decided to enter the international business arena and to attempt to establish its own international sales and service network. The Board of Directors had in mind two target countries, namely Germany and Mexico. But the company lacked financial resources and managerial know-how to establish its own network in these two target markets.

GB's technical know-how was far superior to that of similar companies in Mexico. The problem in this market was that there would be little copyright or patent protection. The maximum license agreement would only be for four years. Royalties[6] would amount to only 4 percent of net sales after deducting the cost of materials and components supplied by GB Ltd. This agreement would produce only £20,000 in royalties if the local license produced annual sales of £1 million. Furthermore, the Mexican government would tax the royalties at the rate of 20 percent. Furthermore, given the maximum agreement time of four years, royalty payments would soon cease too.

The position with the German license was as follows. There would be a small down payment by the licensee and a royalty payment for three years, declining to 3 percent in the second half of a six-year agreement. However, the German company would be allowed to distribute and service other related products as well. Naturally this concerned GB Ltd, as there were no assurances that its services and products would be treated more favorably, and it also reflected a lack of protection.

Task:

Should GB Ltd enter into a licensing or a joint venture with either company? Support your argument.

Key Terms

market entry mode　市场进入模式

export mode　出口模式

intermediate mode　中间商模式

hierarchical mode　全资模式

naive rule　单一规则

pragmatic rule　注重时效规则

strategy rule　策略规则

internal factor　内在因素

external factor　外在因素

mode characteristic　模式特征

indirect exporting　间接出口

direct exporting　直接出口

cooperative export mode　合作出口模式

intermediate entry mode　中间商进入模式

licensing　许可证

franchising   特许经营

joint venture   合资

strategic alliance   战略联盟

franchisee   总经销

franchisor   授予特许者

licensee   领到许可证的人

licensor   许可证颁发者

expropriation of asset   资产征收

acquisition   收购

integrating production   产品一体化

📄 Notes

1. naive   *a.*   单一的，单纯的
2. heterogeneity   *n.*   异质；不同成分
3. pragmatic   *a.*   实际的，注重实效的
4. pedestal   *n.*   基础
5. inertia   *n.*   惯性
6. royalty   *n.*   版税

✍ Exercises

I. Multiple choices.

1. Marketing of business products tends to rely heavily on the strategic element of _____.

    A. advertising

    B. list prices for unique items

    C. short channels of distribution

    D. infrequent customer service contact

    E. individual decision making

2. Which of the following is NOT true of the advantages of indirect exporting?

    A. Limited commitment and investment required.

    B. Local selling support and services available.

    C. Minimal risk.

    D. No export experience required.

    E. High degree of market diversification is possible as the firm utilizes the internationalization of an experienced exporter.

3. Candy-makers Mars and Nestle have applied their names to lines of ice cream. These are examples of _____.

    A. line extension

    B. brand extension

    C. brand licensing

    D. brand mark

4. A partnership in which two or more companies share the work, costs, and rewards of a major project is _____.

    A. a foreign partnership

    B. a trade venture

    C. reciprocal partnership

    D. a joint venture

    E. cooperative industry

5. The strategy components for a firm's marketing mix in the international market, just as in the domestic market, are _____.

    A. product, packaging, and promotional materials

    B. distribution, shipping, and transportation logistics

    C. profitability and market share

    D. product, distribution, promotion, and price

    E. exchange rates and time delays in transportation

6. A significant advantage of using a standardized strategy for all of a firm's markets is _____.

    A. economies of scale that grow out of large production runs

    B. the consideration that is given local tastes and preferences

    C. customized promotional messages for each market

    D. variety in products and promotions

    E. the ability to satisfy varied market segments

7. When Coca-Cola uses a global marketing strategy that includes a single product and a single message, the product/promotion strategy being employed is _____.

    A. product adaptation   B. promotion adaptation

    C. straight extension   D. product invention

    E. dual adaptation

8. On which of the following do international product/promotion strategy decisions NOT depend?

A. Needs of customers in the foreign market.

    B. Competitive conditions in the foreign market.

    C. The nature of the product.

    D. The way in which the foreign customers are used to buying.

    E. The distribution system in the domestic market.

9. Which of the following is NOT a factor in the attractiveness of the US to foreign investors?

    A. High levels of discretionary income.

    B. Political stability.

    C. Well-controlled economic problems.

    D. A positive attitude toward foreign investment.

    E. Good weather.

10. The trend toward foreign ownership of US companies is likely to continue as foreign multinational firms seek to attain control over _____.

    A. prices   B. the supply of employment

    C. demand for all goods   D. distribution channels

    E. engineering and technology

II. True or false.

1. The principal disadvantage of licensing is that it can be a very limited form of participation.

2. Exporting is the most traditional and well-established form of operating internationally.

3. Licensing, joint ventures and importing are points and tools for global market entry and expansion.

4. Large-scale direct expansion may be less expensive and a major commitment of managerial time and energy is unnecessary.

5. Management contracting includes the sharing of risk and the ability to combine different value chain strengths.

6. One of the advantages of joint venture is better control of sales activities compared with other forms of participation in foreign markets.

7. Licensing is an alternative entry and expansion strategy with considerable appeal.

8. Direct exporting takes place through sales by foreign distributors, sales agents, and overseas sales subsidiaries.

9. As export merchants, they are essentially acting as domestic wholesalers operating in foreign markets through their own sales agents or salesforce.

10. International trading companies tend to be large-scale manufacturers and merchants and they are involved in wholesale and retail distribution.

III. Discussion.

1. Describe briefly the different methods of foreign market entry.

2. What are the advantages and disadvantages of barter, counter-trade, and export processing zones as market entry strategies?

Chapter Nine

Competitive Analysis and Strategy

竞争分析和竞争策略

◀ Objectives　学习目标

When students finish this chapter, they should be able to accomplish the following:

☑ To identify the forces influencing competition

☑ To identify the two strategies to achieve competitive advantages

☑ To be able to use the right sub-strategies to gain competitive advantage in global market

Successful marketers are those who can steer their organizations through the turbulent marketing environment, and do it better than competitors. Whilst easy to say, in practice it is not easy to do. Many competitive industries and organizations are very difficult to penetrate, despite all the intelligence techniques that may be available to get information. Any successful organization has to look at the competition, and moreover, be aware how the nature of competition can guide its strategy.

9.1　Forces Influencing Competition　影响竞争的因素

9.1.1　Competition　竞争

Competition in most global product / markets is intense. One way to look at competition is by industry analysis[1]. Competition drives down rates of return on invested capital. If the rate is "competitive", it will encourage investment; if not, it will discourage competition.

As shown in Figure 9-1, the forces influencing competition include：

1. Threat of new entrants

New capacity, a desire to gain market share and position, and new approaches to serving customer needs are what new entrants can bring to an industry. New entrants mean that prices will be pushed downward and margins squeezed, resulting in reduced industry profitability. Eight major sources of barriers to entry are：economies of scale, product differentiation, capital requirements, switching costs, distribution channels, government policy, cost advantages independent of scale and competitor response.

2. Threat of substitute products

The availability of substitute products places limits on the prices market leaders can charge in an industry; high prices may induce buyers to switch to the substitute.

3. Bargaining power of buyers

Customers aim to pay the lowest possible price to obtain the products or services. The buyers' best interests are served if they can drive down profitability in the supplier industry. They can purchase in such large quantities that supplier firms depend on the buyers' business for survival. They are likely to bargain hard for low prices when the supplier's products are regarded as commodities. Buyers will also bargain hard when the supplier industry's products or services represent a significant portion of the buying firms' costs. The willingness and ability to achieve backward integration is another source of buyer power.

4. Bargaining power of suppliers

If suppliers have enough leverage over industry firms, they can raise prices high enough to significantly influence the profitability of their organizational customers. If suppliers are large and relatively new in number, or when the suppliers' products or services are important inputs to industry firms, or are differentiated, or carry switching costs, the suppliers will have considerable leverage over buyers.

5. Rivalry among competitors

Rivalry among competitors refers to all the actions taken in the industry to improve their positions and gain advantage over each other, such as price competition, advertising battles, product positioning, attempts at differentiation, and so on.

The elements of industry structure are suppliers, buyers, new entrants and substitutes.

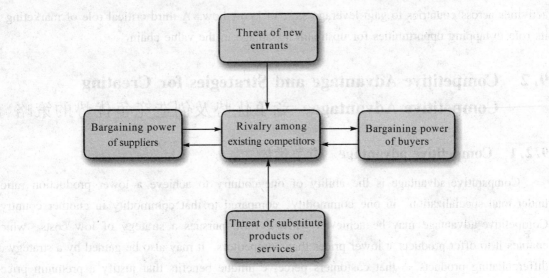

Figure 9-1   The Forces Influencing Competition

9.1.2   Competition analysis   竞争分析

In order to know how best to compete, as well as the analysis given above, one needs to know the way competitors measure themselves, their strategy to date, their major strengths and weaknesses and likely future strategy. In the first of these — knowing the way competitors see themselves — much can be learned from public accounts, interviews and the trade press. Other ways are to have competitive personnel, take part in trade fairs, purchase the competitor's product and take it apart, or indulge in "espionage[2]". In identifying the competitor's strategy to date, it is not enough to believe what they say but to reconstruct their strategy. Evaluating resources is difficult. It is essential to look at their production, marketing, financial and management resources. On the basis of these first three, it is possible to guess the future.

Not all competitors are necessarily bad. Good competitors can absorb demand fluctuations[3], expand the market, increase motivation, and act responsively to the industry. There is, for example, room for all developing countries to take a share in most world markets in commodities, without one country wishing to be too aggressive.

9.1.3   Competitive strategy   竞争策略

Value chain analysis espouses[4] three roles for marketing in a global competitive strategy. The first relates to the configuration[5] of marketing. It may be advantageous to concentrate some marketing activities in one or a few countries. A second role relates to the coordination of activities across countries to gain leverage say, of know how. A third critical role of marketing is its role in tapping opportunities for upstream advantage in the value chain.

9.2   Competitive Advantage and Strategies for Creating Competitive Advantage   竞争优势及创造竞争优势的策略

9.2.1   Competitive advantage   竞争优势

Comparative advantage is the ability of one country to achieve a lower production ratio, under total specialization, in one commodity, compared to that commodity in another country. Competitive advantage may be achieved when a form pursues a strategy of low costs, which enables it to offer products at lower prices than competitors. It may also be gained by a strategy of differentiating products so that customers perceive unique benefits that justify a premium price. Competitive advantage is based on lower production costs and / or quality of market factor differentiation between one country or industry and another in like products.

Two different models of competitive advantage have received considerable attention; they are generic strategies and strategic intent.

1. Generic strategies

Generic strategies are based on the principle that the achievement of competitive advantage is at the core of a superior marketing strategy. There are four generic approaches to outperforming others in an industry — overall cost leadership, differentiation, focused differentiation and cost focus (see Figure 9-2). The first two strategies impact on broad markets; the latter two are to achieve narrow-focus advantage.

1) Overall cost leadership

Here the company works hard to achieve the lowest costs of production and distribution so that it can price lower than its competitors and win a large market share. Based on a firm's position as the industry's low-cost producer in broadly defined markets or across a wide mix of products, this strategy has become increasingly popular in recent years. Cost-leadership advantage can be the basis for offering lower prices and more value to customers. It has been the cornerstone of other highly successful strategies. Cost leadership, however, is a sustainable source of competitive advantage only if barriers exist that prevent competitors from achieving the same low costs.

2) Differentiation

The company concentrates on creating a highly differentiated product line and marketing program so that it comes across as the class leader in the industry. It can be a very effective strategy for defending market position and obtaining above-average returns. To have a differentiation advantage, a firm's product has an actual or perceived uniqueness in a broad market, the uniqueness allows a company to charge a premium price for its products.

3) Focused differentiation

The company focuses its effort on serving a few market segments well rather than going after the whole market. It offers a narrow target market the perception of product uniqueness at a premium price. The world of high-end audio equipment offers a good example.

4) Cost focus

It means offering a narrow target market low prices. When a firm offers a narrow target market lower prices than the competition based on the firm's lower-cost position, this strategy is adopted. In the shipbuilding industry, Chinese shipyards offer simple, standard-vessel types at low prices that reflect low production costs. (Porter, The Competitive Advantage of Nations, p. 39)

If there are few perceived differences between products and their uses are widespread, then the lowest cost firms will get the advantage. This is the case of television sets and many fruit products. If there is a large perceived difference created, then the firm has more price leeway[6]. Focus strategies concentrate on serving a particular segment better than anyone else.

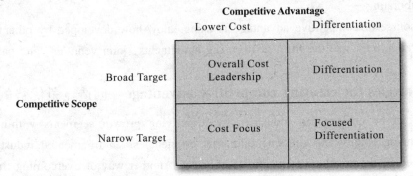

Figure 9-2   Generic Competitive Strategies

5) The life cycle

Successful global strategists have also to be cognizant of the international life cycle. Successful strategies start with a firm base in one region or country, and then expand as opportunities arise. These opportunities have to be explored alongside careful analysis of the life cycle stage in one or another country. Failure to do so may mean that the opportunity has passed, whereas the firm may be under the impression it is still there.

2. Strategic intent

An alternative framework for understanding competitive advantage focuses on competitiveness as a function of the pace at which a company implants new advantages deep within its organization. This framework identifies strategic intent, growing out of ambition and obsession[7] with winning, as the means of achieving competitive advantage. Four successful approaches are as follows.

1) Layers of advantages

A company faces less risk in competitive encounters if it has a wide portfolio of advantages. Successful companies steadily build such portfolios by establishing layers of advantage on top of one another.

2) Loose bricks

A second approach takes advantage of the "loose bricks" left in the defensive walls of competitors whose attention is narrowly focused on a market segment or a geographic area.

3) Changing the rules

A third approach involves changing the so-called rules of engagement and refusing to "play by the rules" set by industry leaders.

4) Collaborating

A final source of competitive advantage is using know-how developed by other companies. Such collaboration may take the form of licensing agreements, joint ventures, and partnerships.

9.2.2　Strategies for creating competitive advantage　创造竞争优势的策略

Success can be achieved in industries by identifying growth segments within an overall market, enhancing quality and stressing operating efficiencies. In fragmented industries success can be achieved by the creation of economies of scale. Another way of overcoming fragmentation is by "positioning" which must be consistent.

We can adopt a classification of competitive strategies based on the roles firms play in the target market. The four main types of positioning strategy are market-leader strategies, market-challenger strategies, market-follower strategies and market-nicher strategies.

（1）**Market leader**：The firm in an industry with the largest market share; it usually leads other firms in price changes, new product introductions, distribution coverage, and promotion spending. Most industries contain an acknowledged market leader. In market leadership the firm must work at maintaining its position, having got there through, say, cost advantage or innovation, by being very responsive to market needs. Competitors focus on the leader as a company to challenge, imitate, or avoid. Some of the best-known market leaders are General Motors (autos), Kodak (photography), IBM (computers), Campbell's (soups), Coca-Cola (soft drinks), Wal-Mart (retailing), McDonald's (fast food) and so on.

To remain market leader, the firms can take any of three actions. 1) They can find ways to expand total demand. 2) They can protect their current market share through good defensive and offensive actions. 3) They can try to expand their market share further, even if market size remains constant.

(2) **Market challenger**: A runner-up firm in an industry that is fighting hard to increase its market share. In the market challenger category, an organization may publicly announce its intention to take over the number one position either by price advantage, product innovation or promotion. Such as in the construction equipment industry, Komatsu successfully challenged Caterpillar by offering the same quality at much lower prices. And Kimberly Clark's Huggies grabbed a big share of the disposable diaper market from P&G by offering a better-fitting diaper with reusable fasteners. The challenger can attack the market leader, which is a high-risk but high-gain strategy that makes good sense if the leader is not serving the market well. IBM entered the personal computer market late, as a challenger, but quickly became the market leader. The challenger also can avoid the leader and instead challenge firms of its own size, or smaller local and regional firms. If the company goes after a small local company, its objective may be to put that company out of business. So, to define its strategic objective is really important for a market challenger.

(3) **Market follower**: A runner-up firm in an industry that wants to hold its share without rocking the boat. The market follower is "allowed" to stay in the market only if the leader chooses to maintain a price umbrella and not maximize share. However the follower may be able to service segments on a more personal level than the leader and hence maintain an industry position.

A follower can gain many advantages. Since the market leader must bear the huge expenses of developing new products and markets, expanding distribution, and educating the market, the market follower can learn from the leader's experience and copy or improve on the leader's products and programs, usually with much less investment. Following is not the same as being passive or a carbon copy of the leader. A market follower must know how to hold current customers and win a fair share of new ones. The follower is often a major target of attack by challengers. Therefore, the market follower must keep its manufacturing costs low and its product quality and services high.

Firms that are second or third in an industry are sometimes quite large, such as Colgate, Ford, and Pepsi Co. These runner-up firms can adopt one of the above two strategies. They can challenge the leader and other competitors in an aggressive bid for more market share (market challengers) , or they can play along with competitors and not rock the boat (market followers) .

(4) **Market nicher**: A firm in an industry that serves small segments that the other firms overlook or ignore. Almost every industry includes firms that specialize in serving market niches. Instead of pursuing the whole market, or even large segments, these firms target sub-segments, or niches. Nichers are often smaller firms with limited resources. But smaller divisions of larger firms also may pursue niching strategies. Firms with low shares of the total market can be highly profitable through smart niching.

Other strategies include " market flanking[8] " — a classical Japanese approach. The competitive position of the industry is very important to the would be global marketer. Intelligence, such as that gathered by the process described, is an essential prerequisite to designing a strategy. Too often developing countries attempt to gain entry into the international market without knowledge of the industry or competitors. The need to properly assess the market and devise a strategy on the assessment is a must to succeed.

The "copy adapt" strategy is a relatively well-tried strategy in which an organization may seek to copy a successful product / market strategy pioneered by another organization and adapt it to local conditions or other markets. Many examples of this strategy exist in less developed countries, where the local populace may simply not have the income to afford the real thing. Typical examples exist in all countries but none more so than in India. One can see agricultural land implements, tractors, ox carts and many other cheaper, adaptations of well known marques, for example, the International Harvester and the Indian Mahindra tractor "look alike".

☞ Cases

Argentina Beef

Beef has been a tradition in Argentina for two centuries. It had always exported salted meet and later chilled beef, but with the establishment of "barriers" internationally the Commonwealth Preference System, and other environmental factors like World War II, Argentina's international beef market contracted and so it standardized the domestic market. Argentina's beef consumption per capita is almost four times that of Western Europe (70 – 80 kgs compared to 15 – 25 kgs).

Despite its domestic orientation recently. Argentina is still the world's third largest beef producer and fourth in exporting terms behind Australia, Germany and the US. Its traditional export markets for lower value products (boned and manufactured-beef) has been lost to subsidized EU supplies and because of other developed country protection measures.

However it has maintained or increased its export of high value products (boneless cute, canned beef, frozen beef) which now account for over 80% of export value. Its export value is now near the $800 million mark although only 10% of its total agricultural exports.

The Argentina beef industry faced all the "macro" forces described by Porter internally and externally, and the threat of new entrants, but survived. This success was not necessarily built on favourable trading conditions but its ability to maintain international competitiveness through rampant inflation, currency over-evaluation, heavy taxation, potential uncertainty and increased competition from substitute products internationally and from the Argentine cereals sub sector which was clamoring for more resources.

Its success was sustained by:

(1) low cost production of quality beef (climate and extensive grasslands);

(2) well developed, flexible and transparent livestock marketing system;

(3) innovations in beef distribution domestically (butcher chain stores, vacuum packing);

(4) development of new international market outlets (Mid East);

(5) debt rescheduling by banks for livestock and trading enterprises.

With recent measures to make the industry viable again, including capacity rationalization, Argentina beef is now back in profit and is exporting a little more now.

🗒 Key Terms

competition analysis   竞争分析

competitive strategy   竞争策略

competitive advantage   竞争优势

comparative advantage   比较优势

generic strategy   一般策略

overall cost leadership   总体成本指导

differentiation   差异

focused differentiation   集中差异

cost focus   成本集中

life cycle   生命周期

strategic intent   策略意图

layers of advantage   利益层

loose bricks   宽松的结构

portfolio   投资组合，业务经营项目组合

collaborating   合作

market-leader strategy   市场领袖策略

market-challenger strategy 市场挑战者策略
market-follower strategy 市场追随者策略
market-nicher strategy 市场补缺策略
copy-adapt strategy 模仿—改进策略

📖 Notes

1. industry analysis 行业分析
2. espionage *n.* 间谍，侦探
3. fluctuation *n.* 波动，起伏
4. espouse *vt.* 支持，赞成
5. configuration *n.* 构造，结构
6. leeway *n.* 回旋余地
7. obsession *n.* 困扰
8. flank *v.* 置于侧面，夹击

✍ Exercises

I. Multiple choices.

1. Smith's Fine Foods is involved in selecting and analyzing a target market and developing a marketing mix to gain long-run competitive advantages. Based on this example, Smith's is creating a _____.

   A. corporate strategy   B. target design
   C. mix strategy   D. marketing strategy
   E. marketing tactic

2. In examining her firm's recently completed market attractiveness-business position model, Jenna Cook finds that the firm's sport sunglasses unit is high on both dimensions. Which one of the following strategies would this placement dictate?

   A. Invest.   B. Harvest.   C. Divest.   D. Maintain.

3. When Sony Corp. purchased Columbia Pictures, it engaged in _____ because its new products were not technologically related to its current products.

   A. product development   B. market development
   C. concentric diversification   D. market penetration
   E. horizontal diversification

4. Seagram Co., which markets alcoholic beverages, acquired MCA, which produces movies

and television shows and owns publishing houses, theme parks, and movie theatres. What type of diversified growth does this acquisition represent?

A. Conglomerate diversification.   B. Integrated diversification.

C. Concentric diversification.   D. Vertical diversification.

E. Horizontal diversification.

5. Kraft purchased Duracell battery division and operates this division as a separate profit centre within the firm. In this example, Duracell is a _____ of Kraft.

A. strategic business unit   B. marketing unit

C. dependent unit   D. corporate unit

6. A _____ is something that an organization does extremely well — sometimes so well that it gives a company an advantage over its competition.

A. competitive advantage   B. sustainable competitive advantage

C. distinctive competency   D. strategic vision

E. marketing opportunity

7. A _____ is created when a company matches its distinctive competency to the opportunities it has discovered in the market.

A. market opportunity   B. market requirement

C. competitive advantage   D. strategic window

E. competitive opportunity

8. Product-portfolio analysis is based on the idea that _____.

A. a firm's market share and market attractiveness are factors for a marketing strategy

B. a firm has a profitable impact on marketing strategy

C. a product's market growth rate and its relative market share are important determinants of its marketing strategy

D. a product's market growth rate and market attractiveness determine the marketing strategy

9. Philip Morris's strategy of cutting prices on its Marlboro cigarettes to enlarge its market share in the increasingly competitive tobacco industry is known as _____.

A. market penetration   B. market development

C. product development   D. product penetration

E. concentric integration

10. The publishers of The Economist developed a campaign to market the magazine to university and college students studying business and management courses. This would best be referred to as a strategy centering on _____.

A. product development   B. horizontal diversification

C. market development   D. concentric diversification

E. conglomerate diversification

II. True or false.

1. The final step in the marketing control process is to compare actual performance and standards.

2. In a period of recovery, the best marketing strategy for Electrolux would be characterized by flexibility.

3. In the beer industry, a few large brewers supply the majority of the market. The brewing industry is an example of the competitive structure: Monopolistic Competition.

4. Post Office Parcel Services firms would most likely have a monopoly for its competitive environment.

5. Essex Office Products has decided to use a particular competitive tool that it feels will have a major impact. Its consultant, Dr. Bell, contends that this particular approach is the one most easily copied by the firm's competitors. The tool in question is: market segmentation.

6. A small hardware store whose only competitor is a huge discount store would be least likely to use the competitive tool distribution.

7. Customer value analysis refers to analysis conducted to determine what benefits target customers value and how they rate the relative value of various competitors' offers.

8. Some basic competitive positioning strategies that companies can follow are: overall cost leadership, differentiation, and focus.

9. While trying to expand total market size, the leading firm must constantly protect its current business against competitors' attacks.

10. Competitor-centered company is a company whose moves are mainly based on competitors' actions and reactions; it spends most of its time tracking competitors' moves and market shares and trying to find strategies to counter them.

III. Discussion.

1. What is the difference between "comparative advantage" and "competitive advantage"?

2. Describe, with examples, a market leader, a market challenger, a market follower, a market nicher, a market flanker and a copy-adapt strategy.

Chapter Ten

Cooperation strategies

合作策略

◄) Objectives　学习目标

When students finish this chapter, they should be able to accomplish the following:

☑ To grasp the definition of cooperative strategies

☑ To list the reasons for cooperative strategies

☑ To describe the benefits of cooperative strategies

☑ To identify the types of cooperative strategies

☑ To list the basic steps in starting a cooperative

Why do people start cooperatives?

For over 150 years, cooperatives have been an effective way for people to exert control over their economic livelihoods, and continue to have a powerful impact on economy. Today, in an era when many people feel powerless to change their lives, co-ops represent a strong, vibrant, and viable economic alternative. Co-ops are formed to meet peoples' mutual needs. They are based on the powerful idea that together, a group of people can achieve goals that none of them could achieve alone. There is a rich history of cooperation in the USA. In Wisconsin, 2.7 million residents (more than half the population) are served in some way by cooperatives. Cooperatives provide a unique tool for achieving economic goals in an increasingly competitive global economy. These goals may include:

- Achieving economy of size;
- Increasing bargaining power;
- Sharing costs of new technology;

- Adding value to agricultural products;
- Gaining access to new markets;
- Reducing risks associated with new enterprises;
- Obtaining new services;
- Purchasing in bulk to achieve lower prices;
- Securing credit from financial institutions.

10.1　What Are Cooperative Strategies?　什么是合作策略?

Cooperative strategies are the forms of cooperation between two or more companies, where the purpose is to enhance the competitiveness of the strategic partners. We often use phrases collaborative agreements, strategic alliances, and global strategic partnerships to name them. The rationale[1] behind such linkages is that every partner must have something valuable and unique to contribute in the cooperative. Especially, in the international markets, the companies can bring, for example, their product-market knowledge, ultimate delivery network, or access to some markets to the alliance, and thereby increase the value of the partnership. The linkages may appear in several forms. It can differ from simple contractual agreement to production agreements, where production stages are shared, or to marketing agreements, where companies cooperate in selling, promoting and delivering the products.

10.2　Reasons to Cooperate　合作原因

Cooperatives in many developed countries, such as the US and Japan, play a vital role in the economy. In the US, over 47,000 cooperative businesses generate $100 billion in economic activity. Nearly 40% of the US population participates in some kind of cooperative. In Japan, Keiretsu exists in a broad spectrum of markets, including the capital market, primary goods markets and component parts markets. Keiretsu influence not only Japan's economy, but the economy in other countries as well. The influence stretches when Keiretsu expands.

Distinctive features of a cooperative come into play right from the start. A group of potential members is not looking for just any possible business opportunity to provide the greatest return on investment. In fact, there is often, but not always, a defensive nature to the reason for starting a cooperative. The group considering the new enterprise is typically responding to an economic problem which has a negative impact on them or to an opportunity requiring more resources or capital than they can individually supply. The problem itself is what catches the group's attention and motivates them to consider and develop a cooperative solution. The individuals involved are looking for the best opportunity as a group to own and operate a cooperative enterprise generating the highest total returns aimed at addressing the common economic problem.

The 4 most important reasons are as follows:

(1) The influence of the global economy and the emergence of a multi-polar economic world.

The influence of the global economy and the emergence of a multi-polar economic world have created a number of companies which have matched, exceeded or approximated the achievements of recognized leaders in each area. The change is dramatic in rapidly evolving industries like computers, where newcomers can ride the wave of new technologies, as well as in mature industries like automobiles, where new entrants can adapt more readily to changing market demands. Howard Perlmutter (of Wharton) has identified 136 industries, spanning the entire alphabet from Accounting to Zippers, where one has to be world scale in order to survive profitably.

(2) The growing complexity of products and services, and their design, production and delivery is another contributory factor.

It is indeed a rare business today which does not rely for its raw materials, marketing or distribution on people with diverse technological or market-specific skills. Developing and assembling all these assets under a single roof is difficult and often not even desirable. The greatest advantages of specialization and scale are usually realized at the component rather than at the system level. Therefore, enterprises may derive the best results by creating a focus on the component while forming ties with one another in order to create and manage system level interdependence. Corning, the giant in the ceramics[2] and glass market, has made alliances so central to its strategy, that it defines the corporation as a network of organizations.

(3) New technologies are creating links between industries that were formerly separate.

Alliances allow specialists in each field to cooperate and to exploit new opportunities much faster than if each were to try and develop industry-specific skills and assets that may be readily available with others. For example, in the emerging multimedia field, computer technology is merging with telecommunications, video and audio technologies. Several groups have been formed to develop Personal Digital Assistants (PDA). AT&T joined with Olivetti, Marubeni and Matsushita in launching EO, a start-up company that developed a PDA to be sold by the partners. In the drugs and pharmaceuticals industry, the rising costs of development which have increased from an average of $16 million and 4 years in the seventies to $250 million and 12 years in the nineties for every new drug released in the market is driving the business leaders to increasing collaborations.

（4）The increasing importance of global scale has created a fertile ground for alliances.

Linkages with local companies in various markets often help a company to spread its costs over large volumes or give it access to skills and assets in different nations. While networks of wholly owned subsidiaries can also be used, regulatory barriers or the need for rapid expansion, sometimes preclude this option.

Research shows that：

① large companies that are active in alliances produce returns 50% higher than those who are not；

② those with the most "alliance experience" produce returns 2x that of novice[3] companies；

③ firms participating in alliances are growing 37% faster than their peers who are not；

④ stock market usually views alliances as a positive development, while M&A is looked upon negatively on the acquirer.

When AOL (American On-Line)[4] formed an alliance with Hughes by investing $1.5 billion to access DirecTV, market capitalization of AOL went up by $21 billion. But when AOL merged with Time Warner, the market capitalization went down by $39 billion.

This impact on market capitalization was one of primary reasons that a lot of com's[5] issued plenty of press releases stating the formation of alliance with company X. Generally, right after a press release the price of the stock went up.

10.3　Benefits of Cooperatives　合作利益

Benefits of any form of cooperative are as follows：
— accelerate product development；
— spread risk / share resources；
— access to new markets, expand customer base；
— increase market presence；
— provide added value to customers；
— access knowledge and expertise outside of your company；
— strengthen reputation — credibility.

10.4　Different Types of Cooperatives　合作公司类型

The cooperative form is highly flexible and adaptable. Several different types of cooperatives exist, each performing a different function. Co-ops also operate in a variety of industries.

10.4.1 Networks 网络

A business network is a group of firms that collaborate to meet common needs, stimulate learning and combine complementary skills to achieve shared objectives and improve the long-term viability of the individual firms. The common bond may range from being in the same industry, to broader common interests such as sharing information about employee training or health insurance programs.

While they may or may not be formally organized, these networks are characterized by a lack of formal or legal business agreements among the individual member firms. The limitations of small firms such as under capitalization, a lack of management depth and marketing ability are well known. These problems are particularly acute in rural areas where many small firms are scattered throughout large geographical areas. In addition, problems of increasing costs and a lack of resources in many small municipalities[6] are creating significant challenges for local governments and economic development officials.

Organizational characteristics of networks

A network ranges from informal social groups to formal associations. The common bond ranges from being in the same industry to a specific mutual interest and the participants, often small to medium sized entities due to industry, location and so on, in it tend to take a long-term view, because the common interest will continue.

Some government, such the US, holds a negative attitude to network or similar organizations. So members of a networks may risk an Anti-trust issues.

10.4.2 Alliances 联盟

Structurally, alliances are a middle way between networks and cooperatives. Alliances are typically limited in size, having two or more entities linked through collaborative agreements[7] for a specific purpose or service such as joint ventures or to provide education programs.

Alliances may range from agreements created for a single short-term purpose, to ongoing long-term relationships. Alliances are typically characterized by a more-or-less formal agreement which may range from a hand shake to a legal contract.

Organizational characteristics of alliances

An alliance has several unique characteristics. First, it has an understanding or at most a contractual agreement, but rarely a separate legal corporation. Second, it often involves two or a small number of entities which are often corporations. Besides, the partners of an alliance may be in different industries but they have a common interest and their skills, talents and capabilities are complementary. An alliance tends to keep a short to medium to long term relationship. It is often organized to provide a very specific task, product or service.

There are many types of strategic alliances, including: 1) Horizontal alliances at the same level in the supply chain; 2) Vertical alliances that link firms at adjacent stages in the supply chain; 3) Domestic and international alliances.

10.4.3　Cooperatives　合作企业

Probably the most widely known and proven of collaborative business organizations are cooperatives. They are usually formed of many entities and are legally constituted, limited liability corporations[8] controlled by their members.

Cooperative members are often in the same industry and have common economic interests which may involve joint marketing, purchasing of supplies and / or the providing of services.

1. What are the different types of cooperatives?

The cooperative form is highly flexible and adaptable. Several different types of cooperatives exist, each performing a different function. Co-ops also operate in a variety of industries.

Given all these factors, different ways of categorizing cooperatives have been developed. This Manual and the Cooperative Development Conference which it accompanies use the following categories.

(1) Agricultural Co-ops[9] include producer, farm supply, and new generation co-ops. These co-ops are formed by farmers and other producers to process and market their products (including agricultural goods, crafts and manufactured products) or to provide supplies needed for their farms and businesses. During the last decade, a movement toward value-added, new generation agricultural co-ops has swelled throughout the upper Midwest.

(2) Consumer Co-ops are formed to buy groceries, financial services, and many other goods and services. Examples include retail food co-ops and credit unions.

(3) Business Co-ops are formed by a group of businesses or organizations in order to purchase supplies or services in bulk. Examples include wholesalers owned by retail hardware stores and grocery stores.

(4) Worker Co-ops are owned by the employees who work in them. Another form of worker ownership is the Employee Stock Ownership Plan (ESOP[10]).

2. Organizational characteristics of cooperatives

(1) A separate, legal, limited-liability corporation;

(2) Members are often in the same industry and have a common economic interest;

（3）Formed for perpetuity[11]；

（4）Usually composed of many entities；

（5）Often used by individuals or proprietors；

（6）Involved in joint marketing of outputs, purchasing of supplies and ／ or providing services；

（7）A wide variety of products and services provided.

3. Factors that lead to partnership success

（1）Mission. Successful strategic partnerships（GSPs）create win-win situations, where participants pursue objectives on the basis of mutual need or advantage.

（2）Strategy. A company may establish separate GSPs with different partners；strategy must be thought out up front to avoid conflicts.

（3）Governance. Discussion and consensus must be the norms. Partners must be viewed as equals.

（4）Culture. Personal chemistry is important, as is the successful development of a shared set of values.

（5）Organization. Innovative structures and designs may be needed to offset the complexity of multination management.

（6）Management. GSPs invariably involve a different type of decision making. Identify potentially divisive issues in advance, and establish clear, unitary lines of authority that will result in commitment by all partners.

10.5 Basic Steps in Starting a Cooperative 合作的基本步骤

The process of forming a new cooperative requires a step-wise approach to arriving at the group's ultimate decision to start the business. In the case of a start-up cooperative, all of the initial members have to be identified as part of the formation process. A critical number of member-owners must agree to move ahead with the decision to participate before the business can start. Unique financing and control features of cooperatives can make the start-up process a complex one.

Typically, the process of forming a new cooperative is very time consuming and involves a number of leaders, advisors, and professionals, as well as organizational support from other entities. The process usually involves many informational and organizational meetings as well as coordination of the involvement of a mix of individuals and organizations.

Six Phases of New Cooperative Development：

1. Identifying an opportunity[12]

- Define critical questions;
- Explore relevant market / economic need;
- Discuss and agree on scope and nature of problem / opportunity;
- Research economic aspects of problem.

2. Building consensus on potential for cooperative[13]

- Study organizational alternatives;
- Hold initial meetings to review scope and nature of cooperative solution;
- Discuss and agree on cooperative approach;
- Create initial budget.

3. Developing trust among potential members

- Identify leadership to champion project;
- Establish steering committee;
- Agree on calendar and tasks;
- Assign tasks;
- Raise seed capital;
- Research market;
- Conduct feasibility study;
- Agree on feasibility and inform;

4. Securing member commitment[14]

- Develop detailed business plan;
- Establish legal identity;
- Create interim[15] board;
- Set up books / accounting;
- Conduct member equity drive and sign-up;
- Retain manager / CEO (Chief Executive Officer);
- Launch cooperative.

5. Involving other stakeholders[16]

- Secure necessary financing;
- Formalize relations with customers or suppliers.

6. Starting up the cooperative

- Hold annual meeting;
- Elect directors;

- Establish committees;
- Secure necessary assets;
- Hire staff.

☞ Cases

Case 1. Japanese Keiretsu

(pl. keiretsu or **kei · ret · sus**: A network of businesses that own stakes in one another as a means of mutual security, especially in Japan, and usually including large manufacturers and their suppliers of raw materials and components.)

See also http://www.rotman.utoronto.ca/~evans/teach363/keiretsu/keiretsu.htm.

Before the WWII, Japan was dominated by four large economy groups with closer historical background: Mitsubishi, Mitsui, Sumitomo, and Yasuda. These were involved in steel, international trading, banking and other key sectors in the economy and controlled by a holding company, which established financial links among the different members. Large, influential banks were part of these conglomerates[17], providing necessary funds.

After the WWII, the allied forces wanted a strong Japan to fight the Korean war and communism in general, they helped to re-establish these companies conglomerates, now called Keiretsu.

Among them, the most important ones are the "financial Keiretsus" (Big Six) with horizontal relationships across industries. The ex-Zaibatsus — Mitsui, Mitsubishi and Sumitomo — belong to this grouping with close-knit relationships among group members. Sanwa, Fuyo and Ikkan are new formed groups with a bank at their core. Usually they only have one enterprise in each business sector to enjoy economies of scale and avoid competition within the group. The "big six" keiretsu are 78% of market share valuation on Tokyo Stock Exchange.

Another form is represented by the "distribution" Keiretsu with vertical relationships, controlling this way, the flow of products, services, prices, etc., from the factory to the consumer. In most cases they are smaller than the horizontal groupings or even part of them. One large company is a member of a horizontal Keiretsu but has its own independent vertical group. Generally, distribution Keiretsus are less influenced by a bank. The advantage of this structure lays on the grounds of many subcontractors working as "buffers" for the core firm in economic downturns. They do so because they can fire their temporary workers at any time opposing to the life-time employment situation in the large companies. As a result the whole group can adapt to changes in the business environment.

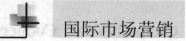

Case 2. Joint venture between Coca-Cola and P&G in the food and beverage industry

The alliance of Coca-Cola and Proctor & Gamble is perhaps the most noted because it was featured in Forbes' "Partner or Perish" article. Coke changed its strategy from traditional acquisition to strategic alliance after its failed purchase of Quaker Oats. To gain fast access to the snack and non-carbonated beverage markets dominated by competitor Pepsi, Coke has created a 6,000 employee, $4 million snack and beverage joint venture with P&G that will include Pringles, Hi-C, and Fruitopia along with Coke products.

Case 3. Joint venture agreement of Rivio with Bank of America for online banking industry

Small Rivio Software did not have the capital to begin marketing its web-based time card, accounting and online banking services. Instead of approaching the capital markets, it enticed Bank of America to contribute $3 million and access to its 1.7 million customers in a joint venture created to market the web-based products.

Case 4. Marketing agreement of OSI Pharmaceuticals with Genentech in the pharmaceutical industry

Modest OSI Pharmaceuticals did not have the capital to begin marketing its anti-cancer agent, OSI-774. Instead of approaching the capital markets, it entered into a marketing agreement with giant Genentech. Genentech provided the capital to begin the marketing until breakeven, and thereafter assumed 50 percent of the costs in exchange for 50 percent of the profits.

Case 5. Product development agreement of Welch Allyn with Baxter International in the health equipment industry

Small Welch Allyn, which had developed a patent-monitor system, entered into a product development agreement with Baxter International to combine the monitor system with Baxter's heart pump to form a single, improved product.

Case 6. Joint venture of Robustion Technologies with Walkington, Inc. to manufacture and market fireplace logs

Robustion Technnologies, which had developed a fireplace log made of spent coffee grounds and the process for producing such logs, entered into a joint venture with Walkington, Inc., which has access to retail giants such as Home Depot, to fund the development of a manufacturing facility and the production and distribution of the logs.

Case 7. Joint venture of giants in the telecommunications industry

Even giants such as Sprint, Telecommunications, Comcast and Cox Communications found the capital markets prohibitively expensive for any of them to individually acquire PCS licenses in FCC auctions. Instead, they formed a joint venture where they pooled their resources and collectively bought the licenses and funded the building of a PCS network.

Case 8. Licensing arrangements of Polo Ralph Lauren in the consumer durables industry

Polo Ralph Lauren has entered into license arrangements with West Point Stevens, ICI Paints and others for furniture and housewares that will be marketed under the "Polo" and "Ralph Lauren" names.

Case 9. Technology sharing agreement between Canon and HP in the copier business

Canon, which had developed the technology toner and toner cartridges, entered into an agreement to share that technology with Hewlett-Packard, which had developed the software and computer chips to operate the cartridges and spurt the toner on product.

Case 10. First auto joint venture established after China's WTO entry

Beijing Motor Co. Ltd. signed a strategy cooperation agreement with Hyundai Motor Co. of the Republic of Korea in Seoul on May for jointly establishing the Beijing Hyundai Motor Co., Ltd.

The joint venture is the first cooperation approved in the field of motor production after China's WTO entry. Hyundai will make the use of Beijing's basis on auto industry and China's huge market, aiming to achieve its strategic goal of becoming the fifth of the world top five auto manufacturers by 2010.

The introduction of Hyundai's capital, advanced technology and management skills will upgrade Beijing Motor's products and services, then promote the development of relevant industries and accelerate Beijing's motor industry to merge into the global market.

☐ Key Terms

cooperative strategy　合作策略
global strategic partnership　全球战略伙伴
global economy　全球经济
multi-polar economic world　多极化经济世界
spread risk　分摊风险

credibility 可信性

capitalization 股本，资本总额

network 网络

horizontal alliance 横向联盟

vertical alliance 纵向联盟

domestic and international alliance 国内国际联盟

raise seed capital 筹集种子资产

Chief Executive Officer（CEO） 执行总裁

collaborative agreement 合作协议

📄 Notes

1. rationale   *n.*   基本原理
2. ceramics   *n.*   制陶术，制陶业
3. novice   *n.*   新手，初学者
4. AOL（American On-Line） 美国在线服务公司
5. com   *n.*   商业组织，公司
6. municipality   *n.*   市政当局，自治市
7. collaborative agreement   合作协议
8. limited liability corporation   有限责任公司
9. co-op   合作企业
10. ESOP   （促进雇员拥有本公司股票的）雇员股票拥有计划
11. perpetuity   *n.*   永恒
12. identifying an opportunity   确定时机
13. building consensus on potential for cooperative   为合作企业的潜能造舆论
14. securing member commitment   确保成员承担义务
15. interim   *a.*   临时的
16. stakeholder   *n.*   资金资助者
17. conglomerate   *n.*   团体

✍ Exercises

I. Multiple choices.

1. Cooperatives take a variety of forms, including _____.

    A. insurance companies and banks

B. service cooperatives and marketing cooperatives

      C. employees and boards of directors

      D. both common and preferred shares

      E. all of the above

2. Cooperatives _____.

      A. lower costs   B. can generate a surplus

      C. allow members one vote each   D. can be publicly traded

      E. all of the above

3. Strategic alliances _____.

      A. spread the ownership, not the risk

      B. are dominated by the institutional partner, not the private partner

      C. spread risk and give the partners something they do not have within their individual organizations

      D. exist between a subsidiary and its parent, not between institutional subsidiaries

      E. are illegal in Canada because of the Tax Act

4. Keiretsu is the term for _____.

      A. a full-line wholesaler in Korea

      B. a producer-customer direct channel in Hong Kong

      C. selling agents and brokers in Japan

      D. vertical integration and a social and economic bond between producers and intermediaries in Japan

      E. a vertical integration of as well as a social and economic bond between producers and intermediaries in Japan

5. One characteristic of networks is _____.

      A. provides services, joint purchasing and/or combined marketing efforts

      B. involves two or a small number of entities

      C. a short to medium to long term relationship

      D. often used by individuals or proprietors

      E. members are often in the same industry and have a common economic interest

6. One of the types of strategic alliances is _____.

      A. exporting   B. licensing

      C. franchising   D. agricultural co-ops

7. Which mode of entry into a foreign market is characterized by an organization allowing others to produce and distribute its goods?

      A. Exporting and importing.   B. Licensing and franchising.

C. Strategic alliance.   D. Wholly owned subsidary.

8. GSP, which creates win-win situations, is a _____ that leads to partnership success.

   A. strategy   B. governance   C. culture   D. mission
   E. management

9. Which of the following is NOT one of the main reasons for people to start cooperatives?

   A. To share costs of new technology.

   B. To gain opportunity to become market leaders.

   C. To reduce risks associated with new enterprises.

   D. To obtain new services.

10. Which of the following belongs to the phase of new cooperative development — starting up the cooperative?

   A. Research economic aspects of problem.

   B. Discuss and agree on cooperative approach.

   C. Assign tasks.

   D. Establish legal identity.

   E. Establish Committees.

II. True or false.

1. Ford Motor Company's marketing strategy in Europe reflects a company that saw Europe as distinctly fragmented into narrow markets within their specific nation states.

2. The United States can be considered as a good example for regional economic integration.

3. Regional economic integration is the political and economic agreement among countries that give preference to member countries to that agreement.

4. Global strategic partnerships will become less important in the Asia-Pacific regions.

5. The WTO allows a departure from its policy to grant the same favorable trade conditions to all WTO members in the case of regional trade agreements (RTAs).

6. The goal of a free-trade area (FTA) is to abolish work permits among its members.

7. Collaborative agreements can be used to refer to linkages between companies to pursue a common goal.

8. Custom unions levy a common external tariff on goods being imported from nonmembers.

9. Changes in the political, economic, socio-cultural, and technological environments are leading to new strategies in global competition.

10. Trade creation allows consumers access to more goods at lower prices and is considered a major benefit of regional economic integration.

III. Discussion.

Visit the following websites and find some information about European Union (EU), the North American Free Trade Agreement (NAFTA), and Asia-Pacific Economic Cooperation (APEC).

ECOWAS is the name for the regional economic group in Africa that represents sixteen countries in the western region of the continent. The Web site gives a great deal of information about the organization. On the About ECOWAS page, you can learn about the mission of the organization as well as the structure of its management. On the page called Presentation of ECOWAS, you are able to load some PowerPoint presentations that describe the group's functions in more detail. (Be patient! It downloads very slowly.) On the ECOWAS Chairmen page, you can see all of the past chairs of the organization and their country of origin since the inception of ECOWAS. The country Web site for each chair is also included and provides a wealth of additional knowledge about the West African region. The last section of the site provides a welcome message from the current Executive Secretary, Lansana Kouyate, along with a vita, quotes, his honors, and his reports to the organization.

1. Who are the 16 member nations of ECOWAS?
2. What is the Mission of ECOWAS?
3. Name the 7 commissions included in ECOWAS.
4. Is the principal focus of this Web site political or economic integration? Explain.

Part IV

国际市场营销组合

International Marketing Mix (4 Ps)

Chapter Eleven

Product Decision

产 品 决 策

🔊 Objectives 学习目标

When students finish this chapter, they should be able to accomplish the following:

- ☑ Product definition and five important characteristics
- ☑ Product classification
- ☑ Product design and product life cycle
- ☑ Product strategies
- ☑ Branding selection
- ☑ Product decisions and some pitfalls in product decisions

11.1   Product and It's Five Important Characteristics
产品和产品的五个特点

11.1.1   Definition 定义

What is a product? A product is anything that can be offered to a market for attention, acquisition, use or consumption and that might satisfy a want or need.

A Revlon perfume, a symphony concert, a National Day vacation tour, a Shinco DVD, a college study consultation — all these are products.

11.1.2   Five characteristics of products 产品的五个特征

When talking about a product, one needs to consider its characteristics. John Fayerweather suggested five important characteristics that are relevant to global marketing product decisions. They are 1) primary functional purpose; 2) secondary purpose; 3) durability and quality; 4) method of operation, and 5) maintenance.

Primary function is the function(s) that a product is firstly designed to have. For example, in high-developed country, the primary function of a mobile phone is to communicate when a person is out of home or office.

While in a less developed country, a mobile phone is not only a communication tool but also a symbol of higher social position. Thus, the product has a secondary function: a symbol of social position.

The third characteristic of a product is durability and quality. For different market, customer will have different requirement for a product's durability. A marketer must offer a product appropriate to the certain market. Quality is also a very important part to be considered. In a country like the US where labor cost is very expensive, a customer would seldom have small home appliances repaired. In this market, a small appliance will be designed without any additional "quality". But if this product is transferred to a less-developed market, the product would most probably be viewed of low quality, as it is not repairable.

The fourth characteristic is method of operation. This indicates that a product should be designed according to the conditions of its target market. For example, in the UK and Australia, drivers sit on the right, while in China, drivers sit on the left. An automobile marketer must take this into consideration when doing product design.

The last characteristic, according to Fayerweather, is maintenance. The availability and cost of maintenance vary in different parts of the world.

11.2　Product Classification　产品分类

11.2.1　Traditional classification　传统分类

Products may be classified according to a variety of criteria[1]. Traditionally, classification of products is based on users, hence the consumer goods and industrial goods.

1. Consumer products

They are products bought by final consumers for personal consumption. Based on how consumers buying them, consumer products can be further classified as convenience products, shopping products, specialty products and unsought products. See Figure 11-1.

Convenience products are those that consumers usually buy frequently, immediately, and with a minimum of comparison and buying effort. They are usually low priced and widely available. Soap, candy, newspapers are in this catalog.

Shopping products are those purchased by consumers after characteristic comparison on such based as suitability, quality, price, and style. Examples include furniture, clothing, used cars, and major appliances.

Specialty products are consumer products with special characteristics or brand identification for which a significant group of buyers is willing to make a special purchase effort. Specific brands and types of cars, high-priced sports equipments and custom-made dresses are among this catalog.

Unsought products are consumer products that the consumer either does not know about or knows about but does not normally think of buying. Typical examples are life insurances and blood donation to the Red Cross.

Convenience products	Shopping products
> Buy frequently & immediately > Low priced > Mass advertising > Many purchase locations fast food, candy, newspapers	> Buy less frequently > Higher price > Fewer purchase locations > Comparison shop clothing, cars appliances
Specialty products	Unsought products

> Special purchase efforts
> High price
> Unique characteristics
> Brand identification
> Few purchase locations
 	
lamborghini, roles
	> New innovations
	> Products consumers don't
	  want to think about
	> Require much advertising &
	  personal selling
	
	life insurance, blood donation

Figure 11-1   Consumer Product Classification

2. Industrial products

They are those purchased for further processing or for use in conducting a business. There are three groups of industrial products: materials and parts, capital items, and supplies and services, as shown in Figure 11-2.

Materials and parts are industrial products that become a part of the buyer's product, through further processing or as components. They include raw materials and manufactured materials and parts. Raw materials include farm products and natural products. Manufactured materials and parts include component materials such as iron, yarn, cement, wires and component parts such as small motors, tires, castings.

Capital items are industrial products that aid in the buyer's production or operations.

Buildings, fixed equipments, portable factory equipment and tools and office equipment are all capital items.

Supplies and services are industrial products that do not enter the finished product at all. Supplies include operating supplies, such as coal, computer, paper, pencil. Business services include maintenance and repair services and business advisory services.

Materials and parts	products that become a part of the buyer's product, through further processing or as components. iron, yarn, cement, wires
Capital items	products that aid in the buyer's production or operations. buildings, fixed equipments, portable factory equipment
Supplies and services	products that do not enter the finished product at all. Supplies include operating supplies, such as coal, computer, paper, pencil

Figure 11-2　Industrial Product Classification

Another traditional method of classifying products is how long a product may exist. Thus, there are durable, consumable, or disposable goods[2].

11.2.2　Products in international marketing　国际市场中的产品

In the international marketplace, the above classification frameworks may also be applicable.

In recent years, with the fast speed of globalized economy, a product with international profit potential is more likely to gain attentions than that with local potentials. Therefore, some researchers further classified products according to their marketing potentials, i. e. local products and international products.

Products that for any reason may be launched within a single national market are called local products. As a local product has limited profit potentials for the company, and a company may have to pay a large amount of money to do the research, it is very difficult for the company to earn the money back in a small potential market. Thus, many companies, especially well-known medical companies prefer to have the products be international products.

Products that are designed to meet the requirements of different international markets and have the potential to be launched in different national markets are called international products.

11.3 Product Design and Product Life Cycle
产品设计和产品生命周期

11.3.1 Product design and the new product development process
产品设计与新产品研发过程

Product design is the process of designing a product's style and function: creating a product that is attractive, easy, safe, and inexpensive to use and services, and simple and economical to produce and distribute.

Eight major steps are necessary for the new product development process. As shown in Figure 11-3, they are idea generation, idea screening, concept development and testing, marketing strategy development, business analysis, product development, test marketing, commercialization.

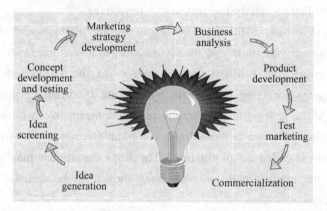

Figure 11-3 New Product Development Process

The systematic search for new product ideas is called idea generation. Any new product designing starts with it. The search must be systematic, or the new product idea will most probably not be good ones for its type of business. Major sources of new product ideas include internal sources, customers, competitors, distributors and suppliers and others.

The second stage is to reduce the ideas generated. This stage is known as idea screening. The purpose of screening is to spot good ideas and drop poor ones as soon as possible. Most companies require their personnel to write up new product ideas on standard form that can be reviewed by a new product committee.

The committee develops a checklist to grade the idea and those surviving ideas can be screened further and find the ideas that would fit the "fair idea" level.

A concept development is a detailed version of the new product idea stated in meaningful consumer terms. It offers the most quality, performance, and features of the product that the consumer may favor.

For a new product, a company may develop several alternative product concepts, find out how attractive each concept is to consumers and choose the best one.

To find out the best concept, concept testing is necessary. Concept testing is the process to testing the new product concepts with groups of target consumers. The concepts may be presented to consumers symbolically or physically.

The next step involves designing an initial marketing strategy for a new product based on the product concept. The strategy includes three parts: The first part describes the target market, market positioning, sales, market share and profit goals for the first few years. The second part is about the planned price, distribution, and marketing budget for the first year. The third part is about the planned long run sales, profit goals and marketing mix strategy.

Business analysis is a review of the sales, costs, and profit projections for a new product to find out whether these factors satisfy the company's objectives.

A good method is to look at the sales history of similar products and should survey market opinion. It should estimate minimum and maximum sales to assess the range of risk.

If the product passes the business test, it moves to the product development. Product development is a strategy for company growth by offering modified or new product to current market segments. It is the process to develop the product concept into a physical product in order to assure that the product idea can be turned into a workable product. The first full-scale working product from a concept is called a "prototype." The R&D department may develop one or more physical versions of the product concept. And then they must be tested. This will consist of functional tests and consumer tests.

If the product passes functional and consumer tests, the next step is test marketing. In this stage, the new product and the marketing program are introduced into more realistic market settings. It lets the company test the product and its marketing program. Three approaches are available for a test marketing: Standard test markets, controlled test market, or simulated test markets.

Standard test markets approach involves finding a small number of representative test cities, conducting a full marketing campaign in these cities. The results would include store audits[3], consumer and distributor surveys, and other. And the results will be used to forecast national sales and profits and discover potential product problems.

Controlled test markets approach let the firm to make the testing marketing in some stores that controlled by several research firms; the company will pay a certain amount of fee for the testing market. Controlled test markets take less time than standard test markets and usually cost less.

Simulated test markets approach is to test new products in a simulated shopping environment.

Consumers are required to behave in a stimulated purchasing environment and then are asked questions for their behaviors. The data are then analyzed by computer and result will gain from it.

Business marketers use different way for test marketing. They may conduct product use tests. To offer products to small groups of potential customers who agree to use the new product. New industrial products also can be tested at trade shows. The distributor and deal, standard or controlled test markets are also possible choices for the company.

Test marketing gives management the information to make a final decision about whether to launch the new product. So the last step for a new product design is to commercialize it, that is, to introduce the new product to the market.

The company must decide on introduction timing and then the place to launch it. Companies with international distribution systems may launch new product through global rollouts.

11.3.2 Product life cycle 产品生命周期

Products have a limited market life. Typically there are 4 stages for the development of a new product: Introduction, growth, maturity and decline. See Figure 11-4.

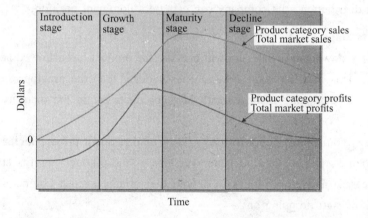

Figure 11-4   The Product Life Cycle (PLC)

1. Introduction stage

A period of slow sales growth as the product is introduced in the market. This stage starts when the new product is first launched. Introduction takes time, and sales growth is apt to be slow.

Profits are nonexistent in this stage because of the heavy expenses incurred with product introduction. Because the market is not generally ready for product refinements at this stage, the company and its few competitors produce basic versions of the product. These firms focus their selling on those buyers who are the readiest to buy. These consumers are sometimes called innovators. The company may adopt one of several marketing strategies for introducing a new product. It can launch the product with a high price and low promotion spending. Such a strategy is very suitable for a limited sized market. Or the company can launch the product with a low price and heavy promotion spending which enables the company to penetrate the market and take the largest market share. The strategy in this stage is very important, as it is the first step in a grander marketing plan for the product's entire life cycle.

2. Growth stage

If the new product satisfies the market, it will enter a growth stage, in which sales will start climbing quickly. It's a period of rapid market acceptance, and substantial profit improvement. The innovators will continue to buy, and early adopters will start to follow their lead, especially if they hear favorable word of mouth. They will introduce new product features, and the market will expand.

Profits increase during the growth stage, as promotion costs are spread over a large volume and as unit-manufacturing costs fall. In the growth stage the firm faces a trade-off between high market share and high current profit. By spending a lot of money on product improvement, promotion, and distribution, the company can capture a dominant position.

3. Maturity stage

A period of a slowdown in sales growth because the product has achieved acceptance by most potential buyers. This maturity stage normally lasts longer than the previous stage, and it poses strong challenges to marketing management. Most products are in the maturity stage of the life cycle.

In this stage, competitors begin to react. They market down prices, increase the advertising and sales promotions, and try to find better versions of the product. Profits stabilize or decline because of increased marketing outlays to defend the product against competition. Some of the weaker competitors start dropping out.

4. Decline stage

When demands are less, technology advances, consumer tastes shift, or competition increases, sales show a downward drift and profits erode, therefore, some firms withdraw from the market. This is the decline stage. As for those remaining companies, they may cut the promotion budget and reduce their prices further.

It is often difficult to designate where each stage begins and ends. Usually the stages are marked where the rates of sales growth or decline become pronounced. Nonetheless, marketers should check the normal sequence of stages in the industry and the average duration of each stage. Cox found that a typical ethical drug spanned an introductory period of one month, a growth stage of six months, a maturity stage of fifteen months, and a very long decline stage — the last because of manufacturers' reluctance to drop drugs from their catalogs. These stage lengths must be reviewed periodically intensifying competition is leading to shorter PLCs over time, which means that products must earn their profits in a shorter period.

11.3.3 International Product Decisions   产品的国际决策

Standardization vs. adaptation

Changes in design are largely dictated by whether they would improve the prospects of greater sales, and thus, over the accompanying costs[4]. Changes in design are also subject to cultural pressures. The more culture-bound the product is, for example food, the more adaptation is necessary. Most products fall in between the spectrum of "standardization[5]" to "adaptation[6]" extremes. The application the product is put to also affects the design. In the UK, railway engines were designed from the outset to be sophisticated because of the degree of competition, but in the US this was not the case. In order to burn the abundant wood and move the prairie debris, large smoke stacks and cowcatchers were necessary. In agricultural implements a mechanized cultivator may be a convenience item in a UK garden, but in India and Africa it may be essential equipment. As stated earlier "perceptions" of the product's benefits may also dictate the design. A refrigerator in Africa is a very necessary and functional item, kept in the kitchen or the bar. In Mexico, the same item is a status symbol and, therefore, kept in the living room.

The following factors are considered very important when a company adapt standardization strategy:

(1) Economies of scale in production and marketing;

(2) Consumer mobility — the more consumers travel the more is the demand;

(3) Technology;

(4) Image, for example "Japanese", "made in".

The latter can be a factor either to aid or to hinder global marketing development. Nagashima (1977) found the "made in USA" image has lost ground to the "made in Japan" image. In some cases "foreign made" gives advantage over domestic products. In China, one sees many advertisements for "imported", which gives the product advertised a perceived advantage over domestic products. Often a price premium[7] is charged to reinforce the "imported means quality" image. If the foreign source is negative in effect, attempts are made to disguise or hide the fact through, say, packaging or labeling. Mexicans are reluctant to take products from Brazil. By putting a "made in elsewhere" label on the product this can be overcome, provided the products are manufactured elsewhere even though its company maybe Brazilian.

Many MNCs vary their product strategy when entering different countries and markets. They do it on the base of the following reasons.

（1）Differing usage conditions. These may be due to climate, skills, level of literacy, culture or physical conditions. Maize, for example, would never sell in Europe rolled and milled as in Africa. It is only eaten whole, on or off the cob. In Zimbabwe, kapenta fish[8] can be used as a relish[9], but will always be eaten as a "starter" to a meal in the developed countries.

（2）General market factors — incomes, tastes, etc. Canned asparagus may be very affordable in the developed world, but may not sell well in the developing world.

（3）Government — taxation, import quotas, nontariff barriers, labeling and health requirements. Non-tariff barriers are an attempt, despite their supposed impartiality, at restricting or eliminating competition. A good example of this is the Florida tomato growers, who successfully got the US Department of Agriculture to issue regulations establishing a minimum size of tomatoes marketed in the United States. The effect of this was to eliminate the Mexican tomato industry that grew a tomato that fell under the minimum size specified. Some non-tariff barriers may be legitimate attempts to protect the consumer. For example, at the beginning of 2002, the EU stopped importing China's honey in excuse of excessive antibiotic in it. Meanwhile Japan, Canada and the United States also have intensified checks on China's honey. Thus, China's agricultural and animal products meet "green trade barriers[10]" since the country entered into the WTO.

（4）History. Sometimes, as a result of colonialism, production facilities have been established overseas. Eastern and Southern Africa is littered with examples. In Kenya, the tea industry is a colonial legacy, as is the sugar industry of Zimbabwe and the coffee industry of Malawi. These facilities have long been adapted to local conditions.

（5）Financial considerations. In order to maximize sales or profits the organization may have no choice but to adapt its products to local conditions.

（6）Pressure. Sometimes, as in the case of the EU, suppliers are forced to adapt to the rules and regulations imposed on them if they wish to enter into the market.

11.4 Product Strategies in International Markets
国际市场产品战略

There are five major product strategies in international marketing, as shown in Table 11-1.

Strategy 1：Product – Communications Extension（Dual Extension）

This strategy is very low cost and merely takes the same product and communication strategy into other markets. However, it can be risky if misjudgments are made. For example, CPC International believed the US consumer would take to dry soups, which dominate the European market. But the company failed because it did not work.

Strategy 2: Product – Communication Adaptation Extended Product – Communications Adaptation

If the product basically fits the different needs or segments of a market it may need an adjustment in marketing communications only. Again this is a low cost strategy, but different product functions have to be identified and a suitable communications mix developed.

Strategy 3: Product Adaptation – Communication Extension

The product is adapted to fit usage conditions but the communication stays the same. The assumption is that the product will serve the same function in foreign markets under different usage conditions.

Strategy 4: Product Adaptation – Communications Adaptation (Dual Adaptation)

Both product and communication strategies need attention to fit the peculiar need of the market.

Strategy 5: Product Invention

This needs a totally new idea to fit the exclusive conditions of the market. This is very much a strategy that could be ideal in a Third World situation. The development costs may be high, but the advantages are also very high.

Table 11-1   Product Strategies in International Markets

Product Strategy	Communications Strategy	Product / Functions Met
1 Extension	Extension	Same
2 Extension	Adaptation	Different
3 Adaptation	Extension	Same
4 Adaptation	Adaptation	Different
5 Invention	New	Same

The choice of strategy will depend on the most appropriate product / market analysis and is a function of the product itself defined in terms of the function or need it serves[11], the market defined in terms of the conditions under which the product is used, the preferences of the potential customers and their ability to buy the product in question, and the costs of adaptation and manufacture to the company considering these product – communications approaches.

11.5 Brand Selection 品牌选择

11.5.1 Brand 品牌

A brand is the distinctive name of design (logo, package, trademark, etc.) that becomes a recognized marketplace image, a way for buyers to distinguish a product from its competitors.

Some companies such as Toyota, McDonald's, Shell Oil, and Sony have established international brand names. They can be recognized pretty soon by new markets. This brings both positive and negative aspects.

On a positive note, if the target markets have no preconceived notion about what the company represents, products of the companies can be very easily accepted by the consumers in those new markets.

But famous brands of big companies sometimes are rejected for local protest. They are also blamed for some serious social and environmental problems.

The fact of the international market is many companies are not equipped with highly accepted brands. These companies have even bigger problems. They have to spend extra time and money to persuade the local government, their distributors and consumers. In a foreign market, more effort would be taken to overcome problems of language and cultural differences.

11.5.2 Brand equity 品牌价值

Brand equity is defined as the added value a brand name gives to a product beyond the functional benefits provided. In another word, it is the value of a brand, based on the extent to which it has high brand loyalty, name awareness, perceived quality, strong brand associations, and other assets such as patents, trademarks, and channel relationships.

Branding is expensive, time-consuming, and can make or break a product. The most valuable brands have a brand equity that is considered an important company asset. Therefore, it's very important to regulate a set of strategy, which is suitable for certain product when confronting all challenges.

11.5.3 Brand extension 品牌拓展

Brand extension is the process of applying an established name to new product lines. This is a risky concept even in one's domestic market, not to mention a foreign market. However, risk can also bring greater success. It's likely for a marketer to attach a brand to a product line already accepted in the new market.

11.5.4 Co-branding 联合品牌

What did you think when you first saw a credit card bearing the name of Jet Airways and Citibank, or logo of Intel on the Compaq or IBM PCs? The answer to the above lies in a single word — Co-branding, which is a happening thing in today's marketing circles.

Co-branding refers to two or more brands enter into a partnership that potentially serves to enhance both brands' equity and profitability. The most successful example of this kind is the display of "Intel inside" logo[12] on the cabinet of most personal computers. Both the computer manufacturer and Intel gain. A marketer must be very cautious when choosing a co-branding partner.

Companies must decide whether or not to brand, whether to produce manufacturer brands or distributor / private brands, which brand name to use, and whether to use line extensions[13], brand extension, multibrands, new brands, or co-brands. And all the challenges come from rival companies and their products.

11.5.5 Branding strategy 品牌策略

In thinking about branding strategy, it must lead to success and sink the rival. At the same time, it should solve the challenges that are met, although it may be difficult. When branding a product, one should pay attention to satisfy following properties of a good brand. The best brand names suggests something about the product's benefits; suggest product qualities; are easy to pronounce, recognize, and remember; are distinctive, and do not carry negative meanings or connotations in other countries or languages.

(1) Distinctive name: A brand name should be chosen on the base of image desired, consumer cultural perceptions, and the marketer's product line.

(2) Attractive symbol or logo: Symbol and logo should be multi-cultural, simple, meaningful and generic.

(3) Customized slogan: Slogan must be meaningful and attractive since it tends to stay in the consumer consciousness for extended periods.

(4) Goodwill creation: Donations and other public relation activity can help to gain brand awareness when entering a new market.

(5) Event association: To establish a close and long-term relationship in the consumer's mind between a favorable event and the product.

It is a little difficult to find out all the challenges of a strong brand at the moment when the product was branded because every brand must suffer a long time period before it becomes so prominent. Maybe it will take 10 years or more. Only the brander knows how many challenges, and what challenges, they had suffered. So, it is necessary to assume what challenges they had met and analyze what challenges they are facing by some research studies.

11.6　Service as a Product　服务产品

A service is an intangible product involving a deed, performance, or an effort that cannot be physically possessed. Service includes rental of goods, alteration and repair of goods owned by customers, and personal services. Service plays a very important role in both country economy and international trade. US is the world's first service economy. More than 75% of the workforce in the private sector is employed in the service industry. Accounts for more than $3 billions in output and contribute 60% of GNP. Between 1980 and 1992, it is reported that the EU created almost 1.3 million new jobs per year in the services sectors — twice the average for the rest of the economy (Eurostat 1995). "Pure" services have a number of distinctive characteristics that differentiate them from goods and have implications for the way in which they are marketed. These characteristics are often described as intangibility, inseparability, variability, perishability and the inability to own a service.

Intangibility: A pure service cannot be assessed using any of the physical senses — it is an abstraction which cannot be directly examined before it is purchased. Measuring quality for services can be very different compared with goods, which has tangible benchmarks against the quality to be measured.

Inseparability: The consumption of a service is said to be inseparable from its means of production. Producer and consumer must interact in order for the benefits of the service to be realized. Both must normally meet at a time and a place that is mutually convenient in order that the producer can directly pass on service benefits.

Inventory: Services cannot be stored. If a producer of a service cannot sell all of its output produced in the current period, he has no chance to carry it forward for sale in a subsequent period.

Inconsistency: For services, variability impacts upon customers not just in terms of outcomes but also in terms of processes of production. For example, lawn care service cannot mow a lawn precisely the same way each time, but need to make the service as efficient and consistent as possible.

Most products are a combination of goods and services. Pure goods and pure services are hypothetical extremes, but which are nevertheless important to note because they help to define the distinctive characteristics of goods and services marketing.

11.7   Product Decision Summary   产品决策小结

Which strategy best fits a company? There is no fixed answer to this question; one should try to analyze the situation before making any decisions.

As well as the above, organizations have also to consider the international product life cycle (described in section one) and the "fit" of the strategy into the company's portfolio[14], strengths and weaknesses. In launching new products into international markets, the international product life cycle concept is crucial. Comparative analysis is a very useful technique for new product introduction. The idea behind this concept is that if underlying conditions existing in one country are similar to those in another, then there is a likelihood of a product being successfully introduced. On the other hand, the international life cycle can work against domestic producers. The introduction of a second country product into a first country which has had a "closed economy" can sometimes kill off local production if that local producer cannot respond to the imported product's competitiveness.

11.8   Some Pitfalls in Product Decisions   产品决策中的误区

1. Product is product
When consumers purchase goods, they purchase the service needed with the goods. When consumers purchase a service, they take it for granted that certain physical goods should be included. Product can not be viewed as pure product.

2. Bigger is better
As far as the differentiation of the product meets the requirements of consumers, the product itself is successful[15]. Consumers pay more attention to fitness than size.

3. All change is good
Coca once tried to modify the ingredients of coca and soon found out it didn't work as the company had expected. They were forced to keep its original formula. This case indicates that sometimes, changes are worse than anything else. It is costly and may damage a brand rather than improve it. Besides, what consumers want is an improved product.

4. Nobody can resist a bargain
Consumers tend to believe that low price means low quality. When the price of a certain commodity decreases dramatically, they may be suspicious about the product. So companies need

to be very cautious each time they want to make use of discounting to attract potential consumers. Brand image is important in the long run.

5. People love luxury

People do prefer luxury in most case, the problem is that they are not willing to or not able to afford it. For a luxurious product, a marketer must take care to direct it to those who can afford it. A luxury oriented product is not likely to have a large market potential.

6. People buy what's good for them

It is only an assumption of a well-intentioned marketer. For if this is the case, the use of seatbelts would not be a legal requirement. The more a marketer tries to secure its products, the high the cost, and the fewer consumers would purchase.

7. The consumer will know our product is better

Many products may have similar functions and appearance, so it's hard for a consumer to figure a particular product out from lots of similar commodities. A marketer must bring the product to consumers via advertising and packaging.

☞ Cases

Case 1.   Why is America's P&G way ahead of Europe's Unilever in China?

One will not find many brands from Europe's Unilever — Lux and Lifebuoy soap, Close-Up toothpaste — on the shelves of Chinese supermarkets. It is more likely to see products by America's Procter & Gamble such as Rejoice shampoo, Crest toothpaste and Tide laundry detergent. "P&G is our largest supplier in terms of sales," says a representative of a large retail chain in Beijing. "Unilever has about one-fifth of P&G's turnover."

Both started operations in the second half of the 1980s, P&G in Guangzhou and Unilever in Shanghai. But while the Americans started small and tied up with just one mainland partner, a unit of the Ministry of Foreign Trade and Economic Cooperation, the Europeans spent big — $800 million over 10 years — on ready-made market share. Unilever formed 12 ventures with an equal number of Chinese entities, each one with its own product line, distribution system and sales staff. "We used the earlier years to get familiar with our Chinese partner," P&G CEO Durk Jager, who once headed the China operation, says of the company's start-from-scratch approach. "We really started investing in China only in 1993 and 1994." Why? The financial controller of a foreign retailer shrugs his shoulders. But he makes a telling observation: "P&G gives us one invoice and its different departments work like a unit. Unilever sends us different invoices and sales people, who sometimes compete with each other."

The lessons are fairly obvious. Although the mainland has more than a billion consumers, they know next to nothing about, and do not care about, international brands. An international brand needs to build awareness and earn consumer trust first and also learn how to work with local partners, and that is easier to do when dealing with just a few of them.

As a matter of fact, Unilever came to China with great caution. The company paid for the high-priced guidance of consultants in drawing up its mainland strategy. The advice it got: team up with local companies that boast solid market share and then use their distribution and marketing systems to sell Unilever products. One of the first ventures was with the maker of Maxam toothpaste, a well-known local brand. Unilever ended up with ventures that made and sold soap, laundry detergent, sanitary napkins, ice cream and other products. It was an unwieldy combination from the beginning, though Unilever was convinced that it could eventually meld the various subsidiaries into a unified and profitable whole.

As a result, the various units tended to work at cross-purposes and even competed with one another. In pursuit of market share, Unilever threw money on promotions and price-cutting. It distributed freezers to ice-cream outlets with the understanding that they would be used only for the Wall's brand. The stores initially carried the pricey ice cream, but they eventually stocked the freezers with cheaper and thus more popular local frozen goods — more affordable, in part, because the domestic competitors did not have to provide their own refrigerators. Unilever joined a price war with local laundry detergents. But it did not pare prices enough — local housewives still preferred lower priced Chinese products to a more expensive imported brand they hardly knew.

Unilever spent on those too, but advertising practitioners in Shanghai say the company's fragmented structure made mounting campaigns[16] difficult. Add to this Unilever's reliance on expatriates[17], who tended to be transferred from their post after three years, just when they were beginning to understand what China was all about. Unilever also has problems retaining local staff. "It is very easy for us to persuade people from Unilever to take another job," says the Shanghai representative of an international headhunter[18]. "We can never get people from P&G. They recruit after graduation and take care of their hires."

Some European firms like supermarket operator Royal Ahold and logistics provider TNT Post have pulled out of China, but Unilever is determined to stay. It is now focused on cost-cutting and wants to raise new money by listing on the Shanghai stock exchange. In November, Unilever announced the formation of a holding company — with only the four Shanghai-linked partners.

For its part, P&G's proposed buyout of its sole partner is nearing completion. That will make the company wholly foreign-owned. China consultants now say this is the way to go, given the expected easing on foreign companies as the mainland signs up with the WTO. Here is the final lesson: be flexible and stay ahead of the curve. This is especially true in China, a rapidly developing economy whose business and trade policies can change almost overnight. Just ask Unilever.

Case 2. PLC of VCD

As we all know, about five years ago, VCD (Video Compact Disk), a typical hi-tech product, was widely accepted by the market / consumers, therefore, it sold pretty well and the prices were ever kept in a considerably high level (¥2,000 – ¥3,000). But only two or three years later, most manufacturers of these products had to lower the prices to not more than ¥1,000 to compete in the markets. Why is there such a contrast in so short a period of time? We may use the PLC (Product Life Cycle) to look into the industry and well illustrate this phenomenon.

Product Life Cycle (PLC) is a course of a product's sales and profits over its lifetime. Commonly speaking, it is made up of four stages: introduction, growth, maturity and decline. With the development of technology, the life cycle tends to be shorter, so firms shall use different marketing strategies according to the stages their products are in.

In China, the price elasticity of consumers' demanding the electric appliances, including VCD, is comparatively large. As a result, most firms consider the price strategy an important means of competition, which will be fully presented in the following two aspects:

(1) When VCD first appeared and was widespread in China, i. e. in the introductory and growth stages of VCD, the prices were certainly very high; but now VCD has experienced its maturity stage and stepping into the declining stage, high-price strategy is no longer appropriate. Instead, price campaign is a common strategy in these two stages, that is to say, firms lower their prices sharply in order to squeeze away competitors and enlarge their market share, so that they can attract the purchase of the laggards. A case in point is the price campaign between several main VCD manufacturers resulting in many bankrupts of small VCD industries.

(2) The sharp price decrease in the last two stages results mainly from the over-productivity of the main VCD manufacturers, which made the supply of VCD more than the demand of markets. Besides, markets' having been saturated led the sales and profits to fall sharply. As a result, some small-sized firms get no profit, even lose money in the competition (esp. in the declining period). In the end, competitors of the latter kind have to retreat from the markets.

On the other hand, PLC still tells us that the product life cycle can be lengthened. As for VCD, it is promising to develop and manufacture its alternative, i. e. CVD, also, DVD is a target of consumers' demand now and in the future. The illustration of this strategy is shown in figure. Only when being able to keep up with the changing of market demand and to meet the customers' demand with new products can an enterprise remain invincible.

Case 3.   The PLC of Wa Haha Children Nutritious Fluid

In 1988, Nutritious Fluid for Children "Wa Haha" was first produced, and the sales increased year by year. In 1993, the sales amounted to 1 billion tubes. After that, sales began to fall annually. In 1994, the innovative of Nutritious Fluid "Wa Haha" for Improving Intelligence had launched into market. But it still couldn't stop the downslide. In 1998, production of the Nutritious Fluid for Children "Wa Haha" almost stopped.

The life cycle of Nutritious Fluid for Children "Wa Haha" lasted ten years, which seems to be a complete product life cycle. But, has Nutritious Fluid for Children "Wa Haha" really come to the end of its lifetime? Are there any chances for this product to come back market?

Industry analysis: Although many of the Nutritious Fluid for grownups in China are of a very short PLC, many other similar products enjoy a long lifetime in the market. Take Wanji American Ginseng Tablet as an example. On the other hand, as the living condition keeps on improving, people hope to enjoy healthy lives; the nutritious industry is now at the rapid growth stage. While in the segment of children's hygienical products, it develops even faster with the promotion of China's only-child policy and other factors. The present Sanjiu Tongtai and Kaiweibao in market are of good sales and profitability. Analysis shows that hygienical products for children are at the stage of growth. The sales decline of Wa Haha Children Nutritious Fluid was not influenced by PLC of the industry.

Competition analysis: Wa Haha Children Nutritious Fluid was an absolute leader of the children nutritious fluids market. Similar products in the market have never gained such great market share. At present, there is no well-known brand in this market, and the competition is not very heated. Analysis shows that Wa Haha's withdraw from the market did not result from lack of competition ability.

Enterprise analysis: The ultimate reason for the decline of Wa Haha Children Nutritious Fluid is the changing of investment strategy. From 1988 to 1993, Children Nutritious Fluid is a dominant product of the enterprise. But after 1994, investment strategy has changed obviously from children nutritious products to beverage industry, which caused the decline of industry scale and market share.

If Wa Haha Co. introduces brand management, and re-packing, re-positioning and re-pricing the product, with the help of strong promotion campaign, it would be most likely to enter the rapid growth stage again.

☐ Key Terms

idea generation   新产品构思

idea screening　新产品筛选

concept development and testing　新产品概念形成和测试

marketing strategy development　新产品营销战略计划

business analysis　新产品商业分析

product development　产品实体开发

testing market　试销

commercialization　商品化

PLC(product life cycle)　产品生命周期

introduction stage　引入期

growth stage　成长期

maturity stage　成熟期

decline stage　衰退期

local product　地方性产品

international product　国际性产品

durability　耐用品

standardization　产品标准化

adaptation　产品差异化

product invention　产品创新

product strategy　产品策略

co-branding　联合品牌

product design　产品设计

marketplace image　市场形象

brand equity　品牌价值

brand extension　品牌拓展

brand strategy　品牌策略

product-communication extension　产品促销拓展

green trade barrier　绿色贸易壁垒

📄 Notes

1. criteria　*n.*　标准(criterion 的复数形式)

2. disposable goods　一次性商品

3. audit　*n.*　盘点

4. accompanying cost　附加成本

5. standardization　*n.*　标准化

6. adaptation   *n.*   改良化

7. price premium   价格贴水

8. kapenta fish   卡朋塔鱼

9. relish   *n.*   调味品

10. green trade barrier   绿色贸易壁垒，是指进口国（主要指发达国家）以保护生态环境、自然资源以及人类和动植物的健康为借口而限制进口的非关税壁垒措施。它依据有关的环保标准和规定，要求进口商品不但要符合质量标准，而且从设计、制造、包装到消费处置都要符合环境保护的要求，不得对生态环境和人类健康造成危害，有效地阻止外国特别是环保技术落后的发展中国家的产品进口，为本国市场形成巨大的保护网，已成为国际贸易中最隐蔽、最棘手、最难对付的贸易障碍之一和贸易保护主义的新形式。

11. The choice of strategy will depend on the most appropriate product / market analysis and is a function of the product itself defined in terms of the function or need it serves …   策略的选择依赖于最好的产品、市场分析，从产品的性能或所满足的需要看，它也是产品的功能之一……

12. logo   *n.*   标志

13. line extension   产品线延伸

14. portfolio   *n.*   业务量，资产组合

15. As far as the differentiation of the product meets the requirements of consumers, the product itself is successful.   只要产品的差异满足顾客的要求，产品本身就是成功的。

16. mounting campaign   固定的广告

17. expatriate   *n.*   海外人员

18. headhunter   *n.*   猎头人，用高薪征聘人才者

✍ Exercises

I. Multiple choices.

1. All but which of the following are subcategories of consumer products?
    A. Capital items.
    B. Convenience products.
    C. Shopping products.
    D. Unsought products.

2. What purpose does the idea-screening phase of the new product development process serve?
    A. To produce a working prototype.
    B. To reduce the number of product ideas from the idea generation phase.
    C. To add new product ideas to those acquired from outside the company.
    D. To develop product concepts from the product ideas.

3. In which phase of the new product development process prior to commercialization does the

company see a huge jump in investment cost?

   A. Business analysis.   B. Marketing strategy development.

   C. Test marketing.   D. Product development.

4. Goods and services that people buy infrequently and with care are called _____ products; goods and services that people buy frequently and without much thought are called _____ products.

   A. convenience; shopping   B. shopping; convenience

   C. convenience; unsought   D. unsought; convenience

5. In which stage of the Product Life Cycle (PLC) is competition at its greatest?

   A. The introduction stage.   B. The growth stage.

   C. The maturity stage.   D. The decline stage.

6. Which of the following is not one of the strategies for extending the life of a product in the maturity stage?

   A. Modify the market.   B. Modify the marketing organization.

   C. Modify the product.   D. Modify the marketing mix.

7. A product is _____.

   A. everything the customer receives in an exchange

   B. the physical object the customer receives in an exchange

   C. the service and idea that is rendered to a customer

   D. anything that can be offered to a market for attention, acquisition, use or consumption and that might satisfy a want or need

8. A brand is best described as a _____.

   A. copyrighted word(s) that gives the manufacturer exclusive ownership

   B. related group of words that describes the product

   C. name, symbol, design, or combination of these that identifies a seller's products

   D. name of the manufacturer of the product

9. McDonald's golden arches, which are prominent on the firm's buildings, packaging, and advertising, represent a _____.

   A. trade name   B. brand name   C. brand mark   D. brand equity

10. Which of the following is NOT one of the unique features of services?

   A. Intangibility.   B. Inseparability.   C. Homogeneity.   D. Perishability.

II. True or false.

1. A company's research and development process is the only way for them to develop new

products.

2. The step-by-step new product development process explained in the text has been used by so many companies over so many years that it is almost failure-proof today.

3. The first full-scale working product from a concept is called a "prototype."

4. When a product has been in the maturity stage of the product life cycle for a period of time, marketing managers have pretty well lost any control of the product to the competitive vagaries that characterize that stage.

5. Brand equity is the added value a given brand name gives to a product beyond the functional benefits provided.

6. The marketing objective for a product in the introduction stage of the product life cycle (PLC) is to promote consumer awareness and gain trial.

7. The goal of VCR manufacturers' advertisement is to maintain brand loyalty and market share; the product category is in the introduction stage of its product life cycle.

8. Products that are used directly in the production of a final product but are not easily identifiable are categorized as component parts.

9. Machines and tools used in a production process but not as part of final products are classified as component parts.

10. Routinely purchased items that do not become part of the final physical product and are treated like expense items rather than capital goods are classified as supplies and services.

11. A desirable feature for a brand name is it can be used as the general name for all products in the category.

III. Discussion.

1. What is a product? What are the features of products?

2. How to classify products traditionally and internationally?

3. What is a product life cycle? Give a brief description of the separate stages.

4. Describe the process of designing and developing a new product.

5. What are the advantages and disadvantages of branding? Why are people willing to pay more for branded product than unbranded products?

6. Web question.

   The concept of a product life cycle identifies four stages in a product's "life cycle": introduction, growth, maturity, and decline. How do companies handle a product that has gone past its maturity stage? Is decline inevitable for all products? Are there any ways to prolong a product's life cycle? If yes, what are the different approaches to do it? Let's look at two products that have been around for more than a century: Arm & Hammer baking soda and Morton Salt. Let us visit the Web sites of these two companies to discover how they have kept their products alive for so long.

First, visit Arm & Hammer's Web site and explore the different sections of this site, paying particular attention to the following:

Product introductions: Arm & Hammer has introduced a host of products that play on baking soda's ability to deodorize and clean. These include A&H toothpaste, detergent, carpet and room deodorizer, air freshener, deodorant, fabric softener, and cat litter deodorizer. The base ingredient in these products does not change, but still the uses are quite different.

New uses of baking soda: A&H's site also has a section where it recommends different uses for baking soda. Click on "Fresh Idea Council" to read about some such uses. For example, it recommends adding baking soda to shampoo to remove residue from styling products in your hair. Also visit the "Tour Our House" section, where the company offers recommendations on how baking soda can be used to deodorize and cleanse a multitude of household items and appliances. The company also encourages readers to send their new ideas and usage recommendations.

Fun uses and usage reminders: The Web site also has a section entitled "Kids' Experiments" where it teaches kids to use baking soda with other household items to "make some great science experiments". The Web site even offers a reminder service where it can send reminder e-mails to users to replace old baking soda (in the refrigerator) with a new pack.

Now visit the Web site of the Morton Salt Company. Again, pay attention to the following:

Product introductions: Morton has used its knowledge of salt and minerals to diversify into water softening products (Morton System Saver) and meat curing products (Morton Tender mix and Sugar Cure mix).

Varied uses of Morton Salt: Visit the section entitled "Household Hints" to find hints on how to use salt to perk up coffee flavor, soothe sore throat, and clean vases, among other uses.

Fun uses for kids: The site also provides a couple of interesting activities for kids that are centered around Morton Salt. For example, there are directions on sculpting with Klaymates and painting with Saltcraft.

(1) Based on what you observed at the above-mentioned Web sites, discuss ways to extend a product's product life cycle (PLC).

(2) What are some other options available to managers to manage products in the decline stage of the PLC?

Chapter Twelve

Pricing

定 价 决 策

📢 Objectives 学习目标

When students finish this chapter, they should be able to accomplish the following:

- ☑ Definition of price and pricing
- ☑ Forces influencing pricing
- ☑ Pricing objectives
- ☑ Pricing products
- ☑ Constrains on international pricing
- ☑ Transferring price and other
- ☑ Pricing internationally
- ☑ Financing of exports

12.1 Price and Pricing 价格和定价

Price is the value of what a consumer exchanges in return for products. It may take the form of monetary exchange, bartered services, or other goods.

Price is the only element in the marketing mix that produces revenue[1]. All other elements represent costs. Price is flexible. It changes very quickly. In a less developed market, price is the major factor affecting buyer's choice. However, non-price factors have an increasing importance recently.

Pricing is an essential part of any business strategy. It is about the marketing activity concerned with the setting of prices for new products and the adjustment of prices for existing products. Pricing creates the revenue to support existing and future opportunities. To price a product or service properly, a firm must first set its pricing objectives, then evaluate the customers' response and other pricing constraints and analyze the potential profit before setting the initial price. As the situation in the market is always changing, so does the pricing strategy. It is necessary to make proper adjustment and adaptation to the price.

Pricing and price competition is the number-one problem facing most marketing executives. The pricing process can be seen in Figure 12-1.

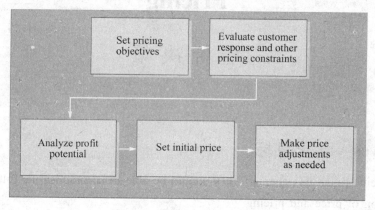

Figure 12-1   The Pricing Process

12.2   Forces Influencing Pricing   影响定价的要素

Pricing is driven by three major forces. They are costs, demands and competition.

Everything has a price and a company cannot sell an item for less than it costs to make or for the company to buy. Costs are very important factors that set the floor for the price that the company can charge. Companies want to charge a price that covers all its costs for producing, distributing, and selling the product, and provides a fair rate of return for its effort and risk. Many companies work to become the "low-cost producers" in their industry. Costs can take two forms: Fixed costs — costs that do not vary with production or sales levels and Variable costs — costs that vary directly with the level of production. Total costs are the sum of the fixed and variable costs at any given level of production. A company can stay in business as long as its price covers variable costs and some fixed costs. The company must carefully watch their costs. If it spends more than competitors to produce and sell its product, the company will have to charge a higher price or make less profit, putting it at a competitive disadvantage.

International pricing must also consider the cost of modifying a product to meet cultural or legal restrictions, tariffs and other taxes, fees to acquire export or import licenses, expenses for the preparation of export documents, charges in the exchange rate for a nation's currency, and transportation costs due to selling to buyers at a greater distance.

Whereas costs set the lower limit of prices, the market and demand set the upper limit. When prices are high, consumers tend to buy less of an item than when prices are low. Lower incomes, higher prices, and needs for other items result in reduced demand for goods or service. Economic conditions, cultural preferences, and legal restrictions in a foreign market will also affect potential demand and the price that can be charged. Pricing freedom varies with different types of markets. Pricing freedom also varies with consumer's perceptions of price and value[2]. When consumers buy a product, they exchange something of value (the price) to get something of value (the benefits of having or using the product). Effective buyer-oriented pricing involves understanding how much value consumers place on benefits. Thus, a company finds it hard to measure the values that customers will attach to a product.

Pricing strategies from competitors are also of great importance. The company needs to learn the price and quality of each competitor's offer and possible competitor's reaction to the firm's pricing moves. Competition gives consumers more choices, which usually keeps prices lower. Competition forces companies to offer special prices to attract customers.

In a word, the three basic factors determine the boundaries of the pricing decision — the price floor, or minimum price, bounded by product cost, the price ceiling or maximum price, bounded by competition and the market and the optimum price, a function of demand and the cost of supplying the product.

There are other factors that influence pricing decisions. These include economic conditions such as boom or recession, inflation, or interest rates; the reseller's policies especially if they do not match the supplier's; the government because of its regulatory power. Besides, social concerns may affect the firm's short-term sales, market share, and profit goals.

However, when a marketer enters international markets, the above-mentioned factors should be considered in a far more complicated background or in a deeper situation. These include regulations in different countries, exchange rates[3] in the world finance market, inflation rates and price control policies; competition in the target market, income levels[4] of different countries, market structure; together with price objectives, production costs, distribution costs[5], profitability[6] of the company itself.

12.3 Pricing Objectives 定价目标

While it is often assumed that the goal of pricing is to generate the most revenue, there are a number of pricing objectives a business pursues, each leading to a different pricing strategy.

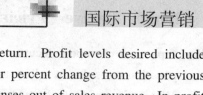

Profitability objectives involve profit levels and target-return. Profit levels desired include satisfactory or maximum profits, expressed in cash amount or percent change from the previous period. Profit is what remains after paying for costs and expenses out of sales revenue. In profit maximization, management sets increasing levels of profitability as its objective. Generally, profit maximization is focused on total output rather than on individual products. In target return, desired profitability is stated in terms of return on sales or investment. Many retailers and wholesalers use a target return on net sales for short-run periods. Cash flow is needed to recover cash quickly, especially with products with short life cycles. Integral to pricing by wholesalers and retailers is markup, an amount added to the cost of a product to cover anticipated operating expenses and provide a desired profit for the period. Manufacturers that are industry leaders often select target return on investment. They can set prices more independent of competition than smaller firms can.

Volume objectives include sales maximization and market-share goals, which are specified as a percentage of certain markets. In sales maximization, management sets an acceptable level of profitability and then tries to maximize sales. This objective can lead to discounting or some other aggressive pricing strategy, such as rebates[7] and sales. Occasionally, organizations are willing to incur a loss in the short run to expand sales volume or meet sales objectives. Market share is a percentage of a market controlled by a certain company or product. Pricing objectives are used to increase market share. If markets aren't growing, the only way for a business to grow is to grab market share from competitors.

Some prices are set to beat competition by beating the pricing leader's prices, hence met competition objectives. To compete effectively, marketers may be the lowest cost producer. Sometimes the companies set their price low to gain market share and prevent competitors from entering the market. They must be willing and able to change the price frequently by responding quickly and aggressively. However, competitors can also respond quickly. Customers adopt brand switching to use the lowest priced brand. Sellers move along the demand curve by raising and lowering prices. Price sensitivity varies among market segments and across different products (necessary products versus luxury). Marketers need to know buyers' acceptable range of prices and sensitivity towards price changes and set their price according to different segments (segment pricing).

Other objectives include social and ethical[8] considerations, status quo objectives, and image goals. Nonprofit organizations and government agencies use social and ethical objectives to cover their costs where possible and to raise money for their activities. Nonprofit organizations use pricing to achieve social goals. Government agencies use price to recoup some or all of their operating costs while delivering needed services. Status quo objectives maintain market share by meeting competitor prices, achieving price stability, or maintaining public image. This is common in industries where the product is highly standardized. Prestige pricing objectives establish a relatively high price to develop and maintain an image of quality and exclusiveness.

In some cases, wholesalers stock up on far more merchandise than they can sell during manufacturers' price promotions, and then resell to customers at higher prices after the promotion is over. This is called forward buying.

The long-run objective of commercial organizations may be taken to be profit maximization. However, in pursuing the objective of profit maximization, a business may adopt several different short-run strategies, including market skimming, market penetration, market holding, or cost-plus/price escalation. Besides, an international marketer also faces the challenge of standardization or differentiation of price in two countries.

12.4   Pricing Products   产品定价

Few organizations can now be pure profit maximizers — there is hardly a sector of industry where competition or potential competition is not prevalent.

12.4.1   Pricing new products   新产品定价

Three frequently encountered price policies are market penetration, skimming and holding for the launch of new products. A low price (penetration) is a volume policy. A high price (skimming) is used if the product is fairly unique, development costs are high and demand is relatively inelastic. Market holding is a strategy intended to hold share. Here products are not based on straight exchange rates at current rates but on what the market can bear.

As shown in Figure 12-2, market skimming price charges the highest price possible over those buyers who most desire the product will pay. Market skimming pricing has several purposes. Since it should provide healthy profit margins, it is intended primarily to recover research and development costs as quickly as possible. This strategy is especially good for limited capacity introductions.

Market skimming is often used in pricing new technological products such as cellular phones and high-definition televisions. Over time, the initial price may be lowered gradually. For a product that prices at skimming price, it attracts market segment that is more interested in quality, status, uniqueness, etc. This strategy is good if competition can be minimized by other means, e.g. brand loyalty, patent, or high barriers to entry.

Generally, the market skimming strategy is particularly relevant to the international marketer who has selected an undifferentiated marketing policy. The marketer can gain a certain profit through, most probably, limited distribution channels with limited commitment. And the market is inelastic.

In market penetration pricing, a relatively low initial price is established for a new product. The price is low in relation to the target market's range of expected prices. The primary aim of this strategy is to penetrate the mass market immediately and generate substantial sales volume and a large market share. A marketer must be very careful before adopting this strategy, for it may lead to a loss of profit.

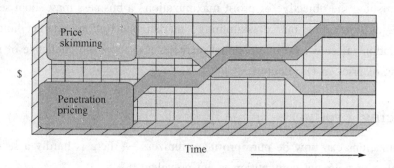

Figure 12-2   Skimming and Penetration Strategy

Market holding pricing is a strategy intended to hold market share. Here products are not based on straight exchange rates at current rates but on what the market can bear. A company sets its price low to gain market share and preventing competitors from entering the market.

12.4.2   Pricing existing products   已有产品定价

When pricing existing products, a marketer will have take into consideration of the existing competition in the market. His pricing freedom would be much more narrowed.

Marketers of raw commodity traded on the international market subject to world prices have no alternative but to take the going price — a price governed by competition, especially on the supply side. They accept market pricing strategy. A market pricing strategy does not mean a low price of a product. If the supplier is one of a few, despite all the problems associated with price fixing, the market may be able to bear a high price. In other cases the product may be so unique that the company should capitalize on its rarity by charging a high price. The problem is, encouraged by the profit margins, more entrants are drawn into the market.

One major feature of international pricing is the increase on the price due to the application of duties and so on. Cost-plus / price escalation takes all these factors into consideration (see Table 12-1).

Table 12-1   Cost-plus Price

Target price in foreign markets	$25.00
Less 40% retail margin on selling price	$10.00
Retailer cost	$15.00
Less 75% importer / distributor marking up cost	$1.96
Distributor cost	$13.04
Less 1.% value added tax on landed value and duty	$1.40
CIF value plus duty	$11.64
Less 9% duty on CIF value	$0.96
Landed CIF value	$10.68
Less ocean freight and insurance	$1.40
Required FOB[9] price to achieve target price	$9.26

If $9.26 is less than the domestic price, and the firm is still interested in the target market, it has a few alternatives: 1) forget about exporting; 2) consider marginal pricing; 3) shorten the distribution channel; 4) modify or simplify product if possible; 5) find an alternative source of supply with lower cost.

Product life cycle pricing strategies recognize that products and product categories generally go through a cycle, including introduction, growth, maturity and decline. During the introductory stage, often there is only one firm in the market, and higher prices are used to recoup initial expenditures. Also a price skimming strategy, such high prices appeal only to those consumers most willing and able to buy the product. During the growth stage prices are lowered as competing products enter the market, and in the maturity stage prices are lowered again as the market becomes saturated. During the final, decline stage, prices are lowered to sell the final inventory.

The pricing strategies and their features of existing products can be see in Figure 12-3.

Pricing Strategies	Features
Market pricing	A price governed by competition, especially on the supply side. Marketers of raw commodity often take this strategy.
Cost-plus / price escalation	Organizations may take into consideration the increase on the price due to the application of duties and so on. This strategy is basically a cost based pricing strategy.
Life cycle pricing	As the product goes from the introductory, growth, maturity and decline, the price must continuously decrease.

Figure 12-3   Pricing Existing Products

12.4.3　Pricing adjustment and adaptation　定价调整

The following are price adjustments[10] based on changing situations.

Businesses offer discounts of all types to buyers who satisfy some criteria that reduce their selling costs. For marketers, strategic discounting can be a powerful tool to increase sales or even out seasonal demand. Discounting can be classified into the following sectors (see Figure 12-4):

Quantity discount is the reduction in the price per unit for purchasing a larger quality. It offers lower prices to customers if they buy in bulk. The cost savings are passed on to the buyer. Cost savings can occur from reduced selling costs; declining fixed costs; declining costs from the suppliers of raw materials; increasing production runs (no increase in holding costs); and shifting storage, financing, and risk taking functions to the buyer. For example, a pack of DIY carpenter toolbox sells at the price of $95 but 2 or more packs for $90.00 each.

Seasonal discount can be used to encourage customers to purchase during off-peak times. This can help to lower inventory levels when demand is down. An example would be coats bought in the summer or swimsuits bought in the winter.

Trade discount is given to such people as distributors or representatives who perform some of the marketing functions, such as selling, storing, and record keeping. For example, a local retailer generally gets 40% – 30% off for the goods and services he takes from his wholesaler.

Cash discount is price reductions offered to customers when they pay for their purchases in cash or pay their bills promptly. This is often used by manufacturers and their distribution channel partners. An example would be 2/10, net /30 where a 2% discount is given if the bill is paid in 10 days; if not, the entire bill is due in 30 days without penalty.

Discount	Definition
Quantity discount	Reduction in the price per unit for purchasing a larger quantity
Seasonal discount	Price reduction offered during times of slow demand
Trade discount	Percentage reduction from list price offered to resellers
Cash discount	Incentive for buyers to pay quickly or a lower price for payment of cash

Figure 12-4　Pricing Adjustments — Discount

As shown in Figure 12-5, promotional discount is temporarily price reduction to increase short-run sales. In this case, the company must decide on loss-leader pricing (product priced lower to attract customers to the store in hopes that they will buy other items at normal markup), special-event pricing, cash rebates, low interest financing, longer payment terms, warranties and service contracts and psychological discounting.

Allowance pricing also has the effect of reducing prices to reward customer responses such as paying early or promoting the product. Trade-in allowance is price reductions granted for turning in a used item when purchasing a new one. Promotional allowance is money paid by manufacturers to retailers in return for an agreement to feature the manufacturer's products in some way.

A recent pricing issue is that of everyday low pricing, where the retailer charges a constant, lower price at all times, with no temporary price discounts. Wal-Mart has led the trend toward everyday low pricing.

Promotional adjustments	Definition
Promotional discount	Short-term discount to stimulate sales or convince buyers to try a product
Loss leader pricing	Setting prices near or below cost in order to attract customers to a store
Trade-in allowance	Discount for providing a product along with monetary payment
Promotional allowance	Price reduction in exchange for the reseller performing certain promotional activities
Everyday low price	The retailer charges a constant, lower price at all times, with no temporary price discounts.

Figure 12-5　Promotional Adjustments

Psychological pricing considers how consumers' perceptions and beliefs affect their price evaluations. Premium (or prestige pricing) uses high prices to convey an image of quality to buyers. Odd-even pricing, the use of $9.99 rather than $10.00, leads consumers to think of the product in the lower (less than $10) category rather than in the $10 to $20 range. Bundle pricing offerers several products as a package at a single price.

Geographic Pricing is used when a company decides on how to price to distant customers. Free On Board or FOB-origin pricing is a geographical pricing strategy in which goods are placed free on board a carrier; the customer pays the actual freight from the factory to the destination. Because the customer picks up its own cost, supporters believe that this method is the fairest way to assess freight charges. Uniform-delivered pricing is a geographical pricing strategy in which the company charges the same price plus freight to all customers, regardless of their location. This is the opposite of FOB pricing. This method is fairly easy to administer and advertise nationally. The averaging method helps distant customers and sometimes discriminates against local or close customers. Zone pricing means that different areas pay different prices on freight but all customers within the same area pay the same freight charges. Basing-point pricing means that all customers are charged freight from a specified billing location. In freight-absorption pricing, the seller pays all shipping costs to get the desired business.

12.4.4　International pricing adjustments　国际定价调整

There are three possible international pricing policies — extension (ethnocentric), adaptation (polycentric) and invention (geocentric).

Extension (standardized pricing) is to set the same global price no matter where the target market is. It is a very simple method but does not respond to market sensitivity. Few firms use this method to price their products in the international trade.

Adaptation (differential pricing) is to set different prices in different markets. The only control is setting transfer prices within the corporate system. It prevents problems of arbitrage when the disparities in local market prices exceed the transportation and duty costs separating markets.

Invention is a mix of extension and adaptation strategy. This takes cognizance[11] of any unique market factors like costs, competition, income levels and local marketing strategy. In addition, it recognizes the fact that headquarters price coordination is necessary in dealing with international accounts and arbitrage and it systematically seeks to embrace national experience.

12.5　Constraints on International Pricing　国际定价限制

12.5.1　Constraints on international pricing　国际定价限制

More and more governments pay much attention to multinational companies' pricing practice. Major international pricing control include：

(1) Price minimum and pricing ceiling. Price controls typically involve the setting of a price ceiling or a price floor. Price ceiling is a legal maximum on the price at which a good can be sold. And price floor is a legal minimum on the price at which a good can be sold.

(2) Specific mark-ups in the distribution channel. Some countries such as Norway set limits the rate of price added to a product during the process of distribution in order to protect

consumers. For example, the health authorities determine pharmacies' maximum markups on prescription drugs.

(3) Manufacturers' profit margins control. Profit margin is simply earnings (or profits) divided by sales, both measured over the same time period. Profit margins are the money left over after paying all of the costs of running the business. A limit on the profit margins helps the consumer to some extend but it will frustrate the development of new technology.

(4) Restrictive trade practice and monopolies. The Monopolies and Restrictive Trade Practices Act, 1969, was enacted to prevent the concentration of economic power to common detriment, control of monopolies, prohibition of monopolistic and restrictive trade practices and matters connected therewith.

Price fixing is to set fixed prices for products of particular types among certain competitors. In the past marketers were able to insist that dealers sell their products at specific prices (resale price maintenance) but the Consumer Goods Pricing Act banned the practice in 1975.

Predatory pricing is to set unreasonably low prices to force competitors out of business.

Price discrimination is the practice of unfairly pricing the same quality, grade, and quantity of goods differently for different customers. Price discrimination that is aimed at reducing competition is forbidden. Marketers can charge different prices when prices are justified by cost differentials; represent a good-faith effort to match competitors' prices rather than to reduce competition; and reflect changing market conditions.

Dumping is the practice of pricing products in host countries below cost or less than their price in the marketer's home country. Nearly every country outlaws dumping.

Deceptive pricing — price that misleads and deceives customers by hiding the true or final price for the product. An example is advertising a price as lower than a fraudulent "regular" price. Another example is bait and switch, where one product is priced very low to lure customers to a store and they're pressured to buy a more expensive product instead. A third example is the misleading promotion of a product at a bargain price when purchased with the same or another product.

12.5.2　Major laws and legislation on pricing　有关定价的主要法律和法规

Laws and regulations governing pricing vary from country to country. The value of the currency of any given country is constantly changing, causing the exchange rate for a product to move up or down. Currency fluctuations may make a product less attractive in a local market, but more attractive in a foreign market.

1. In USA

The Sherman Antitrust Act 1890, which prohibits monopolies or attempts to monopolies and contracts, combinations or conspiracies in restraint of trade.

The Federal Trade Commission Act 1911, which established a commission to investigate unfair methods of competition and issue "cease and desist" orders, that is to say, deceptive pricing.

The Clayton Act 1914 and the Robinson-Patman Amendment 1936, which prohibit price discrimination by ensuring that all members at a given level in the channel of distribution are offered the same terms by the seller.

The Consumer Goods Pricing Act 1975, forbids price fixing.

2. In EU

Treaty of Rome, which supports fair competition, has specific articles that deal with pricing problems.

Article 85 (1) prohibits agreements between firms which prevent, restrict or distort competition within the EU Companies who are against Article 85 may be liable to heavy fines.

Article 86 forbids the abuse of a dominant position within the EU. This includes predatory pricing, limiting production or technical development, a refusal to supply, or discrimination against others to their competitive disadvantages.

12.6　Transfer Pricing and Other　转移价格及其他

12.6.1　Transfer pricing　转移价格

When a company decentralizes, organizing itself into separate profit centers, it is necessary to transfer components or finished products between units. Transfer pricing is used to motivate profit center managers, provide divisional flexibility and also further corporate profit goals. Across national boundaries the system becomes complicated by taxes, joint ventures, attitudes of governments and so on. There are four basic approaches to transfer pricing.

● Transfer at cost: Few practice this, which recognizes foreign affiliates contribute to profitability by operating domestic scale economies. Prices may be unrealistic so this method is seldom used.

● Transfer at direct cost plus overheads and margin. Similar to that in transfer at cost.

● Transfer at a price derived from end market prices: Very useful strategy in which market based transfer prices and foreign sources are used as devices to enter markets too small for supporting local manufacturers. This gives a valuable foothold.

• Transfer at an "arm's length": This is the price that would have been reached by unrelated parties in a similar transaction. The problem is identifying a point "arm's length" price for all products other than commodities. Pricing at "arm's length" for differentiated products results not in a specific price but prices which fall in a pre-determinable range.

1. Financial aspects of international transfer pricing

The transfer pricing can be adopted to minimize tax or import duty liability, or to transfer funds.

(1) Transferring products into a high duty country at very low prices may result in low import duty.

(2) Transferring products into a high tax country at high prices can effectively transfer profits from the high tax country to the low tax country.

(3) Products may be transferred at high prices into a country from which dividend repatriation is restricted or subject to high tax.

(4) It can avoid an accumulation of funds in a country with high inflation rates, or where an early devaluation is thought to be a probability, or where expropriation is feared.

(5) It can be used as a means to concentrate profits.

2. Attitudes to transfer pricing

Many governments see transfer pricing as a tax evasion policy[12] and have, in recent years, looked more closely at company returns. Rates of duty encourage the size of the transfer price: the higher the duty rate the more desirable a lower transfer price. A low income tax creates a pressure to raise the transfer price to locate income in the low tax setting. Harmonization[13] of tax rates worldwide may make the intricacies of transfer pricing obsolete.

Government controls, like cash deposits on importers, give an incentive to minimize the price of the imported item. Profit transfer rules may apply which restrict the amount of profit transferred out of the country.

Although many multinational companies practice transfer pricing, they have various attitudes towards it. Many companies regard it as a means of encouraging and measuring corporate efficiency. Others emphasize the opportunities for financial gain or market manipulation.

12.6.2 Other important price phenomena in international marketing
国际市场营销中的其他价格现象

1. Devaluation and revaluation

Devaluation is the reduction and revaluation an increase in the value of one currency vis à vis[14] other currencies. Under the floating exchange rate system[15], devaluation and revaluation occur when currency values adjust in the exchange rate system in response to supply and demand. The idea behind devaluation is to make the domestic price more competitive and so more of the product can be bought for the same foreign currency. However, it can be negated by the higher price and costs induced by inboard goods and services which make up the export product. If the product is inelastic in demand, prices can be maintained if the competitive position is strong. In revaluation, the revaluing country's prices are more expensive. These price increases may be passed on to the customers, absorbed or the domestic price may be reduced.

2. Inflation and dumping

Inflation is a world wide phenomenon, and requires periodic price adjustments. Inflation accounting methods attempt to deal with the phenomenon. It is essential to retain gross and operating profit margins. Actions to maintain margins are subject to government controls (a typical African situation is where governments use price or selective price controls rather than rooting out the underlying causes of inflation or foreign exchange shortages), competitive behavior and the market itself. Price adjustments may affect the demand for products, and this is the ultimate arbiter of price alterations.

Dumping is the process of pricing exports at a lower level than in the domestic market. Dumping is considered illegal in many countries but it is very difficult to prove the dumping has occurred. Low price may be due to higher productivity and a more efficient firm.

12.7 Financing of Exports 出口融资

Money is anything people will accept for exchange of goods and services. A big difference for a marketer to do business internationally is every country has its own unique medium of exchange; US has the dollar, Mexico has the peso, Japan exchanges the yen, and Thailand uses the baht. If a marketer plans to participate in international trade, he has to take into consideration of different exchange rate all the time as his customer may pay him on another currency. There are various financial methods used in the international trade.

Drafts covering exports may be on sight basis for immediate payment or drawn to be accepted for payment 30, 60 or 90 days after sight. Drafts directed to a bank for collection are accompanied by shipping documents consisting of a full set of bills of lading in negotiable form, airway bills of lading, or parcel post receipt, together with insurance certificates, commercial invoices, consular invoices and any other documents that may be required in the country of destination.

Sales on a consignment basis creates no tangible obligation. In countries with free port or free trade zones, it can be arranged to have consigned merchandise placed under bonded warehouse control in the name of a foreign bank. Sales can then be arranged by the selling agent and arrangements made to release partial lots out of the consigned stock against regular payment terms. The merchandise is not cleared through customs until after the sale has been completed.

The two most common methods are payment under a collection agreement and payment under a letter of credit, also called a documentary credit. In both cases, banks are used as intermediaries and the shipping documents are used as collateral security for the banks. Usually, in international sales, the seller draws a bill of exchange either on the buyer or on a bank. This bill is usually payable a certain number of days after sight, e. g. 90 days after sight.

In the case of a collection agreement the bank in the buyer's country is squarely responsible for effecting payment, whereas in the case of a letter of credit this responsibility falls on the bank in the country of the seller.

Where a collection arrangement is organized the seller hands the shipping documents including the bill of lading to his own bank, the remitting bank, which passes them on to a bank at the buyer's place, the collecting bank. The collecting bank then presents the bill of exchange to the buyer and requests him to pay or to accept the bill. When the buyer has complied, the collecting bank releases the shipping documents to the buyer, who is then able to receive the original bill of lading that enables him to obtain the goods from the carrier on arrival of the ship. The collecting bank is liable to the seller if it releases the shipping documents to the buyer without having received finance from him.

Letters of credit are of particular importance. A letter of credit arrangement will be agreed upon in the contract of sale. The buyer instructs a bank in his own country (the issuing bank) to open a credit with a bank in the seller's country (the advising bank) in favor of the seller, specifying the documents which the seller has to deliver to the bank for him to receive payment. If the correct documents are tendered by the seller during the currency of the letter of credit arrangement, the advising bank pays him the purchase price or accepts his bill of exchange drawn on it, or negotiates his bill of exchange, which is drawn on the buyer. Whichever method used is pre-arranged between the seller and the buyer.

Letters of credit can be revocable or irrevocable, confirmed or unconfirmed. Whether the credit is revocable or irrevocable depends on the commitment of the issuing bank. Whether it is confirmed or unconfirmed depends on the commitment of the advising bank. These commitments are undertaken to the seller, who is the beneficiary under the credit. Hence, there are four main types of letters of credit, namely, the revocable and unconfirmed letter of credit, the irrevocable and unconfirmed letter of credit, the irrevocable and confirmed letter of credit, and the transferable letter of credit.

Cases

Case 1.　　Price war predicted on air conditioner market

Aux Air Conditioner, one of the major air conditioner manufacturers in China, invited 20 counterparts to discuss price cuts in Beijing Tuesday.

Insiders agreed that this move indicated an escalation of the price war in the air conditioner market, China Securities reported Monday.

Aux said the high price has scared Chinese residents off and hindered the development of the air conditioner industry.

Statistics show that China households bought 12 million air conditioners in 2000. But China's 100 air conditioner producers churned out 22 million.

Aux noted that there are two different ways of cutting prices, normal price readjustment and an unreasonable price war. Aux opposes the way of expanding market share with lower-than-normal prices.

"What Aux suggests is to cooperate with major air conditioner makers to put the market into order through price readjustment, and drive low quality air conditioners out of the market," a spokesman for the firm said.

Case 2.　　Who are winners of the heated TV price wars?

In the 20th Century, China's color TV producers launched price wars one round after another, bringing the comprehensive price level of TV sets down to a historic low. Many producers suffered from drastic profit drop and the whole sector went sluggish.

Statistics from China's Ministry of Information Technology (MIT) showed that during the first 10 months of 2000, the total output of color TVs stood at 27.71 million sets, and the sales volume was 29.02 million sets, down 106 per cent and 5 per cent respectively. And, the accumulative stock reached 6 million sets.

On the contrary, sales and profits of foreign TV producers in China were on the rise. Their market shares jumped from the previous some 10 per cent up to over 30 per cent in 2000.

Many industrial insiders pondered where the way out for the country's TV sector was. They said that China's color TV sector is now very fragile. The heated price wars achieved little but brought the sector into dual crises: financial crisis and renovation crisis. More and more receivable payment arose and the companies involved have no ability to invest in R&D and thus made technological renovation impossible.

Case 3.　Are we still giants?

Ever since 1996, China's color TV producers have experienced eight large-scale price wars and numerous small ones.

Price wars did do some good to the country's color TV sector. By launching price wars, the Sichuan-based Changhong acquired more market shares and accelerated the process of making a color TV set a household necessity. The price wars also created more opportunities for Chinese TV producers to explore the overseas market.

"China has 87 color TV producers, whose total production capacity is 50 million sets. Currently, the actual production and sales volume stand at around 35 million sets. China is now the largest color TV producer and seller in the world. The Chinese Government has invested 28 billion yuan (US $3.37 billion) in aggregate to promote the development of this sector, reabsorbing 450 billion yuan (US $54.22 billion) in capital and providing more than 200,000 job opportunities for the country," said an MIT official.

However, there are many loopholes in the development of China's color TV sector. Repeated construction and unreasonable industrial and product structures are the two major problems. What's more, the sector lacks core technologies and the managing, service and marketing methods are comparatively lagging behind.

Statistics showed that price wars made the country suffer a loss of 14.7 billion yuan (US $1.77 billion). Enterprises that took part in the price wars suffered a loss ranging from 300 million yuan (US $36.14 million) to more than 1 billion yuan (US $120 million).

Case 4.　Foreign brands battle up for more market shares

Taking advantage of China's heated price war, many foreign TV brands stole into the Chinese market and became big winners.

Responding to the domestic price wars, Panasonic implemented two price reductions during the Labour Day and Chinese National Day holiday sessions in 2000. And, in July and August, many foreign color TV producers joined the price war initiated by Chinese producers.

With the accelerated process of economic globalization, the domestic market becomes more open. Japanese companies like Sony, Panasonic, Toshiba and Hitachi have all set up offices in China.

Foreign producers have carried out a series of activities to promote their products such as roadshows and price-cutting. Due to their advantages in technology, these producers still enjoyed high profits despite large-scale price reduction.

Case 5. Car price war flares up in Jinan

A new round of car price-cutting is heating up in Jinan, capital of East China's Shandong Province.

It was triggered by the Shanghai Volkswagen Automotive Co. Ltd.'s latest announcement of slashing the price of its Santana sedan to 93,000 yuan (US$11,200) from more than 100,000 yuan (US$12,000).

The Changchun-based First Automotive Works' (FAW) also reduced the price of its Jetta GTX from 137,000 yuan (US$16,500) to 130,000 yuan (US$15,660) at a recent auto exhibition in the city.

Industry insiders said it is possible that the Wuhan-based Dongfeng-Citroen Automobile Co. Ltd. will follow suit and cut the price of its Fukang sedan to 98,000 yuan (US$11,800), to retain its market share.

It is the first time that Shanghai VW has reduced the price of its Santana sedan below 100,000 yuan (US$12,000), according to the sources.

It is said that the price of Passat sedan, also made by Shanghai Volkswagen, has been reduced moderately in Jinan's auto market.

Case 6. Cutting prices will boost cinemas

Cinemas in Beijing this week followed the lead of Chengdu, the capital of Sichuan Province, in slashing their ticket prices.

On Monday the price dropped by around 20 per cent, from an average 30 yuan (US$3.6) to 25 yuan (US$3). Special discounts are offered on Tuesdays when tickets cost 15 yuan (US$1.8).

The discount is modest compared with the 5-yuan (US$0.6) tickets offered in Chengdu.

In the past month, many cities, including Tianjin and Nanjing, have also lowered the price of movie tickets.

The country's cultural centers still seem reluctant to open the doors of their cinemas to more customers.

A cinema manager in Beijing said if prices drop from 30 yuan to 5 yuan, a 10-fold increase in customers would be needed to keep their profits at current levels. He said few cinemas would dare to take the risk of substantially reducing prices.

But cinema operators may be ignoring the basic economic rule that players who cannot make ends meet should be eliminated from the market.

The reluctance to reduce prices means film goers have few options when all cinemas demand the same prices.

But at least they can choose to stay at home and watch a VCD if they feel a film at a cinema is unaffordable.

The moderate price-reduction policy may be expedient to both lure more audiences and keep cinemas alive. But the country's film industry will never mature if it cannot break the monopoly of high prices.

Key Terms

transfer pricing　转移定价

extension（standardized pricing）　价格拓展（标准化定价）

adaptation（differential pricing）　差异定价

invention pricing　创新定价

drafts covering export　出口托收

sales on consignment basis　委托销售

cost-plus / price escalation　成本加成定价

deceptive pricing　欺骗定价

devaluation　货币贬值

dumping　倾销

financing of export　出口融资

total cost　总成本

fixed cost　固定成本

variable cost　可变成本

price elasticity of demand　需求的价格弹性

pure competition　完全竞争

pure monopoly　完全垄断

government monopoly　政府垄断

oligopolistic competition　寡头竞争

monopolistic competition　垄断性竞争

market penetration pricing　市场渗透定价

market skimming pricing　市场撇脂定价

product life cycle pricing　产品生命周期定价

market pricing　市场定价

quantity discount　数量折扣

cash discount　现金折扣

trade discount　中间商折扣

seasonal discount　季节性折扣

promotional discount　推销折让

everyday low pricing(EDLP)　每日低价

trade in allowance　以旧换新折让

promotional allowance　推销津贴

psychological pricing　心理定价

market holding pricing　市场保持定价

predatory pricing　掠夺性定价

price discrimination　价格差别，价格歧视

price objective　定价目标

price fixing　规定价格

inflation　通货膨胀

pricing ceiling　最高定价

revaluation　货币升值

Sherman Antitrust Act　（美国）《谢尔曼反托拉斯法》

The Federal Trade Commission Act　《联邦贸易委员会法》

The Clayton Act　（美国）《克莱登法》

Robinson-Patman Amendment　《罗宾逊—帕特曼法》

The Consumer Goods Pricing Act　《消费品定价法》

Treaty of Rome　《罗马条约》

the experience curve　经验曲线

📄 Notes

1. revenue　*n.*　收入

2. consumer's perceptions of price and value　顾客对价格和价值的认同

3. exchange rate　汇率

4. income level　收入水平

5. distribution cost　分销成本

6. profitability　*n.*　赢利能力

7. rebate　*n.*　回扣

8. ethical　*a.*　伦理的

9. FOB　离岸价

10. price adjustment　价格调整

11. cognizance　*n.*　认识

12. a tax evasion policy   逃税策略

13. harmonization   *n.*   一致

14. vis à vis   相对于

15. the floating exchange rate system   浮动汇率体系

 Exercises

I. Multiple choices.

1. In the broadest sense, price is the sum of _____ that customers exchange for benefits.

   A. dollars   B. currency   C. all the values   D. commodities

2. A company can stay in business as long as its price covers _____.

   A. variable costs and some fixed costs

   B. total costs

   C. fixed costs and some variable costs

   D. all costs plus a small profit

3. With a market holding pricing strategy, a company sets its price low to gain market share and _____.

   A. stabilize the market

   B. prevent competitors from entering the market

   C. help the sale of other products in the product line

   D. gain prestige

4. According to product life pricing strategy, what strategy should be adapted in the introduction stage?

   A. The market pricing.

   B. The market holding pricing strategy.

   C. The market penetration pricing strategy.

   D. The market skimming pricing strategy.

5. While costs set the lower limit on prices, _____ and _____ set the upper limit.

   A. market; demand   B. interest rates; inflation

   C. price; value   D. supply; demand

6. Odd-even pricing is mostly based on _____.

   A. product life cycle pricing   B. competitive pricing

   C. psychological pricing   D. market pricing

7. What is skimming pricing?

   A. Companies set prices to break even on production and marketing costs.

B. Companies segment costs of the component parts that make up the product, then set the price to make a profit.

C. Companies charge the highest price possible that buyers who most desire the product will pay.

D. Companies lower prices to keep the market share during a given period.

8. All but which of the following factors directly affect most companies' pricing decisions?

A. Competition.   B. Government regulations.

C. Gross domestic product.   D. Manufacturing costs.

9. Producers in high-tech industries often use the _____ pricing strategy to recoup quickly research and development costs.

A. cost-based   B. electronic   C. penetration   D. skimming

10. Sales start to decline _____ of the product life cycle.

A. at the end of the growth stage

B. at the beginning of the decline stage

C. during the maturity stage

D. at the beginning of the growth stage

II. True or false.

1. Pricing and price competition is the number-one problem facing most marketing executives.

2. External environmental factors have the greatest effect on pricing decisions.

3. "Forward buying" means that wholesalers stock up on far more merchandise than they can sell during manufacturers' price promotions, and then resell to customers at higher prices after the promotion is over.

4. A firm's total cost is made up of two components: direct costs and variable costs.

5. "Optional product pricing" is adding services to the base product to differentiate it from competitors and justify higher prices and margins.

6. The fact that prices are usually higher (often substantially higher) in foreign markets is called price escalation.

7. The Robinson-Patman Act seeks to prevent unfair price discrimination by ensuring that all members at a given level in the channel of distribution are offered the same terms by the seller.

III. Discussion.

1. What is price? Describe factors that influence price of a product.
2. What are the objectives of pricing a product?
3. What are the pricing strategies in pricing a product?
4. Explain the increasing importance of value-based pricing and contrast it with cost-based pricing.
5. What are the international pricing strategies?
6. What is transfer pricing? What are the attitudes of government to transfer pricing?
7. How does international trade finance? What are the most commonly used payments of international trade?
8. List at least five examples of stores that use their pricing strategies as part of their marketing strategy such as "the lowest price leader". Does any of them discuss offering average prices or high prices? Why or why not?

Chapter Thirteen

Developing Distribution

设 立 分 销

📣 **Objectives 学习目标**

When students finish this chapter, they should be able to accomplish the following:

☑ Distribution definition

☑ Distribution functions

☑ Types of channels

☑ Members in channel

☑ Channel management

☑ Physical distribution

☑ Channel strategy for new market entry

13.1 Definition 定义

Distribution is the process that goods are distributed from the manufacturer to the end user. Different companies may adopt different distribution services according to their marketing objectives and strategies. Some companies have their own means of distribution, some companies deal directly with the most important customers, but many companies rely on other companies to perform distribution services for them.

The term "marketing channel" was first used by Stern and El-Ansary. According to Stern and El-Ansary, channel members should have interdependency[1]. They defined a marketing channel as follows:

Marketing channels are sets of interdependent organizations involved in the process of making a product or service available for use or consumption.

13.2　Functions and Types of Distribution Channels
分销渠道的功能和类型

13.2.1　Functions of channels　分销渠道功能

Intermediaries smooth the flows of products to buyers by performing the key functions of informing, promoting, and physical possession. They can be classified into eight main functions, as shown in Figure 13-1.

(1) Information collecting: gathering and distributing marketing research;

(2) Promotion: developing and communicating offers;

(3) Contact: communicating with prospective buyers;

(4) Matching: fitting the offer to the buyer's needs;

(5) Negotiation: reaching agreement on price and terms;

(6) Physical distribution: transporting and storing the goods;

(7) Financing: getting and using funds to cover the costs of channel work;

(8) Risk taking: assuming the risks the channel work.

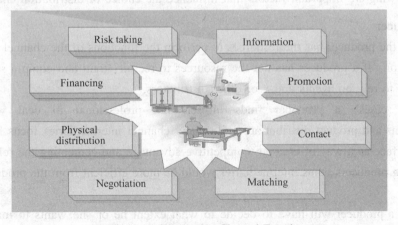

Figure 13-1　Distribution Channel Functions

The information function involves gathering and distributing marketing research and intelligence about the environment for planning purposes. Scanner technology provides a great amount of information. The promotion function involves developing and spreading persuasive communications about an offer. The contact function involves the direct communication between intermediaries especially retailers and buyers. The matching function involves the ability the intermediaries own to match the demand and supply efficiently and economically. The physical possession function consists of the transporting and storing of products. This activity involves the negotiations for reaching an agreement on price and other terms. The risk taking function assumes the risk of the actual transfer of ownership from one organization, carrying the product and receiving payment. The financing function involves acquiring and using funds to cover costs.

Marketing intermediaries increase efficiency in making products available to target markets, smooth the flows of products to buyers from the place of origin. Without an intermediary, each buyer has to negotiate and exchange with each seller. Intermediaries reduce the number of contacts necessary to complete a transaction. A producer will use an intermediary when he believes that the intermediary can perform the function(s) more economically and efficiently than he can. For example, if eight customers want to buy a product from three different manufacturers, they will have to make a total of 24 transactions. However, with an intermediary, the total number of transactions is reduced to 11. Thus, the use of intermediaries is extremely efficient for the consumer and the manufacturer.

13.2.2　Factors that influence the construction of channels
　　　　　影响渠道建设的因素

The following are important factors that influence the choice of distribution channel.

1. Producer

Whether the producer has the resources to perform the functions of the channel is vital for the channel decision. If a producer has not the resources to recruit, train and equip a sales team, the only option is to rely on agents and / or other distributors.

In other cases, a producer finds himself not professional to deal with customer communications and product distribution while many channel intermediaries focus heavily on the customer interface as a way of creating competitive advantage and cementing the relationship with their supplying producers, thus intermediaries would be more efficient from the producer's point of view.

Besides, a producer will have to decide to what extent he or she wants to maintain control over how, to whom and at what price a product is sold. If a manufacturer sells via a retailer, he losses control over the channel and pricing, since different levels of intermediaries are able to make their own decision. On the other hand, direct distribution gives a producer much more control over these issues.

2. Customer

An important market factor is customer characteristics such as number, geographical location, purchasing pattern, purchasing preferences. Their buying behavior will have great influence on the distribution channel decision. How do customers want to purchase the product? Do they prefer to buy from retailers, locally, via mail order or perhaps over the Internet? Another important factor is buyer needs for product information, installation and servicing. Which channels are best served to provide the customers with the information they need before buying? Does the product need specific technical assistance either to install or service a product? Intermediaries are often best placed to provide servicing rather than the original producer.

3. Product

Products characteristics such as bulk, weight, perishability, unit value and serving requirements are important for the marketing strategies planning. Large complex products are often supplied direct to customers (e. g. complex medical equipment sold to hospitals). By contrast perishable products (such as frozen food, meat, bread) require relatively short distribution channels — ideally suited to using intermediaries such as retailers.

4. Intermediaries

The willingness of channel intermediaries to market product is also a factor. Retailers in particular invest heavily in properties, shop fitting, etc. They may decide not to support a particular product if it requires too much investment (e. g. training, display equipment, warehousing). A marketer will also have to pay attention to the intermediary cost. Intermediaries typically charge a "mark-up" or "commission" for participating in the channel. This might be deemed unacceptably high for the ultimate producer business.

5. Environment

Competitors' decision in the market such as competitors' channels, or the degree of exclusivity offered to competitors. Certain governments may lay down specific legal restrictions in order to protect or to encourage foreign marketers. The culture background and customs of a certain market may also influence the structure and strategy decision.

13.2.3   Types of channels   渠道类型

Channels of distribution include consumer marketing channels and business marketing channels. Marketers can choose either a direct distribution channel, which moves goods directly from the producer to the consumer, or an indirect distribution channel, which involves using one, two, three or more intermediary channel levels. Distribution channels can be described by the number of channel levels involved, which is defined the length of a channel. Each layer of marketing intermediaries that performs some work in bringing the product and its ownership closer to the final buyer is a channel level. Figure 13-2 shows several consumer distribution channels of different lengths.

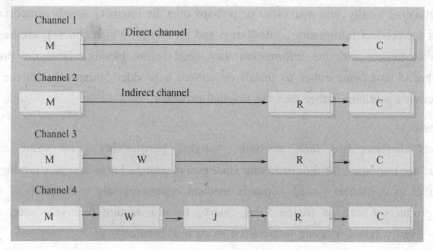

Figure 13-2   Consumer Marketing Channels & Levels

Channel 1, called a direct marketing channel, has no intermediary levels. It consists of a company selling directly to consumers. For example, Avon sell their products door to door or through home and office sales parties; Shanshan sells clothing direct through mail order and by telephone; and many factories sell their machines or equipments through their own stores. The remaining channels in Figure A are indirect marketing channels. Channel 2 contains one intermediary level. In consumer markets, this level is typically a retailer. For example, the makers of televisions, cameras, tires, furniture, major appliances, and many other products sell their goods directly to large retailers such as Wal-Mart and Pricesmart, which then sell the goods to final consumers. Channel 3 contains two intermediary levels, a wholesaler and a retailer. This channel often is used by small manufacturers of food, drugs, hardware, and other products. Channel 4 contains three intermediary levels. In the meatpacking industry, for example, jobbers[2] usually come between wholesalers and retailers. The jobber buys from wholesalers and sells to smaller retailers who generally are not served by larger wholesalers. Distribution channels with even more levels are sometimes found, but less often. From the producer's point of view, a greater number of levels mean less control and greater channel complexity.

Figure 13-3 shows some common business marketing channels. The business marketer can use its own sales force to sell directly to business customers. It also can sell to industrial distributors, who in turn sell to business customers. It can sell through manufacturer's representatives or its own sales branches to business customers, or it can use these representatives and branches to sell through industrial distributors. Thus, business markets commonly include multilevel distribution channels.

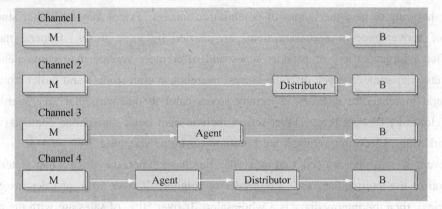

Figure 13-3　Business Marketing Channels & Levels

All of the institutions in the channel are connected by several types of flows. These include the physical flow of products, the flow of ownership, the payment flow, the information flow, and the promotion flow. These flows can even make channels with only one or a few levels very complex.

13.2.4　Members in distribution channel　分销渠道成员

Because the producer and the final consumer both perform some work, they are part of every channel. Members in channel include manufacturer, intermediaries, and consumer. The use of intermediaries results from their greater efficiency in making goods available to target markets[3]. The functions of the manufacturer are to design, produce, brand, price, promote, and sell the product. Marketing intermediaries include wholesalers and retailers. The functions of the wholesaler are to buy, stock, promote, display, sell, deliver, and finance. The functions of the retailer are to buy, stock, promote, display, sell, deliver, and finance.

From the economic system's point of view, the role of marketing intermediaries is to transform the assortments[4] of products made by producers into the assortments wanted by consumers.

Generally speaking, marketing intermediaries include wholesalers and retailers, and each has various forms. Wholesale transactions are all transactions except the transaction with the ultimate consumer. An agent or broker is an intermediary that brings together buyers and sellers but does not take ownership of the products being traded. A wholesaler is a business that buys large quantities of an item and resells them to retailers. A retailer is a store or other business that sells directly to the final user. Retailers are located at shopping malls, open markets, small shops, or large retail stores. Retailers attract the attention of potential customers through product selection, convenience, product quality, sales staff assistance, and special services.

Retailers are in the form of many different kinds of stores. Convenience stores usually locate near other shopping or near the homes of potential customers. Prices may be higher since smaller quantities of convenience or necessary items are carried by these stores. General merchandise retailers offer a larger variety of product types and offer more service than convenience stores. Supermarkets, department store, discount stores, warehouse club stores, and outlet stores are part of the general merchandise retailers. Specialty stores cater to one particular area such as shoes, furniture, clothing, flowers, etc. Direct sellers include mail order, telephone contacts, and door-to-door marketing. Electronic retailers are common on home-shopping TV.

However, it must be noticed that it is the purchaser, not the price, that determines the classification of the intermediary as a wholesaler or retailer. If over 50% of sales are with other intermediaries, then the intermediary is a wholesaler. If over 50% of sales are with the consumer, then the intermediary is a retailer.

International trade may include intermediaries different from domestic companies. An export management company (EMC) provides complete distribution services for businesses that desire to sell in foreign markets. Export trading companies (ETC) are full-service global distribution intermediaries. An ETC buys and sells products; conducts market research; and packages, ships, and distributes goods abroad. Freight forwarders ship goods to customers in other countries. Like a travel agent for cargo, these companies get an exporter's merchandise to the required destination. A customs broker acts as an agent for an importer in conducting customs business on their behalf. It can either be a private individual or a company. It acts as an intermediary that specializes in moving goods through the customs process which involves inspection of imported products and payment of duties.

Packaging is an important part of the marketing process, especially for international trade. When preparing for international shipping, an item should be packaged to avoid breakage, maintain the lowest possible weight and volume, provide moisture-proof surroundings, and minimize theft. Shipments going by land or sea require strong containers.

13.3   Channel Management   渠道管理

13.3.1   Channel strategies   渠道策略

The organization must decide on the amount of market coverage needed to achieve its marketing strategies when set up distribution channel for its product. In terms of number of intermediaries to use, an organization has three basic strategies choices; they are intensive distribution, selective distribution, or exclusive distribution.

For convenience products, where widespread availability is key, the company may opt for intensive distribution. That is to stock the product in as many outlets as possible. Soft drinks, gum, candy, and potato chips are in this catalog; they are sold at grocery stores, gas stations, and neighborhood stores. As channels are usually long and involve several levels of wholesaling as well as other middlemen, the costs of achieving extensive distribution are enormous. In fact, except in social marketing of this nature, it is rare to find organizations, which try for 100% distribution coverage.

For shopping products, where consumers spend some time in the decision process and have some brand preferences, selective distribution may be the best option. Under selective distribution, Suppliers appoint a limited number of retailers, or other middlemen to handle a product line. The distribution channel is usually relatively short with few or no intermediaries between the producer and the organization which retails the product to the end user. Most television, furniture, and small appliance brands are distributed in this manner. Haier , Gree and Glanz use this method to distribute their products.

Exclusive distribution is an extreme form of selective distribution for specialty products where consumers have strong brand preferences and are willing to go out of their way to obtain the product. That is, the producer grants exclusive right to a wholesaler or retailer to sell in a geographic region. This form is often used in the distribution of new automobiles and prestige women's clothing. Rolls Royce dealerships, for example, are limited to only large metropolitan areas where significant portions of their customers reside. In another story, Caterpillar Tractor Company appoints a single dealer to distribute its products within a given geographical area.

13.3.2   Channel conflict   渠道冲突

Managing the distribution channel is by no means an easy task; especially important is minimizing conflict between channel members. Power is not distributed evenly in most distribution channels. Because of this imbalance, conflict often occurs between channel members. Channel conflict is disagreement among marketing channel members on goals, roles, and procedures. Conflict can be horizontal or vertical. Horizontal conflict occurs among firms at the same level of the channel. For example, dealers in a certain city can complain about other dealers in the city who steal sales by being too aggressive in their pricing and advertising or by selling outside their assigned territories. Vertical conflict occurs between different levels of the same channels. For example, a franchiser might come into conflict with its franchisees if it were to build its own subsidiaries in areas previous held by franchise operators. To avoid horizontal or vertical conflict, many companies implement a vertical marketing system (VMS), a planned network of distribution channels designed to reduce conflict among channel members and resolve other distribution problems.

13.3.3 Three major marketing systems 三种主要营销系统

1. Vertical marketing system（VMS）

Vertical marketing system is a distribution channel structure in which producers, wholesalers, and retailers act as a unified system. One channel member owns the others, has contracts with them, or has so much power that they all cooperate. Figure 13-4 shows vertical marketing system.

There are primarily three types of vertical marketing system.

The corporate VMS is a vertical marketing system that combines successive stages of production and distribution under single ownership. Channel leadership is established through common ownership. For example, Bubugao markets telephone and other related equipment through its own chains.

Contractual VMS onsists of independent firms at different marketing levels who join together through contracts to obtain more economics or sales impact than each could achieve on their own. Three forms of franchises are manufacturer-sponsored retailer franchise systems, manufacturer-sponsored wholesaler franchise systems, and service-firm-sponsored retailer franchise systems.

In an administrative VMS, a party who has the strongest power may coordinate successive stages of production and distribution. The party may be a producer or a large retailer. The system depends not on common ownership or contractual ties, but on the size and power of one of the parties.

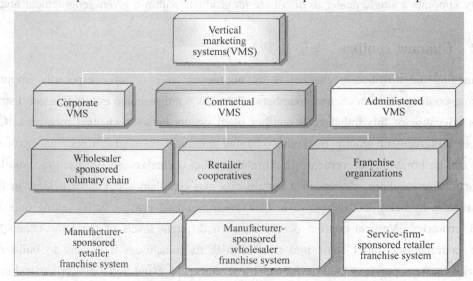

Figure 13-4 Vertical Marketing Systems

2. Horizontal marketing system

As shown in Figure 13-5, another channel development is the horizontal marketing system, in which two or more companies at one level combine their marketing efforts to open new marketing opportunities. By combination, companies enjoy greater capital, improved production abilities and extended marketing resources and accomplish more than just one single company may do. Under horizontal marketing system, potential conflict is greater than in a conventional distribution channel, although profits are infinitely higher.

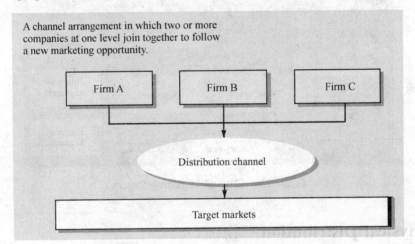

Figure 13-5   Horizontal Marketing System

3. Hybrid marketing system

In recent years, many companies have adopted multi-channel distribution systems according to the different requirements and needs of the companies' marketing strategy.

Hybrid marketing system refers to the situation that single firm sets up two or more marketing channels to reach one or more customer segments. Retailers, catalogs, and sales force form a typical example for the hybrid marketing structure.

As a general rule, companies whose products require tight quality control have short distribution channels while those with products that are less sensitive can afford longer distribution chains.

Hybrid marketing is the identification of marketing actions among diverse groups of an institution, finding ways to achieve coordinated, centralized activities, doing market research, budgeting and expensing actions, doing evaluative research, and executing marketing efforts in well-designed strategic ways. Hybrid, as the word suggests, is blending and balancing efforts designed to serve a wide array of internal and external organizational purposes, in ways that, to the external user, are transparent, coordinated and achieve maximum effect.

Basic marketing tasks are some of the elements of a hybrid marketing structure. These tasks may be quite diverse in nature（some serving faculty and teaching purposes, some alumni, fund raising, admissions, community relations, etc.）.

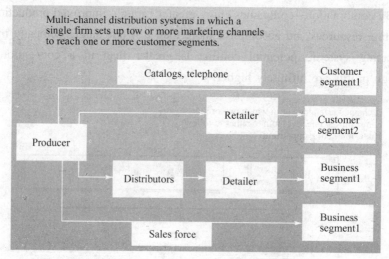

Figure 13-6　Hybrid Marketing System

13.4　Physical Distribution　物流

13.4.1　Physical distribution　物流

Physical distribution refers to the physical requirements necessary to move a product from producer to end-user, it can also be called a marketing logistics system. The starting point for designing a logistics system is to study the service needs of customers. Customers may want several distribution services from suppliers: fast and efficient order processing, speedy and flexible delivery, presorting and pre-tagging of merchandise, order tracking information, and willingness to take back or replace defective goods. In a word, it involves getting the right product to the right customers in the right place at the right time. Many companies today place greater emphasis on logistics because:

（1）customer service and satisfaction have become the cornerstone of marketing strategy;

（2）logistics is a major cost element for most companies;

（3）the explosion in product variety has created a need for improved logistics management;

（4）Improvements in information technology has created opportunities for major gains in distribution efficiency.

If managed effectively, physical distribution can increase customer satisfaction by ensuring reliable, cost-efficient movement of goods through the supply chain.

Physical distribution plays a very important role in international marketing as it must deal with many issues that require high efficiency. It also influences (or to some degree determines) a company's obtaining, maintaining and expanding its market share. Giving a set of logistics objectives, the company is ready to design a logistics system that will minimize the cost of attaining these objectives.

13.4.2 Major logistics functions 主要物流功能

The major functions performed within a physical distribution system include order processing, warehousing, inventory management, and transportation. See Figure 13-7.

(1) Order processing is the method chosen by the organization to receive orders from the customer. It could be by mail, telephone, through salespeople, or via computer or the Internet. Once received, orders must be processed quickly and accurately then shipped to the customer.

(2) Warehousing is the storing of products while they wait to be sold. This storage function is necessary because production and consumption cycles rarely match. Organizations use either storage warehouses or distribution centers to process their products. A distribution center is a large, highly automated warehouse designed to receive goods from various plants and suppliers.

The Web has erased many of the distribution barriers between producers and their potential customers. Many electric commerce sites do not have warehouses because they do not carry inventory. E-commerce distributors dispense with warehouses whenever possible. However, a warehouse enables merchants to exercise more control over service. Amazon. com Inc. sells books online and believes that the warehouse model better serves customers.

(3) Inventory management involves knowing both when to order and how much to order. During the past decade, many companies have greatly reduced their inventories and related costs through just-in-time (JIT) logistics systems. For example, FedEx offers order processing and fulfillment services, streamlined distribution by guaranteeing 48-hour delivery globally, and just-in-time delivery for manufacturers. It's a suite of services that forms the backbone for Web-based companies like Dell. "Inventory velocity has become a passion for us," writes Chairman and Chief Executive Officer Michael Dell in his new book "Direct from Dell" (Harper Business). "In 1993, we had $2.9 billion in sales and $220 million in inventory. Four years later, we posted $12.3 billion in sales and had inventory of $233 million. We're now down to less than eight days of inventory (on hand) and we're starting to measure it in hours instead of days."

(4) Transportation involves the choice of transportation carriers. This affects the pricing of products, delivery performance, and condition of the goods when they arrive — all of which

affect customer satisfaction. The major forms of transportation available are rail, truck, water, pipeline, and air. Recently, with the development of information industry, Internet becomes a new and fast growing transportation carrier.

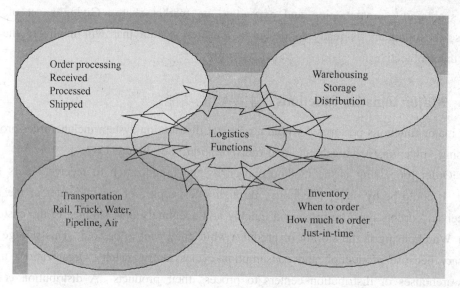

Figure 13-7   Major Logistics Functions

Each shipping method has its advantages, disadvantages and costs (see Figure 13-8). Manufacturers need to balance the total costs of a shipping method with its disadvantages in terms of possible service level.

a. Trucking industry is an important distribution link in almost every country. Trucks are highly flexible in their routing and time schedules. They can move goods door to door. Saving shippers the need to transfer goods form truck to aril and back again at a loss of time and risk of theft or damage, trucks are efficient for short hauls of high-value merchandise.

b. Railroads continue to be a major transportation mode. The products most commonly shipped by rail are bulk products such as automobiles, grain, chemicals, coal, lumber, iron, and steel.

c. Inland water carriers such as barges can efficiently transport bulky commodities. Oceangoing ships are slower than other transportation modes and sometimes affected by the weather, but they are very cost effective for shipping items overseas. Nowadays, ocean going vessels — roll-on-roll-off (RORO) vessels are increasing in number and popularity. They carry standardized containers, thus trucks can roll on and roll off at their destination. Another similar vessel is the lighter aboard ship (LASH) which carry barges stored on the ship and lowered at the point of destination to operate on inland waterways.

d. Pipelines provide a dependable, low-cost method for transporting natural gas, oil products and chemicals form sources to markets. Pipeline shipment of petroleum products costs less than rail shipment, nut more than water shipment. Most pipelines are used by their owners to ship their own products. More than 200,000 miles of pipelines are in operation in the US alone.

e. Air. It is becoming more important as a transportation mode. The use of air transportation for international business activities continues to expand. Air-freight rates are much higher than rail or truck rates, but air freight is ideal when speed is needed or distant markets have to be reached. Air-freighted products are perishables (fresh fish, cut flowers) and high-value, low-bulk items (technical instruments, jewelry).

Today, railroads, ships and barges, trucks, airlines, and pipeline companies are now much more competitive, flexible, and responsive to the needs of their customers. These changes have resulted in better services and lower prices for shippers.

Many shippers use a combination of transportation methods called intermodal transportation to move a shipment. This approach allows shippers to gain the service and cost advantages of various transportation modes. Organizations can contract all of their logistics functions to third party logistics providers such as UPS. These specialized companies are able to offer smaller companies significant economies of scale as they invest the capital needed to build advanced distribution systems for all their customers. An organization can instantly set up a worldwide distribution system without incurring the costs and facing the problems of setting up its own system.

f. The Internet. The number of people who shop and buy products on the Internet is growing; electronic markets allow consumers to directly access manufacturers. As a result, distribution channels are undergoing rapid change. Large orders of high-value products sitting in a warehouse are no longer necessary. Disintermediation becomes possible and it creates a more perfect commercial world as customers are able to deal directly with providers which can eventually weeds out costs and inefficiency. Several electronic merchants are well known for their Internet operations. Cisco Systems Inc. gets just under 60% of its revenue from its Web site, or about 1,000 orders and more than $11 million in sales a day. Both Dell Computer Corp. and Compaq Computer Corp. get $5 million or more daily Internet sales.

The goal of the marketing logistics system should be to provide a targeted level of customer service at the least cost. International marketers face many additional complexities in designing their channels. Each country has its own unique culture and traditions which influence its distribution system. It is very hard to make any change.

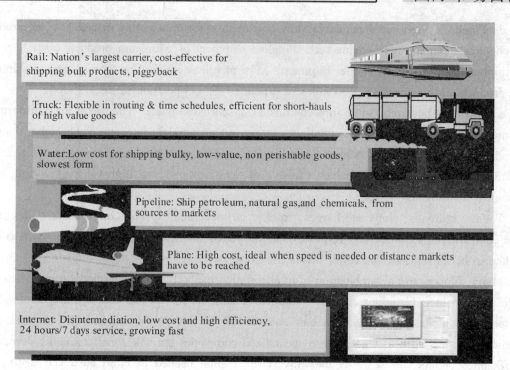

Rail: Nation's largest carrier, cost-effective for shipping bulk products, piggyback

Truck: Flexible in routing & time schedules, efficient for short-hauls of high value goods

Water:Low cost for shipping bulky, low-value, non perishable goods, slowest form

Pipeline: Ship petroleum, natural gas,and chemicals, from sources to markets

Plane: High cost, ideal when speed is needed or distance markets have to be reached

Internet: Disintermediation, low cost and high efficiency, 24 hours/7 days service, growing fast

Figure 13-8   Transportation Modes

13.5   Channel Strategy for New Market Entry
进入新市场的渠道战略

A company, when going international, may find itself in the position of entering a new market. It is often very difficult as distribution becomes a major obstacle. An independent channel agent may be reluctant to take a new product when established names are accepted in the market and the current demands are satisfied. So a company must either provide some incentive to channel agents or establish its own channel to distribute the products directly.

（1）Provide special incentives to independent channel agents. This can be very expensive. The company may offer cash bonus or contest awards for sales. All these are very costly. But the agents know the market better, and they have already mastered the network for distribution and thus, they can efficiently function.

（2）Establish direct distributions. The advantage of this can be to ensure aggressive sales activity and attention to its products. Sufficient resource commitment to sales activity, backed up by appropriate communications programs may, in time, allow a reasonable share of market.

The disadvantages include that training of representative and workforce is time consuming and money costing, that the sales organization will be a heavy loser in the beginning, and the inefficiency of work.

☞ Cases

Case 1.   Selling a CD

Suppose you are a singer and the place is simply where your fans buy your CD. You can also call it distribution.

There are many ways to distribute your CD.

1) Retail

Probably the most difficult is retail (selling your CD in music stores). This is difficult for independent musicians or bands because you usually need to have a relationship with a distributor.

2) Online

Isn't the Web wonderful? You can easily and cheaply set up a web page with your information, sample audio files, show dates, and how to order your CD.

3) In person

Whenever you perform, you should sell your CDs. You can mention that you are selling CDs and where to buy them while you are performing. It is easier if you have a friend to help you. This person can collect the money, hand out the CDs, etc., so you don't have to worry about it during a show.

4) At home

There is nothing wrong with telephone orders!

Case 2.   Dell, a new way of supply

What is one of the biggest differences between the functioning of Dell and Ford? Well, Ford first manufactures a car and then tries to sell it by displaying it on a dealer's lot whereas Dell first sells a PC and then orders the parts to manufacture it! Obviously, Ford's method has several disadvantages — Ford has to continuously guess what customers want, invest a lot of capital in making the inventory available for consumer inspection, and then, once in a while, a dealer has to suffer a "lot rot" — have a vehicle that cannot find a customer. On the other hand, Dell's way of manufacturing almost completely eliminates the need of carrying inventories and at the same time, results in products that are made per consumer specifications and therefore stand a better chance of fulfilling their needs and requirements.

Dell has been an acknowledged leader in supply chain management. It has perfected the art of outsourcing and effective supplier management. Dell is very flexible with its sourcing policies. It has developed strong working relationships with its vendors and now depends heavily on them for components. Ford and GM are trying to follow Dell's example. GM recently announced to spin-off its captive parts maker, Delphi Automotive Systems. Ford is planning a similar move by spinning off its Visteon Automotive Systems. The two companies will get more freedom to outsource from other vendors and also allow these spin-offs to seek business from their competitors.

GM, Ford, Toyota, and Renault are also trying to reduce the time it takes them to make customer specified cars. Currently, these companies can make cars to a customer's specifications, but it takes them weeks or even months to deliver the product. These companies are working towards reducing this time lag to 10 to 15 days (from order placement to the actual delivery of the car)!

Case 3.　Innovative hybrid marketing campaign launches Toyota's clean car for the future

Torrance, CA — the much-anticipated US launch of Prius, Toyota's revolutionary gasoline / electric hybrid car, is underway with the unveiling of an innovative marketing campaign spearheaded by Toyota Motor Sales (TMS) USA., along with Saatchi & Saatchi of Los Angeles and Oasis Advertising of New York.

The teams have created a unique and fully integrated media plan. The campaign theme, "PRIUS / genius", is not only reflective of the new technology, but of the creative web-based marketing approach. The inherent challenge of marketing new technology to a new audience led TMS marketing to utilize a unique tactic. For nearly two years, the campaign has revolved around developing a dialogue with interested consumers. This resulted in a pool of over 40,000 interested consumers or "handraisers" in industry speak. Before arriving in showrooms across the country, nearly 1,800 of the revolutionary Toyota Prius have been sold via on-line purchase requests.

🔲 Key Terms

distribution　分销
direct distribution channel　直接渠道
indirect distribution channel　间接渠道
length of a channel　渠道长度
distribution channels　分销渠道
distribution marketing channel　分销营销渠道
business marketing channel　企业营销渠道

customer marketing channel   消费者营销渠道

intermediary   中间商

wholesaler   批发商

agent   代理人

broker   经纪人

a customs broker   报关行

export management company（EMC）   出口管理公司

export trading company（ETC）   出口贸易公司

freight forwarder   承运商

retailer   零售商

direct seller   直销商

convenience store   便利店

electronic retailer   电视购物商

general merchandise retailer   日用品零售商

specialty store   专卖店

electronic retailer   电子购物店

vertical marketing system   垂直营销体系

corporate VMS   公司式垂直营销体系

contractual VMS   契约式垂直营销体系

administrative VMS   管理式垂直营销体系

horizontal marketing system   横向营销体系

hybrid marketing system   混合营销体系

channel conflict   渠道冲突

horizontal conflict   水平冲突

vertical conflict   垂直冲突

exclusive distribution   独占分销

selective distribution   选择分销

intensive distribution   密集分销

physical distribution   物流

logistic system   物流系统

order processing   订单处理

inventory   存货，库存

transportation   运输

warehousing   仓储

📄 Notes

1. interdependency   *n.*   相互依赖性
2. jobber   *n.*   中间经销商
3. target market   目标市场
4. assortment   *n.*   品种

✍ Exercises

I. Multiple choices.

1. Why do producers give some of the selling job to intermediaries?
   - A. Because this process gives the producer needed control.
   - B. Because intermediaries offer greater efficiencies in getting products to the target market.
   - C. Because intermediaries create greater profits for producers.
   - D. Because consumers expect intermediaries to be involved and would not know how to buy the product otherwise.

2. Channel conflict arises when _____.
   - A. companies opt to bypass the distribution channel and sell directly to big customers, depriving intermediaries of profits
   - B. each member in the channel specializes in performing a narrow function
   - C. channel members disagree about goals and rules, i. e. , who should do what and for what rewards
   - D. consumers disagree about whether to patronize full-service stores, outlet stores, or mail order companies

3. In a vertical marketing system (VMS),_____.
   - A. the channel consists of one or more independent producers, wholesalers, and retailers, each separate business seeking to maximize its own profits, at times even at the expense of other members
   - B. producers, wholesalers, and retailers act as a unified system
   - C. potential conflict is greater than in a conventional distribution channel, but profits are infinitely higher
   - D. all stages of production and distribution are combined under single ownership and determined solely by the manufacturer

4. What is a hybrid-marketing channel?
   - A. Use of multiple channels to reach one or more customer segments by a single firm.

B. A producer buys or sets up its own wholesale and retail outlets.

C. A wholesaler organizes a group of independent retailers to standardize their selling practices and achieve buying economies.

D. Retailers organize their own wholesaling and / or production facilities for buying economies and profit sharing.

5. Major logistics functions include _____.

A. order processing and warehousing

B. inventory and transportation

C. product, price, distribution, and promotion

D. order processing, warehousing, inventory management, and transportation

6. The distribution policy that should be implemented if a product's manufacturer wants to reduce marketing costs and maintain an image of quality and prestige is _____.

   A. intensive   B. selective   C. exclusive   D. restricted

7. In a horizontal marketing system (HMS), _____.

A. the channel consists of one or more independent producers, wholesalers, and retailers, each separate business seeking to maximize its own profits, at times even at the expense of other members

B. producers, wholesalers, and retailers act as a unified system

C. potential conflict is greater than in a conventional distribution channel, but profits are infinitely higher

D. all stages of production and distribution are combined under single ownership and determined solely by the manufacturer

8. Which of the following is NOT an intermediary member of a distribution channel?

   A. Retailer.   B. Advertiser.   C. Manufacturer.   D. Wholesaler.

9. Business firms that operate in the marketing channel between producers and consumers or industrial users are called marketing _____.

   A. intermediaries   B. connections   C. facilitators   D. handlers

10. The use of two or more marketing channels to reach the same target market is referred to as _____.

   A. dual target marketing   B. dual marketing

   C. dual strategizing   D. dual distribution

II. True or false.

1. A wholesaler is a marketing intermediary that takes title to the goods it sells and then

distributes those goods to retailers, other distributors, and sometimes consumers.

2. A generalization that is usually true of marketing channel length is: The more standardized the product, the shorter the channel.

3. When Coca-Cola and Nestle formed a joint venture to market ready-to-drink coffee and tea worldwide, they formed a horizontal marketing system.

4. The use of two or more marketing channels to reach the same target market is referred to as dual channeling.

5. Forcing a dealer to take the full line of products in order to get a strong brand is illegal.

6. Once a firm has defined its channel objectives, it should identify its channel alternatives, i. e. the types and number of intermediaries and the functions that each intermediary should perform.

7. Third party logsitics basically means that firms outsource logistical tasks to independent providers who may adopt one or all of the functions required to get clients' products to market.

8. A direct-marketing channel consists of a manufacturer selling directly to the final customer.

9. Intensive is the type of distribution where there is the use of more than a few but less than all of the intermediaries who are willing to carry a particular product.

10. When retailers develop private brands to compete with producers' brands, the type of marketing channel conflict is vertical.

III. Discussion.

1. What is distribution? What are channels? What are the functions of channels?

2. What are the different types of channels?

3. How are channels structured?

4. Why are intermediaries used in marketing?

5. Tell briefly the intermediaries in both domestic and international marketing.

6. What is logistics system? How does a company deal with its logistic distribution? Briefly describe it.

7. What are the documents that would be prepared for international distribution?

8. Web question.

Banking has gone through metamorphosis in Australia and New Zealand. We tend to think of quite recent milestones such as deregulation of the banking sector in the early 1990s when the financial services sector first comes to mind. However, as the Student Report section of this bank's Web site indicates, ANZ has 150 years of history behind it. The issue for many such organizations is how much of this history is heavy baggage and might best be discarded as the online consumer and business markets beckon. Visit the Student Report section by firstly clicking on About ANZ, and then answer the following questions:

(1) Where did the ANZ first begin?

(2) Did you get lost on the Web site when examining the history of the ANZ?

(3) Does the ANZ conduct online research?

(4) Does the ANZ regard the Internet / Web as an advertising medium?

(5) How do you rate the ANZ. com Web site?

Chapter Fourteen

Promotions

促　销

◀ Objectives　学习目标

When students finish this chapter, they should be able to accomplish the following:

☑ Promotion

☑ Promotional mix

☑ Advertising

☑ Personal selling

☑ Sales promotion

☑ Public relations

14.1　Promotion　促销

It is not enough for a business to have good products sold at attractive prices. Why do consumers buy the televisions they watch, the cars they drive, and even the toothpaste they use?

To generate sales and profits, the benefits of products have to be communicated to customers. In marketing, this is commonly known as "promotion". Consumers buy them primarily as a result of promotion. Promotion is a part of daily life. The clothes consumers choose to wear and the food they choose to eat are almost entirely the result of promotion.

Promotion is one of the major elements of the marketing mix of the business. Promotion is a form of persuasive communication, or getting others to do what marketers want them to do. Its function is that of informing consumers about a product or service and influencing them to buy that product or service. There are many different promotional tools that are used by businesses to enhance the image of the product, such as mailings, speeches, presentations, contests, packaging, films, catalogs, coupons, posters, and even endorsements[1] by famous people. Promotion is an important part of a business's strategy in surviving today's competitive marketplace.

14.2　Promotional Mix　促销组合

To achieve desired sales results, marketers must consider all forms of promotion and decide which ones should be used and in what proportion. Naturally, the aim of every small business owner is to get the most from every dollar spent for promotion. The combination of different forms of promotion is called the promotional mix. The makeup of the promotional mix varies with the product being promoted, the nature of the potential customers, the general market conditions, and the funds available.[2] Promotion mix includes advertising, sales promotion, public relations, and personal selling, etc. See Figure 14-1.

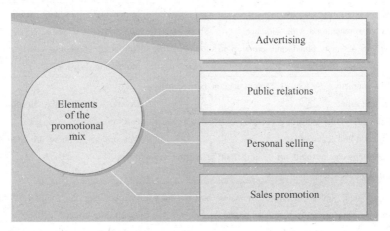

Figure 14-1　Promotional Mix

14.2.1　Elements of the promotional mix　促销组合的元素

The promotional mix elements are advertising, personal selling, sales promotion, and public relations, as shown in Table 14-1.

Advertising is a non-personal sales message that is paid for by an identified company. It promotes the company's products, services, or image and is directed toward a mass audience. The fact that advertising is paid for distinguishes it from free publicity. The non-personal approach of advertising distinguishes it from personal selling. Advertising media are the channels of communication used by advertisers to send their messages to potential customers. Advertising media include radio, television, newspapers, magazines, direct mail, and billboards.

Personal selling is the direct effort made by a salesperson to convince a customer to make a purchase. It is directed toward one person or at a small group through direct communication.

Sales promotion is any sales activity that supplements or coordinates advertising and personal selling. Sales promotion includes free samples, coupons, contests, and other special incentives[3] intended to stimulate sales.

Public relations are the communication of a product, brand or business by placing information about it in the media without paying for the time or media space directly. It builds good relations with the organization's various publics by obtaining favorable publicity, building up a good "corporate image," and handling or heading off unfavorable rumors, stories, and events. For example, when a newspaper covers the opening of a new business, the owner does not pay for it.

Table 14-1　Advantages and Disadvantages of Promotional Mix Elements

Mix Element	Advantages	Disadvantages
Advertising	Good for building awareness Effective at reaching a wide audience Repetition of main brand and product positioning helps build customer trust	Impersonal — cannot answer all a customer's questions Not good at getting customers to make a final purchasing decision
Personal selling	Highly interactive — lots of communication between the buyer and seller Excellent for communicating complex / detailed product information and features Relationships can be built up — important if closing the sale make take a long time	Costly — employing a sales force has many hidden costs in addition to wages Not suitable if there are thousands of important buyers
Sales promotion	Can stimulate quick increases in sales by targeting promotional incentives on particular products Good short term tactical tool	If used over the long-term, customers may get used to the effect Too much promotion may damage the brand image
Public relations	Often seen as more "credible" — since the message seems to be coming from a third party (e.g. magazine, newspaper) Cheap way of reaching many customers — if the publicity is achieved through the right media	Risk of losing control — cannot always control what other people write or say about your product

14.2.2　Push versus pull strategy　推入和拉动策略

The promotional mix is affected heavily by whether the company chooses a push or pull strategy (see Figure 14-2). A push strategy is a promotion strategy that calls for using the sales force and trade promotion to push the product through channels. The producer promotes the product to wholesalers, the wholesalers promote to retailers, and retailers to customers. It involves "pushing" the product through distribution channels to final consumers.

A pull strategy, however, is different as the producer directs its marketing activities toward final consumers to induce them to buy the product. It is defined as a promotion strategy that calls for spending a lot on advertising and consumer promotion to build up consumer demand. If the strategy is successful, consumers will ask their retails for the product, the retailer will ask the wholesalers and wholesalers will ask the producers.

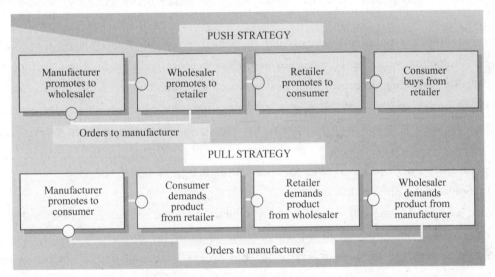

Figure 14-2　Comparison Between Push and Pull Strategies

14.2.3　Steps of developing effective marketing promotion　有效促销的步骤

There are 5 steps to developing effective marketing promotion, as shown in Figure 14-3.

1. Determine the communication objectives

Buyers go through buyer-readiness stages (awareness, knowledge, liking, preference, conviction, and purchase). With pushing strategies, marketers use personal selling to promote their product to retailers and wholesalers, not the end user. They include special incentives such as discounts, promotional materials, and cooperative advertising[4]. Advertising and sales promotions are part of pulling strategies, which build consumer awareness so that the consumer will ask retailers to carry the product. By selecting the appropriate combination of promotional mix elements, marketers attempt to achieve the organization's promotional objectives: to provide information, differentiate a product, increase demand, stabilize sales, and accentuate[5] the product's value.

2. Determine the budget

Marketers must take careful consideration before deciding the amount of money the company wants to spend to achieve its sales goals. Four common methods are used to set the total promotional budget. In the affordable method, organizations simply take care of their business expenses and then determine how much they think they can afford to spend on promotion. In the percentage-of-sales method, the budget is set at a certain percentage of current or forecasted sales. The competitive-parity method of budget setting takes advantage of the collective wisdom[6] of the industry.

Organizations get industry averages and base their promotional budget on those industry averages. Promotion spending is increased when competitor spending increases and decreased when competitor spending decreases. The best approach to setting budgets is the objective-and-task method. According to this approach, the marketer first sets clear objectives for promotion, determines the tasks it would take to achieve the objectives, and then adds up the costs of the tasks.

Several factors need to be considered when setting the promotional budget.

(1) Stage in the product life cycle

When consumers are unfamiliar with a product building early awareness and trial is expensive. As a result, products in the introduction stage of the product life cycle have larger budgets than products in the later stages of the life cycle. Traditional media companies are the single biggest beneficiaries[7] of Internet initial public offerings[8] (IPOs). The primary use of IPO money is marketing a company's brand to consumers and to encourage people to go online.

(2) Market share and consumer base

Market share affects budgets in two ways. First, an organization with a large current market share needs a higher budget as a percentage of sales than an organization with a low market share. High-market-share[9] organizations are the target of competitive actions and defending the large market share is expensive. Second, an organization's desired market share influences the budget. Maintaining market share takes fewer resources than building share. For example, companies that are trying to build market share before and after going public are spending more than ever on advertising and promotion. Increasingly online companies are spending their ad money with long-established branding mediums: radio, TV and billboards. After going public, Internet companies like SOHU. com and Amazon continue to use traditional media to reach the masses of people who aren't yet online. An online company stated that "traditional advertising is a key ingredient in building brand and recognition and promoting the benefits of online retail shopping. "

(3) Competition and clutter[10]

When there are many organizations competing for a share of the consumer's heart and mind, it will take a larger budget to rise above the clutter and be heard by the consumer. In 1998, Barnes & Noble Inc. 's Barnesandnoble. com spent $18. 5 million — mostly in network radio as well as local television — beating out archrival[11] Amazon. com, which spent $17. 7 million.

(4) Frequency

It is the number of times that are exposed to the message. Messages take several repetitions to be comprehended by consumers. Greater frequency requires a larger budget.

(5) Product substitutability

In product categories where consumers don't perceive a great deal of difference between brands, marketers spend a great deal of money to differentiate their brands and create clear positions in the minds of consumers. If brands are perceived as differentiated, budgets may be smaller.

3. Design a message

It is to determine the message's content (rational, emotional, or moral appeals), message structure, and message format.

The effect of the creativity factor in a campaign is more important than the money spent, so creating message and selecting media are two major elements. Messages are changing in accordance with time and marketing concept. A marketer may use inductive method talking to consumers, dealers, experts and competitors to seek for good ideas or deductive method setting framework to generate message to satisfy both producer and consumers. A message must be desirable, distinctive and provable. A marketer would have to pay attention to both the content and the execution of the message. Another important aspect is any promotional message can not overstep social and legal norms. Marketers should not make false claims. They must avoid false demonstrations.

4. Choose the media

Media refers to the entire set of channels through which it is possible to transmit messages to some people or the entire public. The channel can take the form of broadcast (TV and radio), print (newspapers, magazines, direct mail), display media (billboards, signs, posters), or electronic (Internet Web pages, diskette presentations). If the function of a channel is to distribute the same message to many people simultaneously, it is considered a nonpersonal communication channel or mass medium (television, radio, newspaper, magazine, billboard). Newspapers and television represent the largest advertising media categories. No interaction is possible between mass media and their receivers; they carry messages without personal contact or feedback. If the channel is only able to transmit a message to one person at a time it is considered a carrier (telephone). In addition, a carrier permits interactivity (the ability to respond and react) between sender and receiver. In a personal communication channel, sender and receiver communicate directly with each other over the telephone, face to face, through the mail, or through Internet chats. Direct contact with consumers by company salespeople forms a common personal communication channel. The media planner considers whether it would be best to use personal communication channels or nonpersonal communication channels to transmit the message to target buyers. Word-of-mouth[12] influence has a strong effect.

The Internet is an exciting and powerful addition to traditional media. Interactive media represents the fastest growing type of media. Interactive advertising directly involves the viewer, who controls how much information he or she receives. The interactive two-way communications capability of the Internet, combined with its broad and rapidly growing acceptance around the world, has attracted advertisers. The Internet provides a medium for promotion that can be used to identify prospects, collect information profiling[13] those prospects, and execute micro-segmentation promotion delivery strategies. Online promotional content can be tailored to current or past customer behavior, attributes, knowledge or prior buying behavior, or a combination of all three.

5. Measurement and management of the effectiveness of promotion

Good planning and control of promotion depends on measures of its effectiveness. It is better to limit a campaign to one or a few cities first and evaluate its impact before rolling a campaign throughout the country with a very large budget.

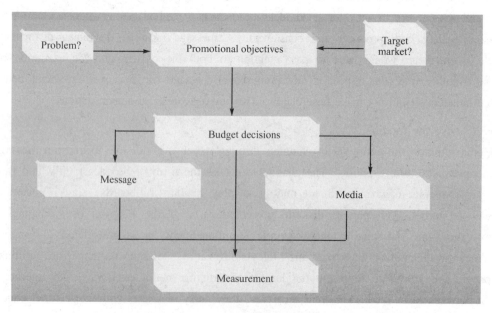

Figure 14-3   Steps of Effective Promotion

14.3　Advertising　广告

14.3.1　Definition of advertising　广告定义

Among all the promotion means, advertising is, to some degree, the most often used elements. Advertising is the process of seizing the consumer's attention. Generally, advertising is any paid form of non-personal presentation and promotion of ideas, goods, or services. It can be an identified sponsor in such media as magazines, newspapers, outdoor posters, direct mail, novelties, radio, TV, bus posters, catalogs, directories[14], programs and circulars. Product advertising places a message to promote a good or service, while institutional advertising promotes a concept, idea, or philosophy.

Advertising is a mass-mediated communication. It is used to reach large numbers of consumers who are geographically dispersed. Products can be dramatized through the use of color, sound, and visuals. It is effective at building awareness, knowledge and a long-term image for the product. On the other hand, advertising is impersonal, expensive, and not adaptable to individual consumers. It is difficult to measure the effectiveness of advertising campaigns.

14.3.2　Major advertising decisions　广告主要决策

As a very important part of promotional mix, major decisions in advertising is similar to that of effective promotion decisions, which also include objective setting, budgeting, message strategy, media strategy and measurement. Some of these are unique in this promotional method.

According to the different objectives, an advertising program can be classified into three catalogs: informative, persuasive and reminding.

Informative advertising is the advertising used to inform consumers about a new product or feature and to build primary demand. It is heavily used in the pioneering period. An informative advertising is telling the market about a new product, suggesting new uses for a product, informing the market of a price change, explaining how the products works, describing available services, correcting false impressions, reducing buyers' fears and building a company image.

Persuasive advertising is very important in the competitive stage; the objective is to build selective demand for a particular brand (later growth and early maturity stages). It is the advertising used to build selective demand for a brand by persuading consumers that it offers the best quality for their money. Specific comparison of one or more attributes with one or more other brands in the product class makes persuasive advertising comparative advertising.

Persuasive advertising is about building brand preference, encouraging switching to the brand, changing buyers' perception of product attributes, persuading buyers to purchase now and persuading buyers to receive a sales call.

Reminder advertising is for mature products (later maturity and decline stages). The objective is to remind people about the brand. Advertising is used to keep consumers thinking about a product. Coco-Cola ads on TV are designed to remind people about Coca-Cola, not to inform or to persuade them. As a reminder advertisement, it is very important to remind buyers that the product may be needed in the near future, tell them where to buy it, keep it in buyers' minds during off-season[15] and maintain its top-of-mind awareness[16].

Media decisions must be coordinated with marketing strategy and with other aspects of advertising strategy. The strategic aspects of media planning involve four steps:

(1) Selecting the target audience toward which all subsequent efforts will be directed;

(2) Specifying media objectives, which typically are stated in terms of reach (What proportion of the target audience must see, read, or hear our advertising message during a specified period?), frequency (How often should the target audience be exposed to the advertisement during this period?), gross rating points (GRPs) or effective rating points (ERPs) (How much total advertising is necessary during a particular period to accomplish the reach and frequency objectives?);

(3) Selecting general media categories and specific vehicles within each medium;

(4) Buying media.

Though difficult and often expensive, measuring advertising effectiveness is essential for advertisers to better understand how well their ads are performing and what changes need to be made to improve performance.

Measurement of advertising campaigns includes two aspects.

1) Communication impact research

Communication impact research seeks to determine whether an advertisement is communicating effectively. It can be done before an ad is put into media (pre-testing) and after it is printed or broadcast(post-testing). Direct rating method asks consumers to rate alternative ads. The higher the rate, the more effective the ad might be. Portfolio tests ask consumers to view and listen to a portfolio of advertisements, taking as much time as they need. Then ask consumers to recall all the ads and their content, aided or unaided by the interviewer. The recall level indicates an ad's ability to stand out and to have its message understood and remembered. Laboratory test uses equipment to measure consumers' physiological reactions — heart beat, blood pressure, pupil dilation — to an advertisement.

All these methods tend to be excessively rational and verbal, and tend to rely primarily on respondents' playback in one form or another. Advertisers should, in the meantime, pay attention to the nonverbal elements, which can be very effective in advertising.

Post-testing is used to measure the increased brand awareness[17], brand comprehension[18], stated brand preference[19], etc. If pre-testing is done, the advertiser can draw a random sample of consumers after the campaign to assess the communication effects.

2) Sales impact research

Advertising's Sales impact research is generally harder to measure than its communication effect. Sales are influenced by many factors besides advertising, such as the product's features, price, availability and competitors' actions.

14.3.3　Advertising Internationally　国际广告

Generally advertising is used primarily for low cost, mass volume consumer products. Products like fertilizers, canned and fresh produce and tobacco — all products which are used by end consumers — are the subject of heavy promotion. In intermediate products like timber, leather and cotton the advertising may be more limited in nature due to the fewer end purchasers of the raw material. Until recently, per capita GNP and advertising were directly correlated, due to the more widespread availability of media and higher incomes, giving a larger potential market for products. This is no longer the case. Optimal levels of advertising occur where the advertising / sales overseas effect is equal to the marginal advertising expenditure[20]. The problem is in estimating the levels of each.

Global expenditure on advertising is believed to be more than US $200 billion, with the US the largest spender and Japan next. Individual companies like General Motors and IBM are each spending billions on advertising per annum. Worldwide, although less in Africa, the average advertising expenditure as a percentage of GNP is around 1.4%. The major expenditure is on the television media, with the USA spending over US $30 billion on this medium. In many less developed countries, however, radio is widely used, especially where television is not available. In these countries, print advertising becomes a major medium. On the other hand, global programs like CNN news and MNet television have dramatically increased the global advertising and direct selling possibilities via satellite.

When organizations advertise across international boundaries, a number of important factors have to be taken into consideration. While the process is ostensibly straightforward, that is someone (seller) says something (message) to someone (buyer) through a medium; the process is compounded by certain factors.

These mitigating[21] factors can be called "noise" and have an effect on the decision to "extend", "adapt" or "create" new messages.

Language differences may mean that straight translation is not enough when it comes to message design. Advertising may also play different roles within developed, between developed and underdeveloped and within underdeveloped countries. In developing countries "education" and "information" may be paramount[22] objectives. In developed countries, the objectives may be more persuasive.

Cultural differences may account for the greatest challenge. However, many, notably Elinder (1961), challenged the need to adapt messages and images, as he argued that consumer differences between countries are diminishing. Changes may be needed only in translation. However, this is only one point of view, as there is no doubt that cultural differences do exist across the world. For example, it would be quite unacceptable to have swim-suited ladies advertising sun care products in Muslim countries.

Three major difficulties occur in attempting to communicate internationally:

(1) The message may not get through to the intended recipient[23], due to a lack of media knowledge;

(2) The message may get through but not be understood, due to lack of audience understanding;

(3) The message may get through, be understood but not provoke action. This may be due to lack of cultural understanding.

Media availability is a mitigating factor. Take for example, television is popular in many countries in American and European countries; however, in Africa a number of countries the extent of its use and time available may be limited though they do have it. Media use and availability, coupled with the type of message, which may or may not be used, is tied to government control. Government may ban types of advertising, as is the case of cigarettes on British television. Intending advertisers should refer to the appropriate codes of advertising practice available in each country.

14.4   Personal Selling   人员推销

Personal selling is the direct effort made by a salesperson to convince a customer to make a purchase. It is a personal (face-to-face, telephone, or Internet chat) presentation for the purpose of making sales and building relationships. Organizations realize that it is much cheaper to retain current customers than to attract new ones, hence the focus on relationship marketing that involves working closely with customers to build lasting relationships over time. Personal selling is the essence of developing relationships because it is directed toward achieving mutually satisfying results between buyer and seller, which sustain and enhance future interactions. Relationships are built upon trust. Therefore, a salesperson must place as much emphasis on the customer's interests as on his or her own interests, have enough ability, knowledge, and resources to meet customer expectations, be honest and show that he or she has "something in common" with the customer.

Personal selling is unique because it involves personal contact. It is the two-way marketing communications tool. It follows the AIDA model, which defines a good message and the stages a receiver should go through. The steps in AIDA are to gain the receiver's attention, to create and hold the receiver's interest, to arouse desire, and to motivate a desired action (purchase). Sales promotion, advertising, and publicity move the prospect toward an exchange decision. Yet, personal selling is the tool that most often brings the buying decision process to a satisfactory conclusion for both buyer and seller.

The strength of personal selling is that it is flexible and provides immediate feedback. The salesperson can ask questions to determine the prospect's level of interest and react quickly to the prospect's wants. However, a personal sales call is expensive. So it is most appropriately used in situations where the target market is concentrated, where products are high in value or orders are large, when the product is technically complex, or when the differential advantage is difficult to explain.

A salesperson personally communicates with the prospect to make the sale and build a relationship. The job of a salesperson ranges from order takers to order getters. An order taker interacts with customers placing an order. Order takers include most retail sales workers. They assist customers in finding what they are looking for and try to interest them in the merchandise. They might describe a product's features, demonstrate its use, or show various models and colors. For some sales jobs, particularly those selling expensive and complex items, special knowledge or skills are needed. Order takers include most manufacturers and wholesale sales representatives. For example, a manufacturer representative may spend much of his time traveling to and visiting with prospective buyers and current clients. He discusses the customers' needs and suggests how his merchandise or services can meet those needs. He may show samples or catalogs that describe items his company stocks and inform customers about prices, availability, and how his products can save money and improve productivity An order getter, however, engages in creative selling of products and is responsible for the entire ordering and relationship-building process.

14.5　Sales Promotion　销售促销

Sales promotion is short-term incentives to encourage the purchase or sale of a product. Targets of sales promotion include the trade (wholesalers and retailers), consumers, and an organization's own sales force. Trade promotion activities re designed to encourage companies, sales forces or other members of distribution channels to sell products more aggressively.

Consumer-oriented sales promotions like coupons, rebates, samples, premiums, contests, sweepstakes, and specialty advertising[24], offer an extra incentive to make immediate purchases.

Sales promotions help boost short-term sales. Consumers can be urged to make stronger and quicker responses. They are effective at inducing trial. However, they may have short-lived effects and may hurt a firm's brand-building efforts in the long run if consumers get used to buying a product on sale and become unwilling to pay regular price for the product. Thus, successful sales promotions must promote customer relationship building in the sense that they support the brand image of the product.

The package is the most important component of the product as a communications device. It reinforces associations established in advertising, breaks through competitive clutter at the point of purchase, and justifies price and value to the consumer. Package cues include color, design, shape, brand name, physical materials, and product information labeling.

Point-of-purchase advertising (POP) displays and trade shows are sales promotions directed to the trade markets. The point of purchase (POP) is an ideal time to communicate with consumers. Accordingly, anything that a consumer is exposed to at the point of purchase can perform an important communications function. A variety of POP materials — signs, displays, and various in-store media — are used to attract consumers' attention to particular products and brands, provide information, affect perceptions, and ultimately influence shopping behavior.

A significant trend in marketing communications has been toward greater use of sales promotion in comparison with advertising. This shift is part of the movement from pull-to push-oriented marketing, particularly in the case of consumer-packaged goods. Push implies a forward thrust of effort whereby a manufacturer directs personal selling, trade advertising and trade-oriented sales promotion to wholesalers and retailers. Pull suggests a backward tug from consumers to retailers as a result of advertising and sales-promotion efforts directed at the consumer. Underlying factors of the shift toward sales promotion include a balance-of-power transfer from manufacturers to retailers, increased brand parity[25] and growing price sensitivity[26], reduced brand loyalty[27], splintering of the mass market and reduced media effectiveness, a growing short-term orientation, and favorable consumer responsiveness[28] to sales promotions.

14.6　Public Relations　公共关系

Public relations (PR) entail a variety of functions and activities that are directed at fostering harmonious interactions with an organization's publics (customers, employees, stockholders, governments, and so forth). It is an efficient indirect promotional alternative. It improves companies' prestige and image with the public. PR uses a variety of marketing communications such as media releases, news conferences, and article placements and story ideas in other media, to generate publicity for an organization. Publicity is the firm's solicitation of verbal and written public discussion and recognition. The message can therefore be positive or negative and is not paid for. News stories and features reported in neutral media have a great deal of credibility[29]. Thus, publicity has greater credibility than advertising.

Larger firms often have their own public relations department, with a public relations officer in charge. The main task of the PR department is to present a positive image of the firm and its products to the public.

A variety of methods are usually employed to create a favorable image with the public: good customer relations; sponsorship of sporting, cultural, community and charitable events and organizations; endorsements from celebrities; free gifts promote both image of firm, and its products.

A company can realize their goal of public relations through: news releases; speeches by executives and senior management; special events (formal press conferences and tours, grand openings); written and audiovisual materials aimed at their target market; corporate identity materials (logos, stationery, brochures); public service activities (charitable donations, sponsorships of events); Web sites, etc.

Cases

Case 1.   Advertising: Volkswagen revamps Beetle campaign

Long perceived as an adorable car, the new Beetle is portrayed as a well-engineered car in the 2001 campaign. Volkswagen of America is taking a different approach to advertise its Beetle model in the new TV, print, and Internet campaign, which focuses far more on practical elements including interior space and safety equipment. For instance, for the first time for the new Beetle, some print ads feature cutaway diagrams showing safety features and headroom dimensions. This new emphasis on the rational is in strong contrast with the emotional, image-oriented approach used in Beetle's previous two campaigns of 1998 and 2000. Such a shift is typical of the changes made by automobile makers when car buyers' enthusiasm declines during economic downturns.

Beetle's change in the direction of advertising campaign is prompted by the decline of sales. From April 1998, when Beetle was brought back to the US, through December 1998, sales totaled 55,842, a far higher figure than estimated. The sales kept increasing and reached 83,434 in 1999. However, in 2000, Beetle sales declined 2.8 percent to 81,134. Then, for the first three months of 2001, Beetle sales fell to 15,019, down 27.5 percent, compared with the corresponding period in 2000.

The consumer research reveals that people wants to know more about the car. In addition, based on results of consumer research, this campaign is also aiming to counter consumers' negative perception that Beetle is a small car without much interior space. In response, Volkswagen is touting Beetle as a roomy, well-made car.

Case 2. Ford Motor gets starring role on WB network

A consistent plight of advertisers is finding media that cutters through the clutter and reaches the target audience. Marketers must fight harder than ever to capture TV viewers' attention as remote controls, the plethora of cable / satellite channels, and digital TV recorders, such as TiVo, Replay and Ultimate TV, allow viewers to easily avoid paid commercial spots. One solution, product placement, is to put the product in the show.

The WB network has created a reality show, "No Boundaries," as a product placement vehicle (pun intended). The star is an unlikely one — a fleet of Ford sport-utility vehicles. In the show a group of individuals compete to finish a difficult outdoor voyage while driving Ford SUV's. Ford is paying for the production costs of the 13 hour-long episodes named after the slogan for its SUV lines. Ford will control eight commercial spots in each hour-long episode, using four for their own products. A Ford SUV is expected to be part of the prize for winning the competition.

Ford is promising that the show will not be an extended ad for their product. Though the final word on programming decisions will be the responsibility of the creative team, they are aware that Ford is the corporate sponsor. They will need to balance Ford's interests against the interests of viewers who may turn off a program that lacks compelling drama. If the show fails, Ford risks its reputation by association.

Case 3. Advertising after 9/11

The advertising industry was already struggling with the softening economy before the 9/11. Now they are also struggling with how to promote to consumers facing economic uncertainty and rethinking their priorities and safety concerns. Market researchers are seeing resurgence in patriotism, connections with family and friends, and old-fashioned values such as community, service, and charity. However, marketers are also seeing a desire to return to normalcy. With each week, people are more eager to see regular advertising and are less desiring of sympathy ads.

Thus, marketers are focusing on appeals of patriotism and escapism. For example, Ford's new slogan is "The Spirit of America" and GM's is "Keep America Rolling." Las Vegas is touting itself as "A Place Where You Can Leave Reality Behind." Likewise, promotion of defiant capitalism is increasing, such as the United Airlines new slogan, "Business as usual. Yesterday a cliche. Today a principle." Additionally, consumers are embracing comfort foods like Nabisco's Oreo cookies and Kraft macaroni and cheese. This holiday season, a return to products that bring families together, such as board games, is anticipated. However, some slogans no longer seem appropriate now. For example, the new theme for the US Air Force, "No One Comes Close," has to be rewritten. Additionally, conspicuous consumption seems less important, replaced instead by a "newly felt claustrophobia of abundance."

Marketers now have to recognize that they will be rewarded for the values they embody as much as for the products they make. For example, Southwest isn't about moving people around; rather, it is in the freedom business of letting people go and see the things they dream of. Likewise, the Air Force is in the winning business. Currently, consumers have intensified needs, which can mean opportunities for marketers if they address them correctly.

Key Terms

promotion　促销

promotional mix　促销组合

advertising　广告

personal selling　人员推销

sales promotion　销售推广

public relations　公共关系

push strategy　推入策略

pull strategy　拉动策略

communication objectives　沟通目标

affordable method　力所能及法

percentage-of-sales method　销货百分比法

competitive-parity method　对手水准法

objective-and-task method　目标及任务法

product substitutability　产品可替代率

inductive method　归纳法

deductive method　演绎法

nonpersonal communication channel　大众传播渠道

mass medium　大众传播媒体

carrier　载体

personal communication channel　个人传播渠道

product advertising 产品广告

institutional advertising 厂商广告

informative advertising 告知性广告

persuasive advertising 说服性广告

comparative advertising 比较性广告

reminder advertising 提醒性广告

media 媒体

frequency 频度

reach 到达率

gross rating points（GRPs） 总视听率

effective rating points（ERPs） 有效视听率

direct rating method 直接分级法

portfolio tests 组合测试法

laboratory test 实验室测试法

AIDA model 爱他模型

order taker 接订单员

order getter 新订单接洽员

point-of-purchase advertising POP 广告，售点广告

publicity 宣传推广

📑 Notes

1. endorsement *n.* 认可，支持

2. The makeup of the promotional mix varies with the product being promoted, the nature of the potential customers, the general market conditions, and the funds available. 促销组合由于促销的产品，潜在的顾客群体，基本的市场状况和资金情况不同而不同。

3. incentive *n.* 激励，诱因

4. cooperative advertising 联合广告

5. accentuate *v.* 强调

6. collective wisdom 集体智慧

7. beneficiary *n.* 受益人

8. initial public offering（IPO） 首次公开发行，首次发行从未公开交易过的公司股票

9. high-market-share *a.* 高市场占有率的

10. clutter *n.* 混乱

11. archrival *n.* 主要竞争对手

12. word-of-mouth　*n.*　口碑

13. profile　*v.*　形成……的轮廓

14. directory　*n.*　姓名地址录，目录

15. off-season　*n.*　淡季

16. top-of-mind awareness　首要意念

17. brand awareness　品牌认知

18. brand comprehension　品牌理解

19. brand preference　品牌偏好

20. marginal advertising expenditure　边际广告支出

21. mitigating　*a.*　减轻的

22. paramount　*a.*　极为重要的

23. recipient　*n.*　接受者

24. Consumer-oriented sales promotions like coupons, rebates, samples, premiums, contests, sweepstakes, and specialty advertising, ...　以消费者为中心的销售推广比如优惠券、回赠、免费试用、赠品、竞赛、有奖销售以及特别广告等……

25. brand parity　对不同品牌的同类产品的认知相似性和差异性的衡量

26. price sensitivity　价格敏感度

27. brand loyalty　品牌忠诚度

28. consumer responsiveness　顾客响应

29. credibility　*n.*　可信度

✍ Exercises

I. Multiple choices.

1. There are four major tools of promotion decisions. These are known as elements of promotional mix. Which of the following is NOT one of them?

   A. Advertising.　　B. Pricing.　　　C. Sales promotion.　D. Public relations.

2. What is the main objective of informative advertising?

   A. To create selective demand.

   B. To keep the brand in consumers' minds during the mature stage of the product life cycle.

   C. To stimulate primary demand.

   D. None of the above.

3. A broad set of communication efforts used to create and maintain favorable relationships between an organization and its public(s) is called _____.

A. public relations　　　　　　　　　B. personal selling

C. advertising　　　　　　　　　　　D. sales promotion

4. There are five specific factors to consider when setting the advertising budget. Which of the following is NOT one of those considerations?

A. Stage in the product life cycle.

B. Market share and consumer base.

C. Competition and clutter.

D. All of the above are considerations.

5. _____ is the number of different persons or households exposed to a particular media schedule at least once during a specific time period.

A. Frequency　　　　B. Reach　　　　C. Impact　　　　D. Audience

6. There are a number of objectives of advertising that need to be considered. Which of the following is NOT one of the objectives of advertising?

A. Entertainment advertising.　　　　B. Informative advertising.

C. Persuasive advertising.　　　　　D. Reminder advertising.

7. To set its total promotion budget, a company can choose between four common methods: _____.

A. the affordable method and the percentage-of-sales method

B. competitive method, parity method, objective method, and task method

C. defining specific objectives, determining the tasks that must be performed to achieve these objectives, and estimating the costs of performing these tasks

D. the affordable method, the percentage-of-sales method, the competitive-parity method, and the objective-and-task method

8. _____ is a paid form of nonpersonal communication about an organization and / or its products that is transmitted to a target audience through a mass medium.

A. Sales promotion　　　　　　　　B. Public relations

C. Advertising　　　　　　　　　　D. Personal selling

9. _____ costs considerably more than advertising to reach one person but can provide more immediate feedback.

A. Advertising　　　　　　　　　　B. Personal selling

C. Sales promotion　　　　　　　　D. Public relations

10. What is the first step in developing an effective advertising message strategy?

A. Developing the "big idea" that will make the advertisement memorable.

B. Determining the media with which to advertise.

C. Deciding on message execution.

D. Identifying customer benefits.

11. Slow feedback, high costs, and difficulty in measuring effects on sales are DISADVANTAGES of _____.

    A. advertising   B. public relations

    C. personal selling   D. sales promotion

12. When producers direct their primary marketing activities at channel members to induce them to carry the product and promote it further down the channel, they are using _____.

    A. integrated marketing communications   B. sales promotion

    C. a pull strategy   D. a push strategy

13. Because the number of valid prospects for boats costing more than $200,000 is limited, the Boyin Yachts is likely to make heavy use of which of the following promotion elements?

    A. Public relations.   B. Personal selling.

    C. Advertising.   D. Sales promotion.

II. True or false.

1. A company's integrated marketing communications mix also goes by the name of promotional mix.

2. Contests, free samples, and coupons are examples of personal selling.

3. Non-personal communication channels carry messages without personal contact or feedback.

4. ACD Corporation sells technical products and its customers are concentrated in a small geographic area. The company will use advertising the most.

5. Companies that use the affordable method base their promotion budget on a certain percentage of current or forecasted sales and / or a percentage of the sales price.

6. Most larger companies combine push and pull strategies to move their products from the manufacturer to the final consumer.

7. When Gin Toy advertises a toy on Saturday-morning television and tells children to ask for the product at their favorite toy store, it is implementing a pull strategy in its promotion mix.

8. While the promotion mix is the company's primary communication process, the entire marketing mix must be coordinated for the greatest communication impact.

9. If a push policy is employed in promoting a product, the firm promotes only to the next institution down the marketing channel.

10. A television commercial demonstrating the versatility of the Mercedes sports utility vehicle would best be classified as product advertising.

11. The main disadvantage with the percentage-of-sales method of setting advertising budgets is that it reverses cause and effect.

12. An evaluation of media impact will help determine the media types to be used.

13. Marketers have found much success using standardized ads in their global advertising.

III. Discussion.

1. What is promotion? What is promotion mix?

2. What are the differences among informative, persuasive, and reminder advertising? In what circumstances might a company use each?

3. What are the push and pull strategies?

4. What is advertising? What are the features of advertising?

5. What are the five Ms in advertising?

6. What are the steps of selecting media?

7. How to evaluate the performance of advertising?

8. Visited the Advertising Age Interactive and read 50 Best Commercials and History of TV Advertising special reports, try to find out the successful product slogan on the websites.

9. Browse through the following websites and discuss what type of advertising each uses and what the purpose of the advertising is.

   a. Tobacco BBS — www. tobacco. org

   b. Nike — www. nike. com

   c. Ford — www. ford. com

   d. McDonald's — www. mcdonalds. com

   e. United Parcel Service — www. ups. com

Part V

国际市场营销的管理

Managing the International Marketing

Chapter Fifteen

Marketing Plan

市场营销计划

📢 Objectives 学习目标

When students finish this chapter, they should be able to accomplish the following:

☑ Introduction to marketing planning

☑ Tools used in marketing planning

☑ International planning approach

☑ Key to successful planning

15.1 Introduction to Marketing Planning 市场营销计划简述

15.1.1 Definition 定义

Marketing planning is a logical sequence and a series of activities leading to the setting of marketing objectives and the formulation of plans for achieving them. It is a management process.

Planning involves where the organization would like to be and how to get there, which involves goal setting and strategy determination. Planning involves three main activities:

(1) Situation analysis — where are we now?

(2) Objectives — where do we want to be?

(3) Strategy and tactics — how can we best reach our goals?

Companies usually prepare annual plans, long-range plans and strategic plans. The annual plan is a short term marketing plan that describes the current marketing situation, company objectives, the marketing strategy for the year, the action program, budgets, and controls.

The long-range plan describes the major factors and forces affecting the organization during the next several years. It would be adapted and updated each year so that the company always has a current long-range strategy.

Companies face the difficult task of selecting an overall company strategy for long-term survival and growth. This selection process is called strategic planning. The strategic planning is the process of developing and maintaining a strategic fit between the organization's goals and capabilities and its changing marketing opportunities. It relies on developing a clear company mission, supporting objectives, a sound business portfolio and coordinated functional strategies.

15.1.2 Advantages of planning 营销计划优点

There are mainly six advantages of adequate marketing planning: it gives rise to systematic thinking; it helps coordinate activities; it helps prepare for exigencies[1]; it gives activity continuity; it integrates functions and activities and; it helps in a continuous review of operations.

The planning task depends on the level of involvement in a country. Exporting and licensing give minimum country involvement but joint ventures involve more in-country activity and give a greater degree of integration and control. Planning can be standardized, decentralized or interactive.

15.1.3 Process of marketing planning 营销计划过程

The process of marketing planning includes the following steps: define missions, set objectives and goals, SWOT analysis, plan functional strategies and monitor plan, as shown in Figure 15-1.

1. Define Missions

The mission provides the organization with a purpose or reason for existence. Five questions should be answered in this sector: What is our business? Who is the customer? What do customers value? What will be our business? What should our business be?

To answer these questions, a mission statement is developed in the company. A mission statement is a statement of the organization's purpose, what it wants to accomplish in the large environment. For example, Xerox, the well known copying and fax and other office machine manufacturer develop a mission statement as "we make business more productive by helping them scan, store, retrieve revise, distribute, print, and publish documents".

A mission should not be too narrow or too broad; it should be based on its relative competency[2].

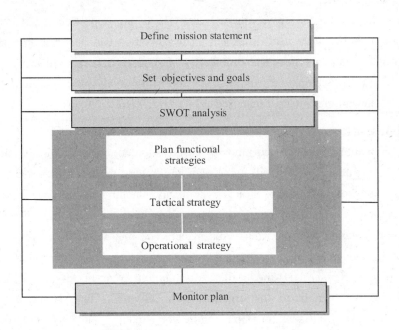

Figure 15-1   The Strategic Planning Process

2. Set objectives and goals

The company's mission needs to be turned into detailed supporting objectives for each level of management. For the different sectors of a business, the objectives are not necessary the same. For example, the Hongta Group[3] is in many business including cigarette production and estate, so the objective for the cigarette production sector is most probably not the same as that of the estate sector.

Objectives are sometimes referred to as performance goals. They focus on desired changes. They are the ends that the organization strives to attain. Generally, organizations have long-term objectives for such factors as return on investment, earnings per share, or size. In addition, they set minimum acceptable standards or common-sense minimums. Objectives elaborate[4] on the mission statement and constitute a specific set of policy, programmatic, or management objectives for the programs and operations covered in the strategic plan. They are expressed in a manner that allows a future assessment of whether the objective has been achieved.

3. SWOT analysis

Analyzing the current market situation is often called a SWOT analysis. It includes making a thorough objective determination of the organization's strengths and weaknesses, assessing organizational resources, and evaluating opportunities and threats. A SWOT analysis of strengths, weaknesses, opportunities and threats will help to focus the assessment, develop organizational competencies, and identify "gaps" between resources available and resources required to meet goals and objectives. External environmental analysis is an opportunity and threat analysis. Opportunities are areas of buyer need in which an organization can perform profitably. They are classified according to attractiveness and probability of success. Threats are a challenge posed by an unfavorable trend or development. Internal environmental analysis is a strengths and weakness analysis of the organization's internal resources.

4. Plan functional strategies

The strategic plan establishes what kinds of business the company will be in and its objectives for each. It is the organization's overall game plan and is long term for usually 5 years. Strategic planning is for the whole company. Strategic company planning is the process of matching an organization's resources with its marketing opportunities over the long run. Then, within each business unit more detailed planning must take place. The major functional departments in each unit must work together to accomplish strategic objectives. These are tactical plans and operational plan. Tactical plans have shorter time frames (usually one year or less) and narrower scopes (specifying details that pertain to the organization's activities) than strategic plans. Tactical planning provides the specific ideas for implementing the strategic plan. It is the process of making detailed decisions about what to do, who will do it, and how to do it. Operational plans are the game plan for a particular product or product line. They support tactical plans and are the tools for executing daily, weekly, and monthly activities. They include policies, procedures, methods, and rules. Operational plans should be done within the context of strategic planning for the entire company and for each strategic business unit (SBU) in the firm.

5. Monitor plan

The last section of the plan outlines the monitors that will be used to control progress. Typically, goals and functional strategies are spelled out for each month or quarter. The practice allows higher management to review the results each period and to spot businesses or products that are not meeting their goals.

The strategic market planning process is based on the establishment of organizational goals and it must stay within the broader limits of the organizations' mission, which is developed taking into consideration the environmental opportunities and threats and the company's resources and distinct competencies.

15.2   Tools Used in Marketing Planning   市场营销计划的工具

The collection of businesses and products that make up the company is called business portfolio. The best business portfolio is the one that best fits the company's strength and weakness to opportunities in the environment. In order to plan the best possible business portfolio, a company must analyze its current business portfolio and develop growth strategies for adding new products or businesses.

Many companies operate several businesses. It is a very important part in the strategic planning to do portfolio analysis. The management will first identify the key businesses (SBU) making up the company. SBU is the strategic business unit which is a unit of the company that has a separate mission and objectives and that can be planned independently from other company businesses. The second step is to assess the attractiveness of its various SBUs and decide how much support each deserves. So most standard portfolio analysis methods evaluate SBUs on two dimensions: the attractiveness of the SBU's market and the strength of the SBU's position in the market. The best known analysis tools are created by the Boston Consulting Group and General Electric.

15.2.1   BCG Matrix   波士顿矩阵法

The BCG Matrix (see Figure 15-2) or the Boston Consulting Group Growth-Share Matrix[5] is one tool that can be used to assess the attractiveness of SBUs. SBUs are classified according to two factors: its market share relative to competitors, and the growth rate of the industry in which the SBU operates. SBUs are plotted on a matrix with two axes. On the vertical axis, market growth rate provides a measure of market attractiveness. The horizontal axis is relative market share that serves as a measure of the company's strength in the market. Plotting a company's SBUs on this matrix allows for some basic resource allocation decisions. It is important to watch the movement of SBUs across the matrix over time. Based on whether each of these is high or low, the four quadrants[6] of the matrix are defined as Stars, Cash Cows, Question Marks, or Dogs.

Question Marks (also called a "Problem Child") are high growth, low share businesses. A question mark requires a lot of cash both to keep up with a rapidly growing market and improve its share position. Strategy must decide between further investment to move question marks to star status (differential advantage) or to phase out the product.

Stars are high growth, high share businesses. They are the market leaders in fast-growth markets and often require heavy investment to build and / or maintain share in rapidly expanding markets. The strategy is to build or even maintain or hold its position as long as possible.

Cash Cows, which should be "milked," are low growth, high share businesses. When the market's annual growth rate falls to less that 10%, the star becomes a cash cow. Cash cows have the ability to generate more cash than can be reinvested profitably in its own operations. Thus, the profits are used for investment in other businesses. The strategy is to defend market share. Also, they are possible candidates[7] for a harvest strategy.

Dogs are low growth, low share businesses. Dogs are often targets for divestment, but may still be profitable and / or contribute to other organizational goals. The strategy is to minimize expenditures[8].

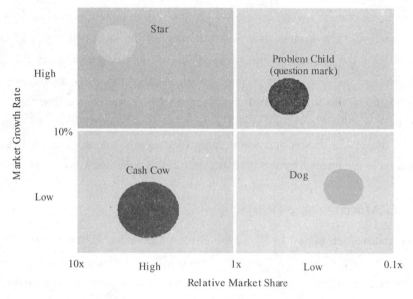

Figure 15-2   The BCG Matrix

15.2.2   General Electric Business Screen   通用电器公司模型

General Electric Business Screen (see Figure 15-3) or GE Strategic Business Planning Grid is very similar to the BCG matrix in the sense that the vertical axis represents industry attractiveness and the horizontal axis represents the company's strength in the industry or business position. The matrix uses two dimensions of three zones each. The most desirable SBUs are those located in the highly attractive industries where the company has high business strength (upper left cell). One difference is that the GE approach considers more than just market growth rate and relative market share in order to determine market attractiveness and business strength. The industry attractiveness index is made up of such factors as market size, market growth, industry profit margin, amount of competition, seasonally & cyclically of demand, and industry cost structure. Business strength is an index of factors like relative market share, price, competitiveness, product quality, customer & market knowledge, sales effectiveness, and geographic advantages. Strategically, the SBUs located in the green cells in the upper left are those in which the company should invest and grow. The SBUs in the yellow cells along the diagonal running from lower left to upper right are overall medium in attractiveness. The strategy is to protect or allocate resources on a selective basis. The SBUs in the red cells on the lower right corner have low overall attractiveness. A harvest strategy

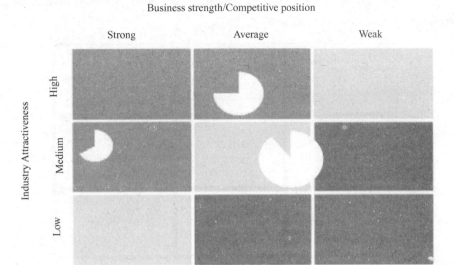

Figure 15-3   General Electric Business Screen

should be used in the two cells just below the three-cell diagonal. These SBUs should not receive substantial new resources. The SBUs in the lower right cell should not receive any resources and should probably be divested or eliminated from an organization's portfolio.

15.2.3   Ansoff Product / Market Expansion Grid   安索夫产品 / 市场发展矩阵

Ansoff Product / Market Expansion Grid (see Figure 15-4) is a portfolio-planning tool for identifying organization growth opportunities. In order to grow, an organization has to consider both its markets and its products. A market penetration strategy suggests that growth is possible by achieving a deeper penetration (sell more) of its present product within a present market. An organization could sell more of its current product(s) to its current customers, attract competitors' customers, or convince non-users to begin using the product, thereby increasing its existing market share. Another growth alternative is to try and identify new markets for its present products. By employing a market development strategy, an organization might identify new markets for its product by determining potential user groups for its current products, seeking additional distribution channels in its present locations, or offering its product for sale in new geographic locations, either domestic or international. Another alternative is to develop new products for an existing target market. Through a product development strategy, an organization might create an augmented[9], or entirely new, product in order to stimulate the current markets and create new ones. Finally, an organization could consider diversification as a growth strategy. The organization develops new products to sell to new markets. Also, it could involve acquiring[10] or starting businesses outside current markets.

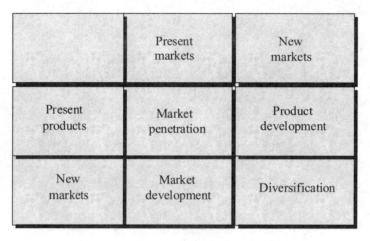

Figure 15-4   Product / Market Expansion Grid

15.3   International Marketing Planning Styles   国际营销计划类型

1. Standardized plans

The issues of centralization and decentralization involve the principle of delegation of authority. When a limited amount of authority is delegated in an organization, it is usually characterized as centralized or, since it is most commonly used and thus standardized . There are different degrees of centralization. These offer a number of advantages:

— Cost savings on limited product range and economies of scale both in production and marketing;

— Uniformity of consumer choice across the world.

There are disadvantages:

— Different market characteristics make uniform products inappropriate, for example, fresh milk products;

— Environmental obstacles disallow standardization; for example lack of refrigerated transport in developing countries.

2. Decentralized plans

When a company finds it difficult to follow the standardized approach or too difficult to follow the different situation in different countries, it would most probably apply for decentralized marketing planning. When a significant amount of authority is delegated to lower levels in the organization, the business is characterized as decentralized.

Decentralized plans take into account the subtleties of local conditions; however, they are usually very costly and resource consuming.

3. Interactive plans

A third approach is the interactive or integrated approach. In this approach headquarters devises branch policy and a strategic framework, and subsidiaries interpret these under local conditions, for example Nestlè. Headquarters coordinates and rationalizes advertising, pricing and distribution.

Within any of the above approaches plans can be either long or short term. Increasingly planning is becoming fairly routine. Most companies operate "annual operating plans" although these are often "rolled forward" to cover a few years hence.

In marketing planning, ultimately, the decision on the type of plan rests entirely on the size of the task, type of task and competence to achieve the task. In exporting flowers, say, to Europe, Zimbabwe would be well advised, with the small quantities involved, to leave the task to those experts in Holland and Germany whose knowledge and competence is far superior. The downside is that some market opportunities may be overlooked.

Table 15-1 shows us domestic planning, internation planning and their characteristics.

Table 15-1　Domestic vs. International Planning

	Domestic planning		International planning
1	Single language and nationality	1	Multilingual/multinational/multicultural factors
2	Relatively homogeneous market	2	Fragmented and diverse markets
3	Data available, usually accurate and collection easy	3	Data collection a large task requiring significantly higher budgets and personnel allocation
4	Political factors relatively unimportant	4	Political factors frequently vital
5	Relative freedom from government interference	5	Involvement in national economic plans; government influences business decisions
6	Individual corporation has little effect on environment	6	"Gravitational" distortion by large companies
7	Chauvinism helps	7	Chauvinism hinders
8	Relatively stable business environment	8	Multiple environments, many of which are highly unstable (but may be highly profitable)
9	Uniform financial climate	9	Variety of financial climates ranging from over-conservative to wildly inflationary
10	Single currency	10	Currencies differing in stability and real value
11	Business "rules of the game" mature and understood	11	Rules diverse, changeable and unclear
12	Management generally accustomed to sharing responsibilities and using financial controls	12	Management frequently un-autonomous and unfamiliar with budgets and controls

15.4 Key to Successful Marketing Planning
营销计划成功的关键因素

In order to operate any type of plan, three types of information are essential:

(1) Knowledge of the market — customers, competitors and government. The environment analysis enables a company to realize its opportunities in the market and threats from its competitors. A better understanding of its current and potential customer positions properly.

(2) Knowledge of the product — the formal product, its technology and its core benefit. Comparative advantage of a company is now a key to success. Product is the base for any comparative advantages. It is essential for a company to understand its technological advantages and its core benefits.

(3) Knowledge of the marketing functions. A company must know how marketing functions and what factors would strengthen the positive effectiveness.

Strategic planning does not mean creating an unwieldy and rigid document. A strategic planning is a roadmap for a company. It sets direction, defines the route, draws a clear picture of the destination and identifies the progress at checkpoints along the way. However, circumstances may intervene to cause some elements to change: the key is to be aware and ready to respond when that happens. On the other hand, changing your strategy often can result in confusion, multiple directions and depleted resources. According to Michael Porter, Harvard Business School, "Strategy must have continuity." It's about the basic value you're trying to deliver to customers and about which customers you're trying to serve. That is where continuity needs to be the strongest. Otherwise, it's hard for your organization to grasp what the strategy is. And it's hard for customers to know what you stand for.

Cases

Case 1.　Understanding business units

Portfolio analysis techniques help managers allocate resources across a number of businesses and markets. These techniques were intended to help corporate-level managers evaluate their different business units as separate businesses. A company may organize its businesses into several strategic business units on the basis of a variety of factors. However, it is assumed that each business unit manages products that are related to each other in some meaningful way. For example, visit Eastman Kodak and scroll down to the section "About the Company" and click on

"About Kodak. " This will take you to a page where you can click on "Business Units" to see how the company is organized into several business units. Then visit Procter and Gamble's site. Click on "About P&G" and then "P&G Products" and explore the links. Find out the philosophy underlying the classification of Kodak's business units and P&G's business units. How are they different? Which of these philosophies do you think is best suited to sensing emerging market opportunities? Why?

Case 2.   A SWOT analysis (abbreviated)

1. Definition

Product development is an essential element of a state tourism strategy and will play a vital role in the future growth of Hawaii's travel industry. To convert unknown attractions into fundamental tourism products, they must be marketed or packaged for easy access and sale to the consumer. Visitor services are an important element of product development. Providing services such as information, literature or access to medical assistance is vital to ensure visitor satisfaction. For international development, special attention must be devoted to services tailored to the needs of visitors from abroad. In a word, product development is any activity that conceives, plans or develops a service or product of interest to travelers.

2. Situation analysis

1) Strengths

(1) Aloha Spirit is real and recognized worldwide as a uniquely Hawaiian attribute. Visitors to the state find a friendly multicultural community.

(2) Hawaii offers a wide variety of activities including many unique cultural and historical experiences.

(3) Hawaii offers a diversity of nature experiences and activities. Its islands possess a natural beauty of land and sea as well as large areas of green space due to active agriculture. Visitors are impressed by stunning mountain and seascapes, sea-life, wildlife, flora and fauna.

(4) Hawaii offers the facilities and infrastructure for development of adventure tourism activities such as hiking, kayaking, biking, river fishing, sailing and horseback riding.

(5) All islands exude an atmosphere conducive to relaxation and romance. Hawaii is known for its low density areas which are appreciated by the discriminating visitor...

2) Weaknesses

Hawaii lacks a clear vision of a sustainable competitive product to promote to the value-conscious traveler. Hawaii has no strategic plan for product development, nor has it defined its target groups and their needs.

Hawaii has a poor service image to overseas travelers from the United States and Japan who have been to Hawaii.

Hawaii has not developed any significant ecotourism product to meet that growing international market.

The visitor industry is not sufficiently integrated into the host culture.

There is a lack of adequate sitting, development and maintenance of facilities for various adventure tourism activities such as hiking, biking, hang gliding, and canoeing.

3) Opportunities

The gaming industry continues to grow.

There is a significant demand for cultural attractions.

Continued growth in the following market segments: golf, health and healing, ocean-related adventure, honeymoon market, adventure tourism (biking, hiking, walking, kayaking, canoeing).

The Meetings, Conventions, and Incentives (MCI) market represents a relatively small proportion of visitors, yet a high proportion of revenues and better utilization of Hawaii's tourism infrastructure.

The significant interest in ecotourism is growing.

4) Threats

There is growing competition for visitors from other destinations and the cruise industry.

Growing interest in activities that are not currently available in Hawaii (e. g. snow skiing, amusement and theme parks) will continue to make Hawaii less of a draw.

3. Objectives and Strategies

1) Objective 1

Develop Hawaii as the world's most desirable visitor destination with a unique and diverse range of facilities, services and activities that reflect the host Hawaiian culture and the multi-ethnic population of the islands.

Recommended implementing strategies:

Regularly obtain and analyze visitor and resident feedback on current products and product standards.

Obtain and analyze non-Hawaii traveler feedback on the Hawaii product.

Identify key Hawaii products with less than desired satisfaction ratings and develop corrective-action programs to improve them.

Establish a system to monitor quality and foster excellence in facilities and services.

Educate industry on ways to incorporate the host Hawaiian culture into the visitor experience.

Integrate Hawaii-made agricultural and manufactured products into all relevant aspects of the tourism product.

Develop, expand and improve the quality of parks, recreational areas, scenic byways, and corridors.

2）Objective 2

Identify and develop new sustainable competitive products compatible with the host Hawaiian culture and the multi-ethnic population of Hawaii.

Recommended implementing strategies：

Identify and address barriers to development of new market niches（e. g. ecotourism, health and wellness）.

Foster the development of attractions and other opportunities to educate visitors about Hawaii's history, people and culture.

Identify new product opportunities with feedback from residents, current visitors and non-Hawaii travelers.

Encourage multi-industry development programs to capitalize on economic synergies and to leverage the resources of the relevant industries.

Key Terms

marketing plan　营销计划
SWOT analysis　SWOT 分析
annual plan　年度计划
long-range plan　远期计划
strategic planning　战略计划
mission statement　使命宣言
business portfolio　经营组合分析
external environmental analysis　外部环境分析
internal environmental analysis　内部环境分析
tactical plan　战术性计划
operational plan　运作计划
SBU（strategic business unit）　战略经营单元
BCG Matrix　波士顿矩阵法
Question Marks　问号
Stars　明星
Cash Cows　现金牛

Dogs　瘦狗
General Electric Business Screen　通用电器公司模型
Ansoff Product / Market Expansion Grid　产品市场发展矩阵
standardized plan　标准化计划
decentralized plan　分散性计划
interactive plans　互动性计划

📄 Notes

1. exigency　*n.*　紧急事件
2. competency　*n.*　能力
3. the Hongta Group　红塔集团
4. elaborate　*v.*　详细解释
5. matrix　*n.*　矩阵
6. quadrant　*n.*　象限
7. candidate　*n.*　候选产品
8. expenditure　*n.*　费用,支出
9. augmented　*a.*　扩张的
10. acquire　*v.*　并购

✍ Exercises

I. Multiple choices.

1. Companies face the difficult task of selecting an overall company strategy for long-term survival and growth. This selection process is called _____.
   A. setting company objectives
   B. creating a mission statement
   C. annual / long-range plans
   D. strategic planning

2. In order to plan the best possible business portfolio, a company must _____.
   A. analyze its current business portfolio and develop growth strategies for adding new products or businesses
   B. analyze its current business portfolio and decide which businesses should receive more, less, or no investment
   C. develop growth strategies for adding new products or businesses to the portfolio
   D. identify its strategic business units (SBUs)

3. The marketing process involves _____.

A. advertising, personal selling, sales promotion, and public relations

    B. product, price, promotion, and place

    C. developing a product, advertising it, and managing distribution

    D. analyzing marketing opportunities, selecting target markets, developing the marketing mix, and managing the marketing effort

4. What elements are the focus of marketing strategy?

    A. Market share position.

    B. Demographic factors.

    C. Superior products, consistent quality and innovative consumer promotion and advertising.

    D. A strong sales force.

5. Marketing mix elements _____.

    A. involve the marketing budget

    B. are a scientific explanation of marketing

    C. are a set of controllable tactical marketing tools that the firm blends to produce the response it wants in the market

    D. address the who, what, when, where, and why of marketing activities

6. The company's strategic plan _____.

    A. reduces the environmental threats a company may face

    B. ensures that the sales force is highly trained and motivated

    C. establishes what kinds of businesses the company will be in and its objectives for each

    D. means that a company's performance is monitored by neutral observers

7. At the business unit level, the focus of strategy is _____.

    A. on the competition

    B. on share prices

    C. on economic value added for the business unit

    D. creating customer value

8. When top-level managers delegate very little authority to lower-level employees, the organization is _____.

    A. centralized   B. decentralized   C. empowered   D. marketing-oriented

9. In essence, all organizations have two types of strategy: _____ is the strategy that the organization decides on during the planning phase, and _____ is the strategy that actually takes place.

    A. planned strategy; realized strategy

    B. intended strategy; realized strategy

    C. intended strategy; implemented strategy

      D. planned strategy; implemented strategy

10. Product, promotion, price, and distribution comprise an organization's _____.

      A. sales   B. marketing program

      C. marketing strategy   D. marketing mix

II. True or false.

1. A business portfolio should be guided by the company's mission statement and objectives.

2. A strategic business unit (SBU) has the same mission and objectives as all other company businesses.

3. An example of a sound marketing objective would be: "Expand consumer awareness by as much as the budget will permit in 2002."

4. The first step in the marketing strategic planning process should be to formulate the marketing mix.

5. Consult-Me Consultants, Inc., has recently been engaged in several special meetings where issues such as business mission, situation analysis, market and growth alternatives, and implementation approaches have been discussed. Consult-Me is apparently engaged in the strategic planning processes.

6. A corn chips offen defines its business as "snack-food" rather than just "corn chips." This is an example of a marketing mix strategy.

7. An example of a sound marketing objective would be: "Expand consumer awareness by 10% in 2002."

8. A high tech company has the business mission of "providing high quality products at a fair price to customers." This mission statement is too broad and does not state the business that the firm is in.

9. Marketing plans that cover a period of more than five years are medium-range plans.

10. In the marketing planning cycle, the final stage is revising / formulating the marketing strategy.

III. Discussion.

1. What is marketing planning? What are the different types of planning?

2. Give a brief description of marketing planning processes.

3. What are the major tools used in marketing planning? Describe them separately.

4. What are the different approaches adapted when making planning internationally?

5. You have been just hired by a small company specializing in soaps and other product.

You are new on the job, and your boss thinks formal strategic planning is an inefficient and ineffective mechanism for small companies. You are determined to change his attitude. Write a memo explaining how formal planning can be used in your company. Search the simplified strategic planning for small to mid-sized companies and find the information to help your explanation.

6. Choose a popular restaurant located near your college. List the strengths and weaknesses that are characteristics of this restaurant; list opportunities and threats that it faces.

Chapter Sixteen

Organizing and Controlling
International Marketing

组织和控制国际市场营销

◀ Objectives 学习目标

When students finish this chapter, they should be able to accomplish the following:

☑ Organization
☑ Marketing control
☑ Manage sales force
☑ Marketing audit and audit process
☑ Case

16.1 Organization 组织

When two or more people work together to achieve a group result, it is an organization. After the objectives of an organization are established, the functions that must be performed are determined.

Organizational structure can be defined as the specification of the jobs to be done within an organization and the ways in which those jobs relate to one another. And the process of creating an organization's structure is called organizing. Personnel requirements are assessed and the physical resources needed to accomplish the objectives determined. These elements must then be coordinated into a structural design that will help achieve the objectives. Finally, appropriate responsibilities are assigned.

16.1.1   The importance of proper organization forms   合适组织形式的重要性

The key to good organizing, planning and controlling in global marketing is to create a flexible structure or framework that enables organizations to respond to relevant differences in the markets in which they operate. Production and marketing systems are interdependent. Furthermore, the activities and economic entities within the network of exchange relationships and any other coordinating mechanisms are complex. Most products and commodity systems exhibit widely different organizational characteristics between countries. Different governments have different programs, horizontal and vertical structural elements can vary, as in terms of access, competitive conditions, parallel marketing channels and the types of contractual and ownership integration. [1]

16.1.2   Forms of organizations   组织形式

The primary formal relationships for organizing are responsibility, authority, and accountability[2]. They enable us to bring together functions, people, and other resources for the purpose of achieving objectives. The framework for organizing these formal relationships is known as the organizational structure. It provides the means for clarifying and communicating the lines of responsibility, authority, and accountability.

Coordination in international marketing is complex and vital. Transaction costs[3] should also be included. The form of appropriate organization depends on a number of factors: company goals, size of business, the number of markets operated in, the level of involvement in the market, international experience, the nature of the product, the width and range of the product line, the nature of the marketing task and the risk involved. In China, many organizational forms are relatively unsophisticated[4]. They are "domestic" based, that is, they may have a small export division within the domestic based operation. Most deal through agents or other machinating houses which have their own organization.

Generally speaking, the international division may be replaced by a variety of structures like a geographical, product, function or strategic business unit approach.

1. Geographical organizational structure

A geographical structure (see Figure 16-1) is one that puts emphasis on regions and physical location to co-ordinate the management of a company. Each region (or division) has the responsibility for almost all of the business functions. Companies that utilize a geographical structure do so for many reasons. This strategy is used to align core competencies[5] with management decision making.

The primary advantage for a geographical structure is flexibility. A division that is autonomous[6] in a region can quickly respond to changes in the environment and allocate its resources accordingly. By keeping control of most of the divisions business functions, the divisions could adjust prices, implement new technology or use a new marketing concept more easily than a functionally organized company.

Secondly, an advantage of geographically organized companies is speed in decision making. Management at each division, with close knowledge of the external environment would be able to make market decisions very quickly. This could result in faster response to everything from competitor price changes or discount opportunities from suppliers.

Employing a geographical structure may be useful when a company is present on different markets — markets that are indeed so different from each other that they have to be served separately.

When every region has its own way of working in each department of the company, production, marketing and selling, it is easy for them to become too independent. They become very autonomous and manage their division the way they want. There is no benefit to sharing information with the rest of the company. This is a big problem. Geographical structure may, due to the lack of communication, lead to losing of control over marketing and sales.

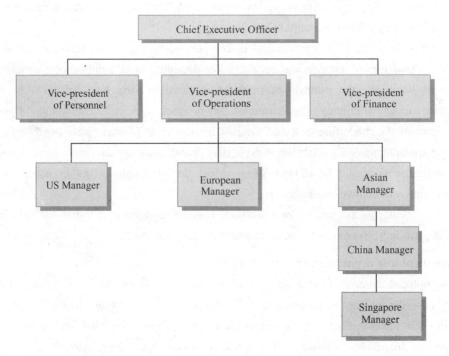

Figure 16-1　Geographical Organizational Structure

2. Product or brand-management organizational structure

A product organizational structure (see Figure 16-2) is a type of a centralized organization structure based on products catalog. In this case departments are responsible for all functions of management associated with a given product. The support functions are placed in product departments. Each department sees progress at all stages of work from input to output, from the materials coming in to the goods going out of the organization. Employees in a department interact with other employees in the same department doing different functions; they learn from each other and see how each contributes to the overall productivity of the department. A symbiotic relationship develops leading to individual and organizational learning. A manager would have responsibility for several if not all processes involved in the manufacture of the product.

Brand management structure ensures focus, and therefore the most effective marketing for each product or service. Having only one person managing all of a company's brands can give short shrift to all and sufficient attention to none. Under brand management structure, each brand manager's sole focus is on his or her brand. In this way, each brand gets the focus, resource coordination, and management it deserves to maximize performance.

In addition, marketing is only one aspect of a brand manager's role. Since the customer's perception of a brand encompasses not only the product itself but also pre-purchase and post-purchase contacts, brand managers must maintain an integrated enterprise view and manage across all functions and geographies.

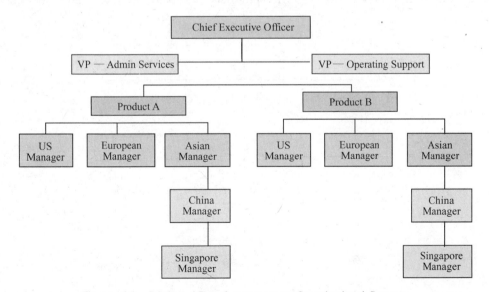

Figure 16-2   Product / Brand-management Organizational Structure

3. Functional organizational structure

The most common form of marketing organization consists of functional-marketing specialists in production, marketing or personnel reporting to a marketing vice-president, who coordinates their activities, as shown in Figure 16-3.

It is quite a challenge to develop smooth working relations within the marketing department, let alone between marketing and other departments. Cespedes has urged companies to improve the critical interfaces[7] among field sales, customer service, and product management groups, since they collectively have a major impact on customer service. He has proposed several ways to form tighter linkages among these three key marketing groups.

Functional organizations have the advantage of being simple to understand with clear lines of command, specified tasks and responsibilities. Staff can specialize in a particular business area such as production or marketing and follow well-defined career paths. This is equally true of human resource specialists who can develop expertise in specific areas such as employee relations or reward management.

However, this form loses effectiveness as the company's products and markets increase. First, a functional organization often leads to inadequate planning for specific products and markets, since no one has full responsibility for any product or market. Products that are not favored by anyone arc neglected. Second, each functional group competes with the other functions for budget and status. The marketing vice-president constantly has to weigh the claims of

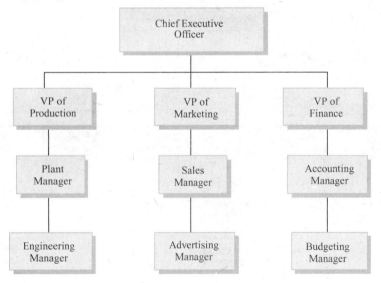

Figure 16-3　Functional Organizational Structure

competing functional specialists and faces a difficult coordination problem.

4. Matrix organizational structure

A matrix organizational structure (see Figure 16-4) combines both process and product management and has both process and product managers. This requires more managers but is justified on the grounds that it results in improved communication and better control. Each employee below the level of process and product managers has two managers, a process manager and a product manager. Each manager can issue work instructions to an employee and dictate when the work is to be done. A matrix structure is said to offer better control for managing the complexity of multi-product manufacturing organizations. This can, however, lead to conflicts when an employee is required to do two tasks at the same time. Instead of introducing more managers, a modern approach would improve communication in other ways and create self-managing work groups.

The big advantage of matrix organizations is that they are great for sharing of information and enabling people to coordinate their efforts with larger organizational goals and strategies.

The problem, of course, is that having two bosses can be confusing, and is a situation that is easily exploited by subordinates, who can pit their bosses against each other. The subordinates can also be unwitting victims of power struggles among the bosses.

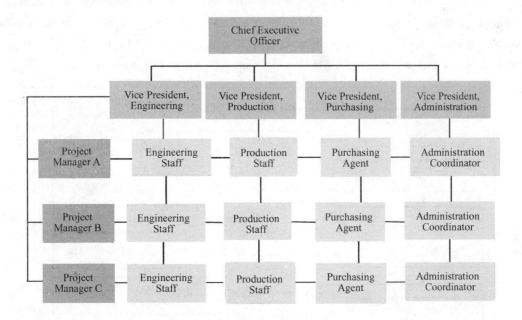

Figure 16-4   Matrix Organizational Structure

The matrix form works best when one dimension[8] is a permanent affiliation[9] (typically functional), and the other is a temporary dimension, such as a client project. So a person is, say, a marketing research analyst, and is presently assigned to the No. 1 project, which will take 6 weeks, and will then be assigned to another project, and so on.

16.2　Marketing Evaluation and Control　市场营销评估与控制

16.2.1　Importance of evaluation and control　评估与控制的重要性

No marketing process, even the most carefully developed, is guaranteed to result in maximum benefit for a company. In addition, because every market is changing constantly, a strategy that is effective today may not be effective in the future. It is important to evaluate a marketing program periodically to be sure that it is achieving its objectives.

Factors like distance, culture, language and practices create barriers to effective control. Yet without control over international operations, the degree to which they have or have not been successful cannot be judged.

Plans are the prerequisite[10] to control, yet these are developed in the midst of uncertain forces both internal and external to the firm. Basically control involves the establishment of standards of performance, measuring performance against standards and correcting deviations[11] from standards and plans. In international marketing the ability to control is disturbed by the distance, culture, political and other factors. Figure 16-5 below illustrates a typical plan / control cycle.

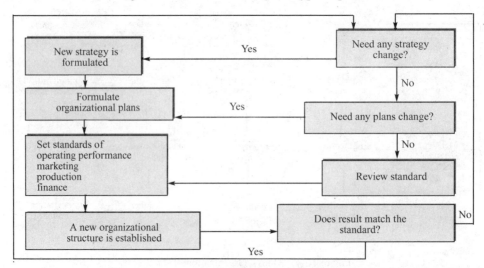

Figure 16-5　Evaluation and Controlling Process

In well developed international operations, headquarters may seek to achieve control over subsidiaries by three types of mechanisms — data management mechanisms, merge mechanisms, which shift emphasis from subsidiary to global performance, and conflict resolution mechanisms that resolve conflicts triggered by necessary trade-offs. In many less developed countries, however, the method of export control takes the form of direct organization by government.

16.2.2　Types of marketing control　控制类型

Generally, there are four types of marketing control, each of which has a different purpose: annual-plan control, profitability control, efficiency control, and strategic control. See Figure 16-6 and Figure 16-7.

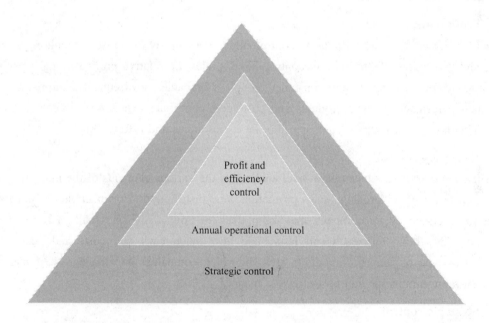

Figure 16-6　Different Levels of Marketing Controls

1. Annual-plan control

The basis of annual-plan control is managerial objectives — that is to say, specific goals, such as sales and profitability, that are established on a monthly or quarterly basis. Organizations use five tools to monitor plan performance. The first is sales analysis, in which sales goals are compared with actual sales and discrepancies[12] are explained or accounted for. A second tool is market-share analysis, which compares a company's sales with those of its competitors. Companies can express their market share in a number of ways, by comparing their own sales to total market sales, sales within the market segment, or sales of the segment's top competitors. Third, marketing expense-to-sales analysis gauges how much a company spends to achieve its sales goals. The ratio of marketing expenses to sales is expected to fluctuate, and companies usually establish an acceptable range for this ratio. In contrast, financial analysis estimates such expenses (along with others) from a corporate perspective. This includes a comparison of profits to sales (profit margin), sales to assets (asset turnover), profits to assets (return on assets), assets to worth (financial leverage), and, finally, profits to worth (return on net worth). [13] Finally, companies measure customer satisfaction as a means of tracking goal achievement. Analyses of this kind are generally less quantitative than those described above and may include complaint and suggestion systems, customer satisfaction surveys, and careful analysis of reasons why customers switch to a competitor's product.

2. Profitability control

Profitability control and efficiency control allow a company to closely monitor its sales, profits, and expenditures. Profitability control demonstrates the relative profit-earning capacity of a company's different products and consumer groups. Companies are frequently surprised to find that a small percentage of their products and customers contribute to a large percentage of their profits. This knowledge helps a company allocate its resources and effort.

3. Efficiency control

Efficiency control involves micro-level analysis of the various elements of the marketing mix, including sales force, advertising, sales promotion, and distribution. For example, to understand its sales-force efficiency, a company may keep track of how many sales calls a representative makes each day, how long each call lasts, and how much each call costs and generates in revenue. This type of analysis highlights areas in which companies can manage their marketing efforts in a more productive and cost-effective manner.

4. Strategic control

Strategic control processes allow managers to evaluate a company's marketing program from a critical long-term perspective. This involves a detailed and objective analysis of a company's organization and its ability to maximize its strengths and market opportunities. Companies can use two types of strategic control tools. The first, which a company uses to evaluate itself, is called a marketing-effectiveness rating review. In order to rate its own marketing effectiveness, a company examines its customer philosophy, the adequacy of its marketing information, and the efficiency of its marketing operations. It will also closely evaluate the strength of its marketing strategy and the integration of its marketing tactics.

Type of control	Prime responsibility	Purpose of control	Approaches
Annual plan control	Top management Middle management	To examine whether the results are being achieved	Sales analysis Marketshare analysis Sales-to-expense ratios Financial analysis Attitude tracking
Profitability control	Marketing controller	To examine where the company is making and losing money	Profitability by product territory Customer group trade
Efficiency control	Line and staff management Marketing controller	To evaluate and improve the spending efficiency and impact of marketing expenditures	Channel order size Efficiency of sales force Advertising sales promotion distribution
Strategic control	Top management Marketing auditor	To examine whether the company is pursuing its best opportunities with respect to markets, products, and channels	Marketing effectiveness rating instrument Marketing audit

Figure 16-7　Types of Marketing Control

16.2.3　Variables influencing control　影响营销控制的因素

A number of factors may influence the control methods. These include:

(1) Domestic practices and values of standardization — these may not be appropriate;

(2) Communication systems — have a heavy influence on control mechanisms — electronic control measures may not always be available;

(3) Distance — the greater the distance, the bigger the physical and psychological differences;

(4) The product — the more technological the product the easier it is to implement uniform standards;

(5) Environmental differences — the greater the environmental differences the greater the delegation of responsibility and the more limited the control process;

(6) Environmental stability — the greater the instability in a country the less relevance a standardized measure of performance has;

(7) Subsidiary performance — the more a subsidiary does, or reports, a non variance, the less likely is there to be headquarters interference;

(8) Size of international operators — the bigger and greater the specialization of headquarters staff the more likely will extensive control be applied.

Regandless the ability to control any international operation, whether it be very sophisticated or relatively unsophisticated, the process will break down without adequate face-to-face and / or electronic communications.

16.3　Manage Sales Force　管理销售力量

16.3.1　From mass marketing to one-to-one marketing 从大众营销到一对一营销

In the past, mass marketing dominated marketing management and strategy for decades. In the 1960s, many firms began to apply principles of segmentation, target marketing, and positioning to create different strategies and marketing programs for different consumer groups. A major change in mindset precipitates a shift from targeted consumer marketing (i. e., marketing to big groups of like-minded buyers) to customer marketing, or a focus on developing relationships with individuals. This approach first gained widespread attention in the 1980s. Ultimately, the sophistication and multiplicity of available technology today enables true one-to-one marketing, as some firms are now able to truly customize offerings for individual users. And customer relationship management is rooted from this trend. Customer Relationship Management (CRM) is a comprehensive business model for increasing revenues and profits by focusing on customers. More specifically, CRM refers to "... any application or initiative designed to help your company optimize interactions with customers, suppliers, or prospects via one or more touchpoints — such as a call center, salesperson, distributor, store, branch office, Web, or e-mail — for the purpose of acquiring, retaining, or cross-selling customers."

16.3.2　Manage sales force　管理营销人员

Sales force is one of the most important elements in the success of many modern sales organizations, as it is the firm's most direct link to the customer. Therefore, management of the sales force is one of the most important executive responsibilities.

Two key points should be made at the outset about sales management today. First, modern companies realize that selling is an indispensable[14] component of an effective marketing strategy. Second, managing a sales force is a dynamic[15] process. Managing a sales force well involves understanding the complexity[16] of selling activities as well as the decisions involved in managing those activities.

A sales manager can use several policies and procedures to influence the aptitude[17], skill levels, role perceptions, and motivation of the sales force. The sales manager must decide what aptitudes are required for the firm's salespeople to do the type of selling involved and to reach the sales program's objectives. Recruiting techniques and selection criteria can then be developed to ensure that salespeople with the required abilities are hired.

A salesperson's selling skills improve with practice and experience. In most cases, though, it is inefficient to let the salesperson simply gain skills through on-the-job experience[18]. Good customers might be lost as the result of mistakes by unskilled sales personnel. Consequently, many firms have a formal training program to give new recruits some of the necessary knowledge and skills before they are expected to pull their own weight in the field. And with the increasing rapid changes in technology, global competition, and customer needs occurring in many industries, training is often an ongoing process necessary to upgrade a sales force's knowledge and skills on a regular basis. The sales manager must determine what kinds of selling skills are necessary for the success of the firm's marketing strategy and sales program. The manager can then design training programs that develop those skills as effectively as possible.

Even after completing a training program, salespeople may run into unusual situations where they face conflicting demands or are uncertain about what to do. Supervisory[19] policies and procedures are needed so salespeople can obtain advice and assistance from management with no undue restrictions on their freedom to develop innovative approaches to customers' problems.

Finally, a salesperson's motivation to expend effort on the job is largely a function of the amount and desirability of the rewards expected for a given job performance. The sales manager should determine what rewards are most attractive to the sales force and design compensation[20] and incentive[21] programs that will generate a high level of motivation. Compensation programs involve monetary rewards. Incentive programs can also include a variety of nonfinancial rewards, such as recognition programs, promotions to better territories or to management positions, or opportunities for personal development. Minolta Business Systems (www. minoltambs. com), for example, offers salespeople who sell 150 percent of their annual quota[22] a trip to exciting locations such as Monte Carlo. Today, salespeople work as part of cross-functional teams. At IBM, for example, the account executive for a client such as EDS (www. eds. com) is the captain of a team involving IBM sales representatives spread out across the globe, as well as representatives from manufacturing, marketing, finance, and other areas of the of IBM. Allegiance, one of the largest medical supply manufacturers and distributors, also uses a team concept with representatives from each product area assisting the salesperson. With the advent of team selling, it has become more difficult to evaluate individual performance and, as a result, to determine appropriate rewards.

16.4　Marketing Audit　营销审计

16.4.1　Definition and requirement　定义和要求

Marketing Audit is the hottest management concept in the new millennium and marketers are getting increasingly conscious about this, no matter small or large sized companies. No chief or head of marketing can afford to stay away from the up-to-date check on marketing process. The marketing audit provides good input for a plan of action to improve a company's marketing performance.

1. Definition

The marketing audit is a systematic examination of every aspect of sales, marketing, customer service, and even operations that affect sales and marketing in order to determine how well and cost-effectively each element helps the firm meet its overall goals. It is essentially an internal assessment. You can perform a simple audit yourself in a relatively short period of time and then develop some high-impact agenda items to improve your marketing performance based on the results of your audit.

Operations globally can be evaluated and improved by a global marketing audit. Audits have a wide focus, are independently carried out, are systematic and conducted periodically. To be successful audits have to have objectives, data, sources of data and a time span and reporting format. Audits can cover the environment, strategy, organization, system, productivity and functions. Unfortunately, as in any attempt to gather global data, all the pitfalls of politics, culture, and language differences arise.

Much of the preceding discussion covers more sophisticated forms of international control, except budgeting which is applicable to all types of exporting or global marketing. As stated earlier, many less developed countries have export controls imposed by governments.

2. Requirements

A marketing audit is a comprehensive appraisal of the organization marketing activities. It involves a systematic assessment of marketing plans, objectives, strategies, programs, activities, organizational structure, and personnel. Such a thorough study of a marketing operation requires an objective attitude. The bank auditors who provide good insight into the marketing audit process, for example, are very cautious and thus very hard to be fooled. A good marketing audit, therefore, is:

(1) Systematic. It follows a logical, predetermined framework and orderly sequence of

diagnostic steps.

（2） Comprehensive. It considers all factors affecting marketing performance, not just obvious trouble spots. Marketers can be fooled into addressing symptoms rather than underlying problems. A comprehensive audit can identify the real problems.

（3） Independent. To ensure objectivity, outside consultants may prepare the marketing audit. Using outsiders may not be necessary, but having an objective auditor is essential.

（4） Periodic. Many organizations schedule regular marketing audits because marketing operates in a dynamic environment.

16.4.2   Audit process   审计过程

Usually, audit includes marketing environment audit, marketing strategy audit, marketing organization audit, marketing systems audit, marketing productivity audit and marketing function audit. The first step of an audit is a meeting between company executives and the auditor to agree on objectives, coverage, depth, data sources, report format, and time period for the audit. They decide on the audit objectives, report format, timing, and other matters.

1. Team organization

An auditing team is necessary. Auditors may come from both the organization or a professional audit services company. Audits generally are conducted by outside consultants that have the experience and objectivity to analyze every detail of the organization's fundraising operations; make recommendations for change; and, where necessary advise the re-organization / revision process. Audits are best conducted by outside consultants rather than staff who usually lack the necessary objectivity and may possess a bias toward the organization and its management. Audit team members must talk to field sales personnel, sales management, customers and suppliers as well. Creative auditing techniques should be encouraged and explored by the auditing team.

2. Data collecting

Gathering data is one of the major tasks in conducting an audit. A detailed plan of interviews, secondary research (including statistic data, newspaper, yearbook, etc.), review of internal documents, and so forth is required.

The information collected includes:

（1） Environment information such as environmental trends, population trends and their expected affection to the existing and planned strategy, expected social and psychological patterns (attitudes, lifestyle, etc.);

（2） Objectives such as the marketing objectives of the business, the possible alter to fit changing environmental variables, the consistency of the objectives, etc. ;

（3）Strategy which includes the relationship between objectives and strategies, sufficiency of resources to implement the strategies, the company's weaknesses, etc. ;

（4）Product decisions about the development of new products and analysis of present products;

（5）Pricing decisions, influences of competitors and the concerns of channel members;

（6）Distribution decisions about the selection, evaluation motivation and drop of channel member, channel structure and other issues;

（7）Promotion decisions about the promotion mix decisions, salespeople selection, monitoring, and evaluation, the payoffs associated with promotional efforts.

Some typical questions in Market Information are "How is marketing research information transmitted to, and used within, the business unit?" and "Is a global information system in place?"

Activities and Tasks concentrate on "How are tasks scheduled, described, and planned? How are the responsibilities of individuals determined?" and "What spans of supervision, reporting relationships, and communication patterns exist? How are they evaluated?"

Personnel's information is also an essential part for the audit process. The level of competence attained by personnel in each position, the state of morale, motivation.

Figure 16-8 shows us questions for a marketing audit to answer about your firm.

A marketing audit should generally answer the following questions about your firm.

✔ Does your firm have a strategic marketing plan? If so, is it evaluated on an ongoing basis?

✔ Does your marketing department gather routinely information on competitors?

✔ Is your marketing department equipped to develop or to act on new service concepts or ideas?

✔ Are proposals or client inquiries handled expeditiously?

✔ Does your company have centralized marketing resources under one authority?

✔ Does your marketing manager have sufficient authority to implement change in operating or delivery procedures?

✔ Is your marketing department structured in an effective manner relative to operations?

✔ Is your marketing function of sufficient size and experience in relation to the company?

✔ Is there adequate interaction between marketing and other departments, divisions or branch offices?

✔ Is there an appropriate "mix" of marketing vehicles(e.g.advertising, sales, promotion,) networking and trade shows)?

Figure 16-8　Questions for a Marketing Audit

Many methods are used to collecting information, then, the audit team will analyze the information and make their judgment.

3. Presenting the report

A report is the final and formal result of an audit. After data collection and analysis, the audit team should prepare for a report. This report will include the main findings, and major recommendations and conclusions as well as major headings for the further study and investment.

Cases

Case 1. Organization of Coca Cola in China market

Coca Cola establishes its China market organization and each section's functions as follow.

Marketing department: Major functions include integrated planning of brand and enterprise's image, promotion idea collection and promotion campaign planning, and relevant budget decision making and implementing monitoring.

Operation department: Major functions include implementation of planning and other decisions made by the management, product distribution and channel expansion, daily transform of feedback collected from markets.

Quality control department: Major functions include all round quality control to guarantee the credit of its products. For example, all products relevant to the production of Coca Cola would be under the strict quality control system. Those products that can pass the inspection will get certificate. Continuers and strict control over quality has been acted through out the whole process of production from the purchasing of raw materials to the output of final products. It doesn't aim to control the rate of waster but to improve the quality of all products.

Finance department: Control of the cash flow and storage of the products as well as professional inspections of slots of marketing distribution channel.

Administration department: To ensure the fluency and efficiency of communication of business, especially to keep good relationship with news press and eliminate all the possible negative influence.

Case 2. Boeing company and its unique organizational structure

As a key element of transforming, the Boeing Company has established a corporate architecture that continues operational performance improvements, while investing capital wisely in new growth opportunities.

The Boeing World Headquarters focuses on shareholder value, develops the strategic direction of the company and allocates the human and financial resources needed to implement the company's business strategies. Shared Services Group focuses on infrastructure and support across Boeing to allow all business units to focus on revenue generation and growth, adding value by consolidating processes and leveraging the buying power of the entire enterprise.

The research and development organization — Phantom Works — acts as the technological glue for the company, developing and transitioning technology and expertise to the products and business processes. Company Wide Process Councils provide leadership to ensure that best practices, tools and processes are shared and implemented across the company.

The six operating business units remain responsible for day-to-day operations and continued solid business performance, driven by economic profit targets that directly align with the shareholders' interests. The result is a company with enormous capability and enormous opportunity.

Case 3.   An example of sales analysis

The managing director of the Huasheng Canning Company is told by the marketing manager that sales are up half a million units on the target and that revenues are five percent above budget. This would be cause for celebration. Or would it? Before answering this question the managing director would wish to look at these figures a little more analytically. The operating results might look those presented in Table 16-1.

Table 16-1   Operating results for a canned product

Canned Produce	Planned	Actual	Variance
Sales (units)	5,000,000	5,500,000	+ 5000,000
Price per unit ($)	3.50	3.40	− 0.10
Total revenues ($)	17,500,000	18,700,000	+ 1,200,000
Total market (units)	10,000,000	12,000,000	+ 2,000,000
Share of market	50%	46%	− 4%
Variable costs @ $2.5 per unit	12,500,000	13,750,000	+ 1,250,000
Profit contribution ($)	5,000,000	4,950,000	− 50,000

It can readily be seen that, although sales have exceeded expectations, the planned price was not achieved and so the product made a lower contribution than expected. In this case the price mechanism would need investigating, as would the estimates of market share. Whilst the Canning Company recorded an increase in sales of ten percent, the market as a whole was twenty percent above target. Seen in this light, there is more cause for concern than for celebration.

Case 4. Wal-Mart and its management of sales force

Wal-Mart insists on partnership and team-work between managers and employees. Wal-Mart has no superstar; it has average people operating in an environment that encourages everyone to perform way above average. Managers go around the store almost 90% of the day to communicate with associates — praise them for well-done job, discuss how improvement can be made, and listen to comments and good suggestion. And it is said 99% of the best ideas came from its employees.

1. Recruitment

In-store employees at Wal-Mart consist of two categories: managers (full-time) and associates (hourly). Managers are hired in one of three ways:

(1) People from other retail companies with outstanding merchandising skills are recruited (10%) ;

(2) College graduates (30%) ;

(3) Hourly associates move up through the ranks (more than 60%).

Current associates can find information and apply for another jobs internally through Internet. People who seek for job can search job information and apply for the part-time, full-time jobs at any time through online system. Their jobs are very well specialized and described according to department and division. For example, their jobs are very well specialized in Store Support such as Accounting Office Associate, Layaway Associate, Department Manager Claims / Reclamation Associate, Customer Service, Fitting Room Associate, Customer Service Manager, Courtesy Desk Associate and People Greeter. Job responsibilities are described very accurately. At Wal-Mart, managers are often recruited internally, but associates are recruited externally.

2. Training

All managers have to complete structural management training programs that consist of on-the-job training and bookwork. Areas studied include management topics such as internal / external theft, scheduling, store staffing, retail math, merchandise replenishment and the Wal-Mart's " keys to supervision " series, which deals with interpersonal skills and personnel responsibility.

All new associates who are hired must complete a " new hire " checklist and a three-day orientation, and they are immediately placed in positions for on-the-job training. No formal training is provided from Wal-Mart headquarters for hourly associates. Store managers train and supervise employees. Video film, computer based training, satellite television, and retail management seminars are popular technique. Topics vary from new cash register functionality to security policies. We can conclude that the company trains the employee in very short-term and tasks specific contents.

3. Salary and bonus

Management positions are salaried. Store managers receive additional compensation based on their store's profit. Assistant store managers receive additional compensation on the company's profitability. All other personnel are compensated on an hourly basis with the opportunity of receiving additional incentive bonuses based on the company's productivity and profitability. People who suggested successful ideas for sales gain, cost reduction and improved productivity receive not only some bonus but also company-wide recognition such as Saturday morning meetings at headquarters or the personal praise of the chairperson. Shrinkage bonuses are implemented to control losses from theft and damage. If stores hold shrinkage below the corporate goal, every associate in that store receives up to $300. A very successful incentive program is its Volume Producing Item contest, whereby departments within a store do special promotions and pricing on items they want to feature. The contest is initially among departments within a store; contest results are compared at both the store-to-store and region-to-region level. This program helped boost sales and sell slow-moving items. It also encouraged employees to be innovative.

☐ Key Terms

geographical structure　地域性结构

product or brand-management organizational structure　产品／品牌管理组织结构

functional organizational structure　功能性组织结构

matrix organization　矩阵结构

share of market　市场份额

marketing audit　市场审计

promotion decision　促销决策

pricing decision　定价决策

distribution decision　分销决策

product decision　产品决策

environment information　环境信息

annual-plan control　年度控制

profitability control　利益率控制，收益率控制

sales analysis　销售分析

market-share analysis　市场份额分析

marketing expense-to-sales analysis　营销费用与销售额对比分析

financial analysis　财务分析

efficiency control   效率控制

strategic control   战略控制

mass marketing   大众营销

one-to-one marketing   一对一营销

Customer Relationship Management(CRM)   顾客关系管理

📄 Notes

1. Different governments have different programs, horizontal and vertical structural elements can vary, as in terms of access, competitive conditions, parallel marketing channels and the types of contractual and ownership integration.   不同的政府从平行或垂直的角度，做出不同的规定，从而规范行业进入，竞争情况，平行营销渠道以及契约与所有权整合类型等各个方面。

2. accountability   *n.*   可记账性

3. transaction cost   交易成本

4. unsophisticated   *a.*   单纯的，单一的

5. core competencies   核心竞争力

6. autonomous   *a.*   自治的

7. interface   *n.*   界面

8. dimension   *n.*   空间的维数

9. affiliation   *n.*   联系

10. prerequisite   *n.*   先决条件

11. deviation   *n.*   偏差

12. discrepancy   *n.*   差异

13. This includes a comparison of profits to sales (profit margin), sales to assets (asset turnover), profits to assets (return on assets), assets to worth (financial leverage), and, finally, profits to worth (return on net worth).   这包括利润与销售额（利润率）之比，销售额与资产总值（资产周转率）之比，利润与资产总值（资产收益率）之比，资产总值与价值（财务杠杆作用）之比，最后是利润与价值（净值收益）之比。

14. indispensable   *a.*   必要的，不可或缺的

15. dynamic   *a.*   动态的

16. complexity   *n.*   复杂性

17. aptitude   *n.*   倾向

18. on-the-job experience   在岗经验

19. supervisory   *a.*   监管的,管理的

20. compensation   *n.*   补偿
21. incentive   *a.*   激励的
22. annual quota   年度定额

Exercises

I. Multiple choices.

1. If you were a marketing manager, under which type of organizational structure would you most likely be working if your firm were a large business with centralized marketing operations?

    A. The organization by type of customer.   B. The functional organization.

    C. The organization by regions.   D. The organization by products.

2. A firm that markets diverse products would most likely base the organization of its marketing department on _____.

    A. products   B. regions   C. functions   D. types of customers

3. Organizing a marketing unit by regions works well for a company that _____.

    A. produces and markets diverse products

    B. is small and has a centralized marketing operation

    C. markets products nationally and internationally

    D. has several groups of customers whose needs and problems are different

4. An appliance manufacturer that sells to large retail stores, wholesalers, and institutions would probably organize its marketing unit on the basis of _____.

    A. sub-regions   B. national divisions

    C. types of customers   D. functions   E. products

5. Marketing managers at London Equipment Company are involved in establishing marketing performance standards, evaluating performance, and reducing the differences between actual and desired performance. These marketing managers are engaged in _____.

    A. the marketing control process   B. marketing systems design

    C. the marketing audit   D. marketing evaluation

6. Organizational structure is defined as which of the following?

    A. Specification of the jobs to be done and ways in which those jobs relate to one another.

    B. Specification of the jobs to be done and how those jobs shall be performed.

    C. Specification of the jobs to be done.

    D. Specification of how performance is to be measured.

7. Which of the following are the chief determinants of an organization's structure?

A. The organization's purpose, mission, and financial structure.

B. The organization's purpose, mission, and strategy.

C. The organization's purpose, financial structure, and human resources.

D. The organization's mission, financial structure, and human resources.

8. The process of establishing performance standards, comparing performance to established standards, and reducing any discrepancies between desired and actual performance is known as _____.

A. total quality management   B. marketing implementation

C. marketing control   D. external marketing

9. All of the following are types of marketing control discussed in the text EXCEPT _____.

A. annual-plan control   B. profitability control

C. efficiency control   D. effectiveness control

10. Which of the following are the important area to be included in a marketing audit report?

A. Political-legal factors

B. Megan's customers

C. Marketing systems and technological factors

D. All of the above should be included

11. The marketing audit does all of the following EXCEPT _____.

A. setting performance standards   B. exploring opportunities

C. providing an overall database   D. gathering information

12. A sales component analysis is also called a(n) _____.

A. profitability analysis   B. sales response function

C. marketing audit   D. sales situational analysis

E. microsales analysis

13. The _____ is a systematic, critical, and unbiased review and appraisal of the basic objectives and policies of the marketing function, and of the organization, methods, procedures, and people employed to implement the policies.

A. marketing audit   B. performance audit

C. benchmark audit   D. standardization audit

14. A major tool of marketing controls which is comprehensive, systematic, independent, and a periodic review of the company's environment, objectives, strategies, and activities to determine problem areas and opportunities is called _____.

A. marketing plan   B. strategic plan

C. marketing audit   D. profitability plan

15. The process of developing and maintaining a strategic fit between the organization's goals and capabilities and its changing marketing opportunities is called _____.

    A. annual planning   B. long-range planning

    C. strategic planning   D. market auditing

16. A marketing audit is _____.

    A. an examination of costs and expenditure involved in marketing

    B. a "snapshot" of the firm's current marketing activities

    C. a check on the cost-effectiveness of the firm's marketing expenditure

    D. none of the above

II. True or false.

1. The Matrix organizational structure uses teams whose members report to two or more managers.

2. Small and medium-sized firms most commonly use matrix organizational structure.

3. The process of creating an organization's structure is called organizing.

4. A marketing control process provides feedback on how well a marketing strategy is working in the marketplace.

5. With regard to "marketing organization", firms that focus their attention on developing a coordinated marketing mix for each brand are examples of matrix organizations.

6. The hard task of selecting an overall company strategy for long-run survival and growth is called marketing control.

7. The marketing audit is a comprehensive, periodic examination of a company's environment, objectives, strategies, and activities to determine problem areas and opportunities.

8. A marketing audit is a control device used primarily by large corporations to study past performance.

9. Gabble's Granola has set up a committee to formally study its current status and capabilities and its future expectations. Gabble's Granola is conducting a marketing audit.

10. A marketing audit should evaluate a company's whole marketing program on a regular basis.

11. A planning manager from corporate headquarters finds that his eastern region has no effective method of allocating resources or evaluating goals and performance of the marketing organization. He suggests that the region should prepare a marketing audit.

12. A marketing audit should be conducted by the person who is most familiar with each of the firm's marketing plans.

13. A marketing audit should help determine if the company's marketing objectives are reasonable.

III. Discussion.

1. Describe briefly the different organizations of a company in different stages.
2. What control methods can a company adopt to evaluate its current position?
3. What are the factors that would influence a company's control?
4. Draw an Organization Structure diagram for the university (or for the School or Department or organization in which you are studying or working). You may not be aware of the complete structure, particularly at the top of the organization, so concentrate on the structure for the School or Department. Given that the total task of an organization has to be split into smaller parts, consider the different ways in which a university could be split.
5. What is marketing audit?
6. Why is it important to make marketing audit?
7. Describe the major process for a marketing audit. How to guarantee the objectiveness of a marketing audit?
8. What are important when preparing a marketing audit report?

Part VI

电子商务与网络营销

E-commerce and Online Marketing

Chapter Seventeen

Basic Knowledge of E-commerce

电子商务简介

◀ **Objectives**　学习目标

When students finish this chapter, they should be able to accomplish the following：

☑ Definitions of e-commerce

☑ History of electronic commerce

☑ Present situation and development trends

☑ Benefits of electronic commerce

☑ Cases

17.1　Definitions of E-commerce　电子商务的定义

Recently, consumers can purchase almost anything from the Internet. If they are interested in personal computers, they can visit the Dell[1] Web site. Dell is the world's leading direct computer systems company. It has more than 26,100 employees working in 33 countries around the globe. Their concept — direct customer contact — has made Dell one of the most successful companies of the 1990s. If someone wants to get a book recently published in a foreign country; it is not necessary to visit the bookstore in that country; they can take a look at the Amason. com. The virtual bookstore keeps most of the latest books published by different presses around the world. By a simple click, the consumer completes the purchase. In addition, many people have used Yahoo Web site already. Yahoo also is electronic commerce. One can go shopping from Yahoo. One can search information from Yahoo. One can send and receive e-mails from Yahoo. Because of electronic commerce, life becomes easy and enjoyable. Electronic business is the general term for buyers and sellers using electronic means to communicate and transact with one another while an electronic market is a sponsored Web site.

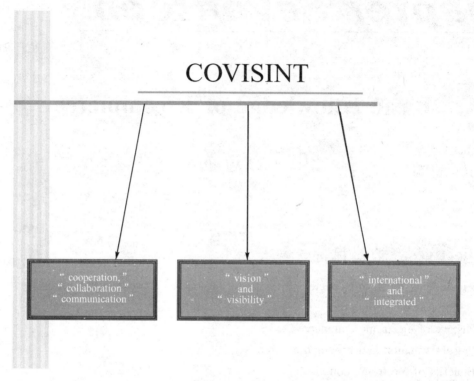

Figure 17-1   Covisint

Besides, leading companies are drawing on powerful new business to business (B2B)[2] applications and network based services to exchange information, interact, and transact with customers and suppliers throughout their value chain. They are redefining existing relationships and creating compelling new ones, reaching new markets, maximizing revenues, and reducing costs. Electronic commerce has become collaborative[3] commerce. For example, according to General Motors purchasing chief Harold Kutner, GM has purchased about $300 million of goods through an automotive industry e-marketplace called "Covisint[4]" (see Figure 17-1). This year the total volume between all the participating automotive members of the exchange should reach approximately $50 billion.

Many people are convinced that the day in which everything from groceries to clothing to movies is bought over the Internet is not far away.

17.1.1　Definitions　定义

As e-commerce is such a new, growing field, a definitive definition has not yet been established.

According to Electronic Commerce Resource Center[5], The electronic commerce is "a broad term describing business activities with associated technical data that are conducted electronically." and "... The goal of Electronic Commerce is to mold the vast network of small businesses, government agencies, large corporations, and independent contractors into a single community with the ability to communicate with one another seamlessly across any computer platform." On the other hand, the American National Telecommunications and Information Administration (NTIA)[6] uses a broader definition that includes the end consumer who participates via electronic shopping. They note that, at its broadest level, electronic commerce can mean any use of electronic technology in any aspect of commercial activity. Thus electronic commerce means the use of a National Information Infrastructure (NII)[7] to perform any of the following functions (quoted from the NTIA Office of the Assistant Secretary, 1995):

- Bring products to market (e. g. Research & Development via telecommunications);
- Match buyers with sellers (e. g. electronic malls, Electronic Funds Transfer);
- Communicate with government in pursuit of commerce (e. g. electronic tax filings);
- Deliver electronic goods (e. g. information).

Although different definitions are given from different points of view, one may safely summarize that e-commerce includes not only the sale and purchase of products and services through the internet, but also the provision of information and the establishment of contact with external supplies and bodies. e-commerce targets customers by collecting and analyzing business information, conducting customer transactions, and maintaining online relationships with customers. It also provides a foundation for launching new businesses, extending the reach of existing companies, and retaining customer relations.

E-commerce can be divided into e-sales, e-communications, e-marketing, e-chain, e-market research and security.

E-sales is a global Web-based solution that helps sales professionals in the field be more productive through online services, applications, and processes. These services make them more efficient, effective, and better able to interact with customers. A personalized portal provides the field with relevant information about customers and their day-to-day business planning, so they can manage their business more effectively. E-sales also improves customer satisfaction by streamlining processes, consolidating multiple systems, and reducing the number of time-consuming tasks.

E-communication, short of electronic communication, has come to signify all forms of communication transmitted by computer over network connections (e. g. Intranet, Ethernet, and Internet). There are three main types of e-communication, each of which is represented by several different forms: e-mail (electronic mail), chat (real time "conversations"), and Newsgroups / Usenet groups. Each of these forms has developed over the years along with the rapidly developing computer technology.

E-marketing is the strategic process of creating, distributing, promoting and pricing goods and services to a target market over the internet or other digital tools such as fax machines, computer modems, telephones and CD-ROMS.

E-chains refers to the emergence of applications facilitating easier capturing, tracking and payment for commodity flows in digital forms. As supply chains grow in volume and complexity, producers and intermediaries are moving away from "paper based" data exchange to digital intermediation. This trend has been present for decades as a result of the rise of more affordable, accessible and integrated computing systems and the rise of the Internet as a virtually costless medium enabling instantaneous collaboration and sharing of data spanning all elements of the supply chain among producers, supply chain intermediaries and end users.

The Internet is providing an efficient channel for faster, cheaper and more reliable collection and transmission of marketing information even in multimedia form. E-market research done on the Net, ranges from client-specific moderated focus groups conducted via chat rooms to interactive surveys placed on Web sites; it can be fulfilled through personal interviews, telephone survey and mail survey.

Comparing to many other e-commerce activities, e-security exchange has a sligntly longer history. In 1961, the US Congress authorized the Security and Exchange Commission (SEC) to conduct a study of fragmentation in the over-the-counter market. The SEC proposed automation as a possible solution and charged the NASD with its implementation. On February 8, 1971, NASDAQ, the word's first e-security exchange company, began trading. When it came to 1994, NASDAQ surpassed the New York Stock Exchange in annual share volume. As the world's largest electronic stock market, NASDAQ is not limited to one central trading location. Rather, trading is executed through NASDAQ's sophisticated computer and telecommunications network, which transmits real-time quote and trade data to more than 1.3 million users in 83 countries. Without size limitations or geographical boundaries, NASDAQ's "open architecture" market structure allows a virtually unlimited number of participants to trade in a company's stock.

Figure 17-2 shows us an e-security exchange process.

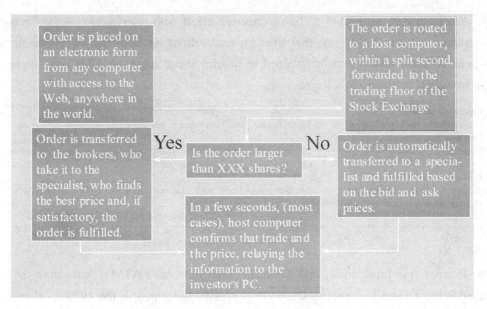

Figure 17-2   E-security Exchange Process

17.1.2   Differences between traditional and Internet marketing
电子商务营销和传统市场营销的区别

A traditional marketing, from a communications standpoint, is primarily a one-way medium. Internet marketing, on the other hand, is a two-way medium. The customer or prospect makes the choice about whether they want to view the material, what parts of the material they want to view, and when they want to view it; furthermore, they have the capability to let the marketers know what they think of it. As such, the content has to be much richer, and more consumer-focused and benefit-focused than marketers might find in traditional marketing materials. The Internet demographic[8] is also somewhat different from the market in the offline world. Internet users are, at this time, primarily male, young or youngish, well educated, and affluent[9]; however, these demographics are rapidly changing, sometimes so fast the surveys can't keep up with the actual changes. The trend is toward more women, seniors, and families joining the Internet community. The current changing demographic is something marketers will need to keep in mind as marketers make the Internet marketing plans.

17.2   History of E-commerce   电子商务简史

Although electronic commerce is often thought of as a recent development, it has actually evolved slowly over a long period of time (see Figure 17-3). The first business telephone transactions date from the late 1800's. The first credit cards were issued midway through the 20th century. American Airlines started its first pioneering effort with reservations — the "request and reply" system — in the 1930s. At that time, a reservations agent would telephone the central control point where inventory was maintained to inquire about space available on a flight, and a response would be returned via teletype.

Communication		
Phase 1	ftp; gopher; news	File transfer; communication to academic and computer enthusiasts
One-way marketing		
Phase 2	Mosaic	Simple World Wide Web vanity pages for market information dissemination; basic customer service
Customer interaction		
Phase 3	World Wide Web	Simple transactions; basic communication to / from company
Organization and process transformation		
Phase 4		Transformation of business processes and new lines of business

Figure   17-3   A Brief E-commerce History

The Internet, electronic mail, and automatic teller machine (ATM)[10] date from the 1960's. One major form of electronic commerce, EDI[11], was implemented in the 1970's. However, the arrival of nearly ubiquitous[12] personal computers and data communications networks in the 1990's has given electronic commerce an enormous boost (see Figure 17-4). Already, it affects such large sectors as communications, finance and retail trade (altogether, about 30 per cent of GDP). It holds promise in areas such as education, health and government. The largest effects may be associated not with many of the impacts that command the most attention (e. g. customized products, the elimination of middlemen) but with less visible, potentially more pervasive effects on routine business activities (e. g. ordering office supplies, paying bills, and estimating demand), that is, on the way businesses interact.

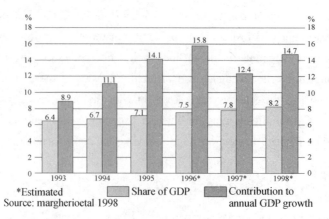

Figure 17-4   US ICT Industry Shares of GDP & Contribution to Growth Percentage

17.3   Present Situation and Development Trends
目前的状况和发展趋势

17.3.1   Present situation   现状

Today's on-line customer tends to respond positively to messages aimed at providing information and negatively to messages aimed at having too much clutter. A consulting firm called Euromonitor noted that the global shopping market was approximately $ 166 billion in 1994. Electronic shopping, including CD-ROMS, accounted for $ 300 million in sales. In 1999, according to the announcement from CommerceNet and Nielsen Media Research, the number of Internet users in North America reached 92 million — 55 million of whom shop online. Women also contribute significantly to the growth in electronic commerce. In 1995, the total volume of online marketing was about US $200 million. When it came to 1998, the volume was about US $5 billion. By 1995, 20% of all Internet users had already used credit cards to purchase something and almost two thirds planned to in the future. About 7% of Internet server operators had sold products or services over the Internet and one third plan to in the future.

Generally speaking, the US still takes the lead of the e-commerce both in technology and practices. Another recent survey of medium-sized businesses based in the central US by the Midwest Business Monitor indicates that 30 percent of them now regularly use the Internet for business purposes and that two-thirds are either on-line now or plan to be in the future. So both the demand for electronic commerce and the supply of electronic commerce are building rapidly.

17.3.2   E-commerce in China   电子商务在中国

The Chinese government pays great attention to the digital commerce development. The government tries its best to encourage the infrastructure construction. The number of the Internet users has risen since in 1980s. Till 2001, there are 26,500,000 total Internet users in China. Among them, 4,540,000 use leased line[13] connections, 17,930,000 are dial-up users[14] and 4,030,000 use both. Besides computer users, there are 1,070,000 people who use other equipment (e. g. mobile terminals and information electrical appliance). In the 1990s, the Chinese government enacted "golden bridge", "gold card" and "golden gate" projects[15]. Since 1994, the China Security Exchange Net[16] covers the whole country. More than 300 stock exchange companies participated in the project. Till 1997, China issued more than 55. 6 million credit cards, and more than 600 millions non-banking IC cards and other debt cards.

However, according to the State Development Planning Commission, among the 15,000 state owned middle or large sized enterprises, only 10% of which basically realized information electronicalization. While in the over 10 million small and middle sized enterprises, only a small number of enterprises started their initial steps to do businesses online. These would greatly holdback the development of e-commerce in China.

17.3.3 Outlook 前景

The potential for growth of electronic commerce is very large and very rapid. Early adopters of electronic commerce will tend to be better educated, higher income consumers. The most rapid adopters are home-based business owners with Internet or on-line service access, according to Data Quest.

The latest research from the Royal Institute of Chartered Surveyors (RICS) predicts that in twenty years time the majority of shopping will be done online. "People are already turning to E-commerce," an RICS spokesman said. "In the near future, an awful lot of routine household goods will be bought on the Internet. Some of the conventional high street chains, like Marks & Spencer and Sainsbury's, are already in trouble. The high street needs to change radically," he said.

Another recent report points out that the value of goods and services sold via B2B electronic markets will reach US $2.7 trillion by year 2004, representing some 27% of the overall B2B market and almost 3% of global sales transactions (Gartner Group, 2000). This growth is slated to occur in the context of a global market for B2B transactions worth US $953 billion, growing to about US $7.29 trillion by 2004 (Gartner Group, 2000). With more corporate procurement completed online every month, the number of virtual marketplaces in the United States has soared from 300 in June 1999 to more than 1000 in 2000 (Girishankar, 2000). It is clear that by offering lower prices and a wider range of suppliers, electronic markets are changing the traditional way of commerce and marketing. Sales through direct and on-line marketing channels have been growing rapidly. In fact, Internet traffic is now doubling every 100 days and it is estimated that electronic commerce will exceed $300 billions by the year 2002.

17.4   Benefits of E-commerce   电子商务的优点

E-commerce provides a widely adopted and popularly embraced technology platform that is making the business management trends of the 90's possible to implement. While the trends started in the late 80's, they are now being realized and transformed by this enabling technology.

The major benefits that the new electronic commerce provides are:

- elimination of errors;
- improved customer service;
- rapid turnaround times;
- elimination of paper documents and printed publications;
- reduced cost;
- increased competition among sellers;
- increased knowledge among consumers;
- reduced need for inventories.

As a result, many well-known corporations are proponents and developers of electronic commerce technology. For example, Wal-Mart now makes over 90 percent of its purchases from suppliers electronically. Both Ford and General Motors require their suppliers to handle all ordering transactions electronically through EDI. IBM operates a large Value-Added Network (VAN) called Advantis that supports EDI and other forms of electronic commerce. Both UPS and FedEx allow customers to track the progress of their shipments via the Internet. Mastercard, VISA, Microsoft, and Netscape Communications are all involved in the development of secure Internet electronic commerce for the World Wide Web.

One reason so many companies and government agencies are interested in the development of extensive electronic commerce is because of its potential to shift or eliminate costs, for example, from the purchaser to the vendor or from the seller to the buyer. When a vendor uses EDI, the purchaser lowers its costs of procurement by avoiding such expenses as answering phones, cutting checks, and postage. And when a consumer conducts a transaction using secure Internet electronic commerce, he / she assumes the cost of the infrastructure needed to conduct the transaction (e. g. a personal computer, a modem, Internet access, etc.). Another reason that electronic commerce is gaining momentum so quickly is that it facilitates the re-engineering of business processes to make them simpler, more efficient, and less costly.

Table 17-1 shows us e-commerce impact on various distribution costs.

Table 17-1   E-commerce Impacts on Various Distribution Costs (dollar)

	Airline Tickets	Banking	Bill Payment	Term Life Insurance Policy	Software Distribution
Traditional system	80	1.08	2.22 – 3.32	400 – 700	15
Telephone-based system		0.54			5
Internet-based system	10	0.13	0.65 – 1.10	200 – 350	0.2 – 0.5
Saving (%)	87	89	71 – 67	50	97 – 99

☞ Cases

Case 1.   The power of search engines（www. signpost. co. uk）

Signpost is one of the leading "premier" UK hotel guides, well respected by business travelers and the public in general. Its printed hotel guide is in wide circulation and the Signpost logo is sought after by upmarket hotels across the UK.

The company now facing a big problem. Its Web site was only being seen by a handful of visitors each month and as more and more people were switching from printed guides to the Internet and his business was suffering quite badly.

A specified analysis identified that the company relied heavily on a database system that was invisible to search engines; the company was advised to redesign of the site removing the misapplied database system.

The entire site was rebuilt as a series of search engine friendly static pages, linked together with a user-friendly navigation system. The company is thus able to be listed top 10 hotels on major engines across a wide range of competitive keyword phrases（most in the number 1 spot）.

Case 2.   Sohu. com in China（http：//www. sohu. com/）

SOHU. COM（NASDAQ：SOHU）http：//www. sohu. com, one of the top three Chinese search engine in China was founded by Chairman and CEO Zhang Zhaoyang in 1996 as Internet Technologies China. It launched Sohu. com in 1998 and changed its name the next year. Zhang owns about 26% of the company. The com is China's premier online brand and indispensable to the daily life of millions of Chinese who use the portal for their e-mail, SMS messaging, news, search, browsing and shopping, in the office, at home or on the road. The Web site's massive use base and strong brand presence in China make SOHU. COM the platform of choice for corporate clients to promote their business. With over 50 million registered users at the end of September 2002, SOHU has the largest online user base in China. It is a household name among the 300 million people living in urban centers. SOHU, with its exclusive focus on the China market, is operating in a high-growth industry under compelling market conditions. The Chinese Ministry of Information Industry（MII）predicts that the Internet sector will grow to 200 million users by 2005. China's economic growth is expected to remain robust in coming years as the country is opening up further under the terms of WTO membership and preparations intensify for the 2008 Beijing Olympics.

Case 3.   Amazon. com（http：//www. amazon. com/）

Amazon. com opened its virtual doors in July 1995 with a mission to use the Internet to transform book buying into the fastest, easiest, and most enjoyable shopping experience possible. It still maintains its founding commitment to customer satisfaction and the delivery of an educational and inspiring shopping experience with its customer base and product offerings grown in its early days. Today, Amazon.com is the place to find and discover anything a customer wants to buy online. Millions of people in more than 220 countries have made the company their leading online shopping site. It offers various products including free electronic greeting cards, online auctions, and millions of books, CDs, videos, DVDs, toys and games, electronics, kitchenware, computers and more. Along with its extensive catalog of products, it also offers a wide variety of other shopping services and partnership opportunities. The amazon.com family of Web sites also includes Internet Movie Database (www.imdb.com), the Web's comprehensive and authoritative source of information on more than 250,000 movies and entertainment programs and 1 million cast and crew members dating from 1891 to 2005.

Case 4.   Covisint.com (http://www.covisint.com/)

On February 25, 2000, DaimlerChrysler, Ford Motor Company and General Motors jointly announced plans to combine efforts and form a single global business-to-business supplier exchange. Each company brought together its individual E-business initiatives to avoid the burdens suppliers would endure if asked to interact with redundant proprietary systems.

The goal was integration and collaboration, promising lower cost, easier business practices and a marked increase in efficiencies for the entire industry. This new organization was temporarily named NewCo. In May, 2000, "NewCo" becomes Covisint. On January 1, 2001 in the US and in July, 2001, in Europe, Asia-Pacific and Latin America, it officially began providing services and the technology services, whose business-to-business applications and communication services connect the global automotive industry. It provides its customers with a common connection to their suppliers and customers based on common business processes.

Covisint works with manufacturers, suppliers and industry trade groups worldwide to define and implement effective common processes for the industry. Once connected through Covisint, the customers are able to reduce costs, increase efficiency, enhance quality and improve time to market.

Covisint was formed by DaimlerChrysler, Ford, General Motors and Renault-Nissan. Since its inception, PSA Peugeot Citroen has also joined the initiative. It has headquarters in Southfield, Michigan, and offices in Amsterdam, Tokyo, Frankfurt, Paris and Brazil.

The company buy $300 billion in goods and services every year, and their suppliers make $700 billion to $800 billion in purchases a year.

📓 Key Terms

e-commerce 电子商务

e-sales 电子销售

e-communications 电子沟通

e-marketing 网络营销

e-chain 电子供应链

e-market research 网上调查

e-security exchange 电子证券交易

📄 Notes

1. Dell 戴尔电脑公司

2. business to business（B2B） 企业对企业电子商务

3. collaborative *a.* 合作的

4. Covisint 汽车零件交易网站，由福特、通用和克莱斯勒联合发起组建的汽车行业联合采购网站。

5. Electronic Commerce Resource Center 电子商务资源中心

6. National Telecommunications and Information Administration（NTIA） （美国）国家电信与信息署

7. National Information Infrastructure（NII） 国家信息架构

8. demographic *a.* 人口统计学的

9. affluent *a.* 富裕的

10. automatic teller machine（ATM） 自动柜员机

11. EDI（Electronic Data Interchange） 电子数据交换，无纸贸易

12. ubiquitous *a.* 普遍存在的

13. leased line 租用线，专线

14. dial-up user 拨号上网用户

15. "golden bridge", "gold card" and "golden gate" projects 金桥、金卡、金门工程

16. China Security Exchange Net 中国证券交易网

✍ Exercises

I. Multiple choices.

1. Electronic _____ is the general term for buyers and sellers using electronic means to communicate and transact with one another while an electronic _____ is a sponsored

Web site.

   A. business; communication   B. marketing; communication

   C. business; markets   D. marketing; data interchange

2. Sales through direct and on-line marketing channels have been growing rapidly. In fact, Internet traffic is now doubling every _____ and it is estimated that electronic commerce will exceed _____ by the year 2002.

   A. 100 days; $100 billion   B. 100 days; $300 billion

   C. 2 years; $300 billion   D. 12 months; $100 billion

3. Today's on-line customer tends to respond positively to messages aimed at _____ and negatively to messages aimed at _____.

   A. providing information; having too much clutter

   B. only selling; providing information

   C. home banking; insurance sales

   D. providing information; only selling

4. A free e-commerce news site provides a variety of information except _____.

   A. free newsfeeds   B. free newsletter   C. open forum   D. free product

5. The major benefits that the new electronic commerce provides are _____.

   A. elimination of errors   B. rapid turnaround times

   C. reduced cost   D. increased knowledge among consumers

   E. all of the above

II. True or false.

1. E-marketing is a generic term used to describe all marketing channels facilitated by the Web.

2. One reason so many companies and government agencies are interested in the development of extensive electronic commerce is because of its potential to shift or eliminate costs.

3. Electronic commerce has become collaborative commerce.

4. China still takes the lead of the e-commerce both in technology and practices.

5. In the 1990s, the Chinese government enacted "golden bridge", "gold card" and "golden gate" projects to promote e-commerce.

6. Traditional marketing, from a communications standpoint, is primarily a one-way medium.

III. Discussion.

1. What are the major benefits of e-commerce?

2. What are the differences between traditional and online marketing?

3. How do you think about the future of Chinese e-commerce?

4. Web site questions

There is a free e-commerce news site that provides a variety of updated articles and resources for people interested in this topic. First, this site offers three key resources: (1) Free Newsfeeds (this provides free breaking news headlines on e-commerce topics by offering Web masters a means to automatically update e-commerce content on their Web sites), (2) Open Forums (this two-way open community forum is a place where one can exchange views on issues of interest, as one can join discussions on a variety of technological and news articles dealing with e-commerce), and (3) Free Newsletters (one can sign up for a variety of free newsletters dealing with technological and e-commerce topics, such as e-commerce Times Weekly Newsletter and Daily Cybercrime and Security Report). Second, the site offers 12 sections with articles on different topics: (1) Front Page, (2) More News, (3) Special Reports, (4) Industry Guide, (5) Small Business, (6) B2B, (7) I-marketing, (8) Opinion, (9) Enterprise, (10) CRM, (11) Stock Index, and (12) Cybercrime. Finally, the site allows one to look at NewsFactor Sites by Topic and highlights other possible news sites.

1) One of the things that makes e-commerce such a useful Web site is that several of its key sections are updated each day. Which sections are these?

2) What type(s) of articles is / are found in the Enterprise section versus the other sections? What about the Cybercrime section?

3) What stocks are tracked in the Stock Index and what else is discussed in this section?

4) What articles does the CRM section cover and how does this vary from the other sections, such as I-Marketing?

5) What is covered in the Industry Guide section?

6) What are the differences between the Front Page, More News, Opinion, and Special Reports sections?

Chapter Eighteen

E-commerce Marketing

电子商务营销

📢 **Objectives** 学习目标

When students finish this chapter, they should be able to accomplish the following:

- ☑ Major categories of electronic commerce
- ☑ E-marketing strategies
- ☑ Key barriers to electronic commerce case
- ☑ Cases

18.1 Major Categories of E-commerce 电子商务的主要类型

It is useful to think of two main types of electronic commerce — that conducted between two organizations (e. g. client and vendor transactions) and that conducted between an organization and its final customers (e. g. consumer to business transactions). The first is the province[1] of one type of electronic commerce, Electronic Data Interchange or EDI. Business to consumer transactions are going to be mainly facilitated over the Internet's World Wide Web (WWW) and through emerging technologies such as e-cash. Although EDI is the most established form of EC at this time, consumer-oriented electronic commerce has far more potential for growth because of the size of the market it can serve.

Providing information in electronic form on-line or in some other retrievable fashion (e. g. through fax-back technology) is an integral part of electronic commerce.

18.1.1 Business-to-business electronic commerce 企业对企业电子商务

The Internet can connect all businesses to each other, regardless of their location or position in the supply chain. This ability presents a huge threat to traditional intermediaries like wholesalers and brokers. Internet connections facilitate businesses' ability to bargain directly with a range of suppliers — thereby eliminating the need for such intermediaries.

There are, however, tremendous opportunities as well as threats for companies regardless of their position in the supply chain, which include:

1. Providing information

McKesson is shifting from its position as a drug distribution business to a new position of value added provider in the health care industry. Its product is information, not drugs. By exploiting its massive database of information on sales and units for pharmacies, that information package is provided to improve the financial performance of pharmacies.

2. Purchasing and selling

General Electric's Trading Process Network allows suppliers to download GE's request for proposals, view part specification diagrams, and communicate with General Electric to complete the transaction. GE is expanding this network to help other companies buy and sell from each other and is investigating a transaction fee business model.

3. Moving to an Internet platform

Banks, like Bank of America and Wells Fargo, are conducting trials to investigate whether EDI functions for business-to-business transactions can be moved to the lower cost Internet platform.

4. Supplying extra net services

Companies with established Intranet[2] systems are beginning to provide subsets of their intranets to strategic customers, partners, or trading partners — such as General Electric's Trading Process Network. Federal Express is leveraging its existing infrastructure for rapid package delivery to provide web-based complete order fulfillment services to businesses.

Business-to-business electronic commerce dominates the total value of E-commerce activity, accounting for about 80 per cent at present. This share is probably conservative, as three firms — General Electric, CSX and NEC — report conducting over US$20 billion in business-to-business electronic commerce. This exceeds all the business-to-consumer sales estimates for 1995 – 1997 by a large margin as well as most estimated e-commerce totals.[3] Because the economic factors affecting the adoption of e-commerce between businesses are much different from those affecting business-to-consumer e-commerce, business-to-business e-commerce is likely to maintain or enlarge its advantage for the foreseeable future.

EDI（Electronic Data Interchange）— Critical Tools of B2B E-commerce

EDI is a fast and dependable way to exchange business documents using computer-to-computer communication between different companies. Literally, EDI are the standards that convert the format of a transmitted document into the format of a receiver's computer.

Benefits of EDI include：

- Reduced paper-based systems；
- Improved problem resolution；
- Improved customer service.

Historically, EDI has been used to improve only discrete[4] processes such as automating the accounts payable function or the funds transfer process. The new focus for EDI, in electronic commerce, is bridging the external and internal business processes which will enable companies to improve their productivity on a scale never seen before. Companies can now enter orders, purchase, do accounts payable, transfer funds, link to suppliers, distributors, customers, banks, and transportation.

Using the Internet as an EDI communication channel could reduce the cost of setting up an EDI relationship and increase the possible trading partners because it is a low cost network and so many companies are already hooked up to the Internet.

18.1.2   Business-to-consumer electronic commerce   企业对用户电子商务

Although business-to-business electronic commerce represents the bulk of all electronic commerce, most attention and speculation about e-commerce has focused on the business-to-consumer segment. With household transactions typically accounting for over half of all domestic final demand, this is not surprising. Moreover, as business PCs and networks are saturated, it is natural for the focus of attention to turn to the household.

Companies are rushing to take advantage of this market. The kinds of business-to-consumer services delivered over the Internet are shifting：

1. One-way marketing

Corporate Web sites are still prominent distribution mechanisms for corporate brochures, the push, one-way marketing strategy.

2. Purchasing over the Web

Availability of secure Web transactions is enabling companies to allow consumers to purchase products directly over the Web. Electronic catalogs and virtual malls are becoming commonplace.

3. Relationship marketing[5]

The most prominent of these new paradigms is that of relationship marketing. Because consumer actions can be tracked on the Web, companies are experimenting with this commerce methodology as a tool for market research and relationship marketing:

- Consumer survey forms on the Web;
- Using Web-tracking and other technology to make inferences about consumer buying profiles;
- Customizing products and services;
- Achieving customer satisfaction and building long-term relationships.

An early example of a company that has leveraged the power of Internet interactivity to revolutionize customer relationships is Firefly. Firefly has created its products through Web-tracking technology. What would have been a conventional audio and video distribution company is now literally creating a custom product[6] for each of its customers, based on the customer's profile[7] and buying behavior[8].

The popular press has largely focused on e-commerce merchants that sell tangible products (e. g. books, wine, flowers, computers). However, with the possible exception of computers, the largest segments involve intangibles (e. g. entertainment, software). This confirms the experience of France Telecom's Minitel service, which has engaged in electronic commerce over a closed network for well over a decade and where the main beneficiaries have been intangibles (OECD, 1998). This makes intuitive sense: when the product cannot be physically examined, traditional commerce has no advantage over the convenience of electronic commerce.[9]

The largest segment of business-to-consumer e-commerce involves intangible products that can be delivered directly to the consumer's computer over the network. It is composed of five broad categories: entertainment, travel, newspapers / magazines, financial services, and e-mail.

Entertainment, which includes adult entertainment, online games, music and video, is the largest category of products sold to consumers. Forrester Research estimates that adult entertainment alone accounted for 10 per cent of all 1996 business-to-consumer e-commerce ($50 million) and would triple to $137 million in 1997, just behind computer products and travel. Firms that track visits to Web pages and analyze the keywords typed into search engines confirm the popularity of adult material. One respected source of information on Web-use reports that while adult sites account for 2 to 3 per cent of the 200,000 commercial Web sites, they account for 10 to 20 per cent of all searches by search engines.

"Pay-for-play" online games and online distribution of music each generated revenues of roughly $50 million in 1996 – 1997 (http://www. forrester. com, 12 April 1997). Online gambling is an entertainment area with large, but poorly understood activity. Most of this activity is on sites located in off-shore havens such as Grenada, home of Sports International. According to one estimate, over $30 billion worth of gambling is conducted on line (Schwartz, 1995). If so, gambling would be the largest single electronic commerce activity. While this estimate seems high, one Internet gambling firm, Interactive Gambling and Communications Corp., had 1996 revenues of $58 million (Brunker, 1997).

Travel services, particularly airline reservations, are another major category of business-to-consumer e-commerce. A European Commission policy paper on electronic commerce in 1996 credits travel services with over half of all electronic commerce. Jupiter estimates at $276 million in 1996 online revenues for travel (air, hotel, car rental, cruises, vacation packages, as well as advertising on travel-oriented sites). This estimate may be conservative, according to Anderson, (1997) and Faiola and Ginsberg (1998).

Online newspaper: More than 2,700 US newspapers post an edition on line, and 60 per cent of them have a daily print circulation of less than 30,000 (Schavey, 1998). Estimated revenue for this segment is around $20 million, an indication that relatively few newspapers and magazines have begun to charge readers. Many of the early, high-profile entrants have had to significantly modify their strategies because readers balk at paying.

Financial services are an important business-to-consumer category. Because many firms engaged in online activity also provide traditional financial services, revenue estimates are difficult to obtain, but one stock brokerage, E * Trade, reported $148 million in revenues in 1996 from 50,000 active accounts and $2.8 billion in assets. Another, Charles Schwab & Co., performs nearly two-fifths of all of its trades online, has tripled the number of online accounts to 1.3 million in the last two years, and has doubled assets to $92 billion in one year (1997–1998). By one estimate, online trading of stocks accounted for 17 per cent of all retail stock activity in 1997, double the 1996 share.

Banking is also enjoying significant e-commerce activity. A recent Ernst & Young survey of 130 financial services companies in 17 countries found that 13 per cent of the firms were using the Internet for transactions with customers in 1997 and that 60 per cent intended to do so by 1999. Nearly a quarter of the 100 top US banks offer online access to accounts. Europe appears to be significantly ahead of the United States in this area; for example, nearly every major German bank is reportedly already online and Finland has established an extensive network banking system.

While e-mail receives less attention than many of the new e-commerce services appearing on the Internet, it is arguably one of the "killer apps" (an application which users find so useful that it is the reason for going on line and subsequently using other services). Nearly two-thirds of all US businesses with a computer have e-mail. About 15 per cent of the US population has access to e-mail, and as users become more accustomed to the Internet, use of e-mail increases on average to about 25 messages a day. As a share of all messages (e-mail plus mail), e-mail has moved from less than a fifth in 1988 to almost half in 1994.

To date, the main tangible products sold electronically have been electronics (including computers), books, clothing and food / drink. Each currently generates $100 – $200 million worth of business-to-consumer sales. Many of these categories are dominated by traditional retailers that have established electronic commerce operations (Dell in the United States, La Redoute in France, Marks & Spencer in the United Kingdom, and supermarkets in the Netherlands). Behind these broader categories are specialty-item merchants (books, flowers, and music CDs) that add value by providing a wider selection, more information about a product, or convenience. As Wal-Mart's decision to make 80,000 items available online shows, however, a wide variety of products can be sold over the Internet. Even some of the most tangible of all house-hold items (groceries, houses, cars) are now sold electronically. Chrysler estimates that 1 – 2 per cent of all of its sales were done via online services in 1996; and JD Power, a marketing firm specializing in the auto industry, estimates that 16 per cent of people buying a new car or truck in 1997 used the Internet as part of the purchasing process (Margherio et al., 1998).

Drivers / inhibitors for business-to-consumer electronic commerce

Factors influencing growth in business-to-consumer electronic commerce differ significantly from those that affect business-to-business electronic commerce. They are more likely to limit its growth and to hold it to 10-20 per cent of the overall total in the near term. While competition may force businesses to engage in business-to-business e-commerce, the business-to-consumer segment faces barriers such as concerns about security of payment, potentially fraudulent merchants, privacy of personal data, and difficulty and expense in accessing e-commerce merchants. In addition to these legal and psychological barriers, three economic factors will have a large impact on the growth of business-to-consumer electronic commerce: ease and cost of access, convenience, and the appeal of mass customization.

18.1.3 Intra-company e-commerce 企业内部电子商务

As new tools of e-commerce, intra-company e-commerce, such as TCP/IP connectivity and web browsers, has finally enabled the building, sharing and use of information within companies. Intra-company applications of Web-based technology are called intranets. Figure 18-1 gives us a brief idea about the intranet growth in the middle 1990s. Companies are embracing intranets at a phenomenal growth rate because they achieve the following benefits.

- Reducing cost — lowers print-intensive production processes, such as employee hand-books, phone books, and policies and procedure.

- Enhancing communications — effective communication and training of employees using Web browsers builds a sense of belonging and community.

- Distributing software — upgrades and new software can be directly distributed over the Web to employees.

- Sharing intellectual property — provides a platform for sharing expertise and ideas as well as creating and updating content — "Knowledge Webs". This is common in organizations that value their intellectual capital as their competitive advantage.

- Testing products — allows experimentation for applications that will be provided to customers on the external Web.

- 90% of corporations are now evaluating intranet solutions.
- At the beginning of 1996, nearly one out of four Fortune 1000 companies already used an internal Web server.
- Business Research Group predicts that 70 percent of all US corporations will have an Intranet by January of 1997, up from 55 percent in June 1996.
- Forrester predicts that the intranet server business will reach $1 billion by the year 2000. (Filed: 22-Jul-96 Source: Business Research Group, Newton MA)
- Zona Research Inc. predicts that worldwide intranet software sales will increase 16-fold in three years.

Figure 18-1   Intranet Growth in 1990s

18.2   E-marketing Strategies   电子商务营销策略

18.2.1   Principles of e-commerce: "free", "information", and "privacy"
电子商务三原则:"免费"、"信息" 和 "隐私"

We can define the unique culture of the Internet by three words "free", "information", and "privacy". Of course, the Internet has changed dramatically from the days it was the sole playground of grad students and computer geeks, but some of the culture has remained. Marketers need to understand its peculiarities, and then leverage these to land sales.

"Free" is always attractive. And "free is beautiful" is deeply imbedded in the online culture. Many net users still expect something "free" from their net surfing. So when planning a company's Internet strategy, "free" should play an important part in it. Offer something free and the world will beat a path to the door. Better yet, offer many things free, and become a Destination Site. Then sell them something while they pass by.

Information is the second secret weapon to attract large number of visitors. Never underestimate information for business people and serious shoppers are driven by their need for information far more than their desire for games and chat. This means that the site must be information rich. Don't worry about offering too much information; there's no such thing. But one needs to offer the information in digestible chunks and provide a carefully designed navigation system to get your visitors quickly where they want to go. Tell the visitors as much as possible, assure them that what they can get from the Web site would be as much as that they can from a real office. If one fails to do so, one would most probably lose your potential customers and push them to the competitors as well.

Privacy involves the security issue of e-commerce. As e-commerce transfers information electronically, the security of the information becomes a very important part to the whole transaction. Besides, how a . com company will guarantee the confidentiality of the information from its customer needs improvement. Privacy is now the toughest public policy issue confronting the industry. Critics worry that marketers may know too much about the customers' lives, and that they may use this knowledge to take unfair advantage of consumers.

18.2.2　Direct marketing　直接营销

Direct Marketing can be defined as "communications where data are used systematically to achieve quantifiable marketing objectives and where direct contact is made, or invited, between a company and its existing and prospective customers". It is the targeting of customers in an individual manner where subtle differences in behavior could be used to develop a uniquely tailored customer relationship. The traditional mass-marketing, however, treats all customers within a segment alike, e. g. a standard advertising campaign is produced to address everyone. The need for this change in focus has arisen because consumers are thought to be more discerning, thoughtful, and individualistic.

Direct marketing is based on developing an on-going relationship with customers in order to maximize their loyalty, value and, consequently, profitability over time. In the first instance, it addresses what is relevant and timely to the customer or potential customer and develops ongoing direct communication channels with that individual as their relationship with the organization grows.

Direct marketing is not particularly new; in fact, it has its origins in the mail-order industry. It can use a large number of channels for reaching prospects and customers. These include face-to-face selling, direct-mail marketing, catalog marketing, telemarketing, TV, and others. In 1990s, electronic communication and advertising media are showing rapid growth indeed. The creation of the "information superhighway" promises to e-commerce. Some market research company has predicted a brilliant future of direct marketing in e-commerce:

(1) Faster change of prices. E-commerce can customize the price for many services.

(2) Disintermediation. electronic shopping will change the role of place in the marketing and

result in the decline of intermediaries between customers and manufactures.

（3）Customerization. Customers will have instant access to information about competitive products.

It can cost up to 5 times as much to obtain a new customer as keeping an existing one. New customers will, however, always be needed to replace lapsed ones. The process to achieve this goal is called customer acquisition. In developing a customer-acquisition campaign, a seven stage process can be defined including: objective setting; segmentation and profiling; targeting; media selection; communication of the offer; fulfillment; and response analysis.

As soon as customers have been acquired, their details and purchase behavior will have to be recorded by means of a database. This can then be used to attain additional customers and to build relationships with current customers. A number of issues need to be addressed before the database is implemented. Then the appropriate database can be established. Once the database has been developed the information can be segmented and developed to provide a uniquely tailored service for each identified segment. It is possible to draw a distinction between four groups of customers each possessing their own response characteristics and this helps define their attractiveness, with the help of database.

A well established database and the good relationship between customers and marketers enable e-commerce's booming in 1990s and is still growing in a very high speed.

18.2.3   Basic marketing elements of e-commerce   电子商务营销要点

1. Build a Web site

To design a Web site, companies will need to answer a number of questions about how and why consumers will use their sites, which would make them identify the target customers of their companies and the market segments. It also helps companies to decide the online marketing models and contents these Web sites can afford, and the structure of the contents as well. Of course, the most important part is to make the customers identify the product / service the organizations can provide and pay appropriate attention to. Marketers will also need to acquire a number of design tools to build a consumer-ready site.

2. Provide appropriate access to the Web sites

Currently, the market for e-commerce among consumers is restricted to those with knowledge of and access to PCs. There are a number of other potential on-ramps to Internet-based commerce for home-based applications, including Televisions. Gaming systems have already been adopted by consumers as an interactive medium for entertainment. However, sales of the highly touted WebTV have been disappointing to date. Video as well as audio telecommunications is required to make the telephone a viable on-ramp to e-commerce. However, the telephone is a device almost every consumer has and uses for commerce. Telcos are aggressively building and providing higher bandwidth capabilities. Pagers and cell phones are rapidly being adopted as wireless communication devices.

3. Guarantee secure, convenient and flexible payment / transaction systems

Financial institutions have been using electronic funds transfer to debit or credit accounts for more than 20 years. The emerging e-commerce industry demands new payment systems that complete the entire business and financial transaction over the Internet.

Some of the new systems include:

(1) Electronic cash. Based on "digital signature" cryptography, banks can enable customers to decode currency encoded with the bank's key. Customers need to set up an account and maintain enough balance in the account to back purchases.

(2) Electronic checks. Digital equivalent of the paper check process, including a signature (computed number that authenticates the check's owner), endorsement by payee, and payment.

(3) Smart cards[10]. Handle multiple functions, such as storage off special marketing awards, access to multiple financial accounts, and other personal shopping and payment preferences.

(4) Promoting.

Online promotions include: purchase demo / receive samples; hear testimonials from satisfied customers; survey the consumer about the product / packaging / pricing or the Web site itself; start regular communications with the consumer via e-mail; focus on the benefits of the product; and introduce a loyalty program that rewards repeat purchases.

18.3　Key Barriers to E-commerce　电子商务的主要障碍

Although Electronic commerce develops very fast in the recent decade, there are, however, quite a few barriers to its further developments. Here listed below are some major barriers to this new marketing field.

1. Lack of standards

Some standards necessary for electronic commerce to emerge and thrive have not yet gelled. The recent agreement among major electronic commerce players to develop SET should speed development.

2. Lack of interoperability

If electronic commerce systems cannot "talk to each other", they automatically become less useful. This has been a problem in the development of EBT systems.

3. Lack of security

At present, lack of security is perhaps the key concern slowing the development of electronic commerce. However, rapid developments in secure transactions technology, certification, and encryption are making this concern less important.

4. Potential for fraud and crime

The potential for fraud and crime in electronic commerce is large, but thought to be no larger than the potential with traditional commerce. For instance, the percentage of credit card numbers stolen off the Internet (even before the deployment of SET) is no larger than that stolen in telephone transactions or in-store transactions.

5. High up-front costs[11]

The costs of developing and implementing electronic commerce systems can be large. Costs include hardware, software, system development, systems maintenance, and communications and these costs occur at both ends of an electronic commerce transaction. However, the costs saved and other benefits realized through the use electronic commerce should pay back the up-front costs.

6. Lack of legal and regulatory systems

The technologies of electronic commerce are evolving much more quickly than the social framework needed to support them. A good example is in the area of digital signatures. Few states have laws that make digital signatures legally binding. Of course, new developments like e-cash raise all sorts of opportunities for people to circumvent national currency systems and taxation systems.

7. Lack of uniform access

Businesses and individuals that do not have access to computers or data communications networks like the Internet will have limited ability to use electronic commerce or electronic government. Traditional channels of distribution will have to exist beside electronic channels, at least for the foreseeable future.

Cases

Case 1. Why liquor marketers like the Web

LEAD STORY — DATELINE: Advertising Age Online, September 4, 2001.

Liquor advertising is tricky these days, with most television networks closed to spirits advertising. That is why many of these brands are turning to the Internet to do some brand building. Some of these sites offer games and chat rooms, while others are banner ad-heavy and offer lots of brand history and recipes. Just in the past year and a half, many liquor companies have turned to the Web in a big way for their marketing and advertising efforts. There have been people hired just to handle Web strategy for these brands. The sites are giving these brands the chance to capture visitors and get them to enter sweepstakes and other loyalty-building games.

Another tactic used in this strategy is to send consumers to the site by putting the Web address on the packaging. This helps to let consumers know that there is a site out there for their favorite hard liquor. Once they go there and realize that they're being entertained, at the same time, they may be unaware that they are being educated on a brand. There is also the advantage that the Web is "world wide" and advertisers get a lot of bang for the buck by reaching consumers that are in all corners of the world where their product may be exported.

Case 2.   The future of online ads

LEAD STORY — DATELINE: E-commerce Times, September 7, 2001.

Online ads are starting to look increasingly like television ads. Additionally, online ads have the advantage of measurability over television advertising. There are three issues though that are impeding the widespread use of online ads. First, only two of the top twenty advertisers spend more than one percent of their budgets online (Walt Disney and Microsoft which both have online properties). The majority of firms buy online ads out of their direct mail budget, which is the smallest part of the media plan typically. If firms would instead utilize the television budget, there would be a lot more potential for online ads. A second issue is the spread of broadband. While the lack of broadband access in many homes limits the use of streaming multimedia advertising, broadband access is increasing at the rate of 440,000 new US households a month. In the meantime, the Interactive Advertising Bureau (IAB) has issued guidelines for using streaming media ads, such as design them with stop buttons so consumers can halt them if needed. The final issue is the need to reduce the clutter of online ads and instead determine means in which online advertisers can get consumers' attention and build a strong impression on consumers. For example, several firms have effectively developed opt-in games that both increase awareness and help them develop a customer e-mail list for future one-to-one contact. Thus, while the majority of online users understand the need for online ads, marketers need to use them more effectively to enhance their future use.

Key Terms

business-to-business electronic commerce　企业对企业电子商务

business-to-consumer electronic commerce　企业对用户电子商务

e-cash　电子货币

electronic check　电子支票

intangible products　无形产品

intra-company e-commerce　公司局域网电子商务

net neighborhood　网上邻居

network banking system　网络银行系统

online ads　在线广告

stock brokerage　证券经纪业

streaming multimedia advertising　流媒体广告

tangible product　有形产品

testing product　试销产品

Data Communication Network　数据通信网络

Notes

1. province　*n.*　范围

2. Intranet　*n.*　企业内部互联网

3. This exceeds all the business-to-consumer sales estimates for 1995 – 1997 by a large margin as well as most estimated E-commerce totals.　这远远超出了对 1995—1997 年所有的 B2C 营业额，同时也是所有电子商务总额的预计。

4. discrete　*a.*　分散的

5. relationship marketing　关系营销

6. custom product　定制产品

7. customer's profile　消费者特征

8. buying behavior　购买行为

9. … when the product cannot be physically examined, traditional commerce has no advantage over the convenience of electronic commerce.　当不能对产品进行实际检测时，传统的商业无法匹敌电子商务带来的便利。

10. smart card　智能卡

11. up-front cost　前期成本

✍ Exercises

I. Multiple choices.

1. Mass marketing is concerned with _____ while one-to-one marketing is more concerned with _____.

   A. the individual customer; the average customer

   B. two-way messages; one-way messages

   C. economies of scale; economies of scope

   D. customer retention; customer attraction

2. The original form of direct marketing is _____.

   A. face-to-face selling   B. direct mail   C. kiosk marketing   D. catalog marketing

3. Today's on-line customer tends to respond positively to messages aimed at _____ and negatively to messages aimed at _____.

   A. providing information; having too much clutter

   B. only selling; providing information

   C. home banking; insurance sales

   D. providing information; only selling

4. _____ connect a company with its suppliers and distributors.

   A. Intranets　　　　　　B. Internets　　　　　　C. Gorenets　　　　　　D. Extranets

5. If the GAP takes laser measurements of its customers, enters the data into a database, and then produces custom fit jeans for the customer upon demand, the GAP is most likely using which of the following techniques?

   A. Digitalization.　　　　　　　　　　B. Disintermediation.

   C. Customization.　　　　　　　　　　D. Market Segmentation.

6. If a retailer or wholesaler has been cut out of the distribution process because suppliers or consumers have chosen to use new e-commerce alternatives, then a process of _____ has just taken place.

   A. disintermediation　　　　　　　　　B. customization

   C. customerization　　　　　　　　　　D. product differentiation

7. E-markets are "_____," rather than physical "marketplaces."

   A. Bazaars　　　　　B. Click-and-brick　　　　C. Marketspaces　　　　D. Brick-and-mortar

8. Internet buying benefits final buyers and business buyers in many ways. Which of the following would be the BEST example of one of these buyer benefits?

   A. E-marketing offers greater flexibility.

   B. Increases speed and efficiency of ordering.

C. Product access and selection.

    D. The Internet is a global medium.

9. Which of the following would NOT be a benefit to a seller for participating in e-commerce and / or using the Internet to complete transactions?

    A. It is easy and private.

    B. Customer relationship building.

    C. Reducing costs and increasing speed and efficiency.

    D. The Internet is truly a global medium.

10. According to information provided by a recent PRIZM report, Americans with the greatest access to the Internet are those that would be considered to be _____.

    A. innovative blue-collar workers

    B. early adopting, upscale Americans

    C. late majority, middle-income Americans

    D. early majority, lower-to middle-income Americans with time on their hands

11. Rather than simply completing transactions, _____ gives sellers greater control over product presentation and allows them to build deeper relationships with buyers and sellers by providing value-added services.

    A. intranet marketing   B. product marketing   C. mass marketing   D. direct marketing

12. All of the following would be considered to be sources of e-commerce revenue EXCEPT _____.

    A. licensing, patents, and trademark income

    B. advertising income

    C. membership and subscription income

    D. transaction commissions and fees

13. _____ sites typically offer a rich variety of information and other features in an effort to answer customer questions, build closer customer relationships, and generate excitement about the company.

    A. Corporate Web   B. Marketing Web   C. Sales Web   D. Advertising Web

II. True or false.

1. Direct marketing involves one-way connections aimed at consumers.

2. Direct marketing is convenient, easy, and private.

3. Direct marketing is poor in building customer relationships.

4. Internet marketing has the advantage of reducing costs.

5. Direct marketing sales have grown at about 4% annually.

6. A customer mailing list and a customer database are the same.

7. Companies use their databases to identify prospects.

8. Telemarketing is the major direct marketing communication tool.

9. Direct mail marketing involves only selling catalogs to customers.

10. Three new forms of direct mail are fax, e-mail, and voice mail.

III. Discussion.

1. What are the features of direct marketing?

2. What are the major catalogs of e-commerce?

3. What are the basic elements of e-commerce? Which do you think is the most important element from the point of a customer?

4. What are the key barriers to the development of e-commerce?

5. How are E-commerce marketing different from traditional marketing?

6. Web question.

　　Amazon was the first to utilize the Internet as a medium of selling books, followed by Barnes & Noble in 1997. Your task is to examine the above sites very carefully focusing on 1) searches for the same common and specialized books, 2) analyses of service depth and quality and 3) charges for books and deliveries. Finally, on the basis of your analysis you should recommend to a friend or relative one or both of the sources to buy books. Connect to each site and spend at least 5 – 10 minutes trying to understand the "personality" of each competitor as it might be revealed through its positioning statement and its overall professionalism. Usually companies use the "About us" section to provide this kind of information. What is the way each company "explains" its mission and itself? What does this statement tell you about how marketing-or consumer-oriented each company is?

　　Now let's choose a book in both of these sites by the author's name. What is your perception of each site? How about if you misspell the author's last name? Which one has the capability to steer you into the right direction?

　　Assume you were not very sure about what this particular book was all about. What support services does each site provide to help you evaluate the book?

　　Now let's compare what the details of pricing and shipping the book in terms of timing and charges are.

　　Lastly, let's compare the variety of other product / services both sites offer. What is the significance of variety to you as a potential consumer? Is it good or bad?

Appendix A

Relevant Web Links

相关网站链接

Chapter One   International Marketing Briefing

☞ http://www. marketingpower. com — a website offers latest information about international marketing, both theory and practice

☞ http://www. consumerpsychologist. com — about consumer and marketing

☞ http://www. glreach. com/ — a website about international marketing study, including papers and news

☞ http://www. themanagementor. com/EnlightenmentorAreas/mrkt/Bps/PLC. htm — about PLC marketing strategy

☞ http://eastlib. east. asu. edu/Thesaurus/Topics/00000118. htm — about marketing in China

☞ http://www. asiamarketresearch. com/china/news. php — about marketing in China and news

☞ http://www. econ. iastate. edu/classes/econ355/choi/mul. htm — about MNCs, give you a general idea about the company

Chapter Two   Three Basic Theories of International Trade

☞ http://www. utdallas. edu/ ~ harpham/adam. htm — about Adam Smith and study on him and his theory

☞ http://www. econlib. org/library/Smith/smWN. html — about the famous book *Wealth of Nations*

☞ http://www. themanagementor. com/EnlightenmentorAreas/mrkt/Bps/PLC. htm — about PLC marketing strategy

☞ http://www. mises. org/tradcycl. asp — a website about the theory of trade cycle in Australia.

Brief introductions to some latest books and recommended books

☞ http://www. bized. ac. uk/virtual/economy/library/glossary/ — a very good glossary offered by Biz/ed, a business and economics service for students, teachers and lecturer

☞ http://www. pharmacoepi. de/EPRG-Questionnaire/questionnaire. html — an example questionnaires of EPRG scheme for a company.

Chapter Three   The Role of Economy

☞ http://www. swlearning. com/pdfs/chapter/ — reviewing world economic trends and local market conditions confronting global traders today and tomorrow

☞ http://www. mhhe. com/business/marketing/ — supplying many latest books of marketing

☞ http://www. worldbank. org/ — supplying related information about "world bank"

☞ http://ollie. dcccd. edu/mrkt2370/Chapters/ch2/2env. html — concerning about the environment of marketing, including economic, cultural, political ones, etc.

☞ http://jws-edcv. wiley. com/college/bcs/redesign/student/resource/0 ,12264 ,-0471230626- BKS-1783-8554-2616-,00. html — shows many cases of global economic environment

☞ http://www. internet-marketing-research. net/barrons_marketing. php—supplies a sample chapter of the macro economic environment in Iran

Chapter Four   The Role of Governments

☞ http://www. wto. org/ — concerning about WTO

☞ http://www. apec. org/ — concerning about APEC

☞ http://www. grida. no/aeo/322. htm — introducing Africa political environment

☞ http://www. jrc. es/iptsreport/vol25/english/MED6E256. htm — introducing a chapter on free trade area

☞ http://www. ustr. gov/reports/nte/2002/japan. PDF — concerning about trade barriers of Japan trading with U. S.

Chapter Five   The Role of Culture

☞ http://www. grida. no/climate/ipcc/ books — concerning about climates

☞ http://www. virtualtourist. com/ — concerning about local customs

☞ http://www. amahonolulu. org/differences. html/ — concerning about culture differences

☞ http://www. swlearning. com/swhome. html/ — supplies one chapter which concentrates on the cultural factors that influence customer preferences and behavior

☞ http://www. bbc. co. uk/worldservice/people/features/world_religions/index. shtml — introducing world religions

Chapter Six   International Marketing Information System and Research

☞ http://www. brescia. edu/academics/syllabus/spring04/mkt307/kotler05_exs. PPT—supplying some related PowerPoint of MIS

☞ http://college. hmco. com/business/pride/marketing/2000e/students/recap/6. html— introducing many definitions of marketing research

☞ http://ollie. dcccd. edu/mrkt2370/Chapters/ch3/3mtstart. html — supplying a chapter on marketing research

☞ http://www2. una. edu/nslindsey/MK360/Mk% 20360% 20ch7. ppt — providing PowerPoint of marketing research

☞ http://www. accd. edu/sac/mgt/mrkg/Chapter% 206. htm — showing a chapter of marketing research and information system

Chapter Seven   Segmentation, Targeting and Positioning

☞ http://www. nku. edu/ ~ shank/chapter7. htm — providing internet exercises on segmentation, targeting and positioning

☞ http://www. exemplas. com/customers/346_11385. asp — about criteria which can be used to segment markets

☞ http://som. csudh. edu/depts/marketing/rberry/503% 20International/Introduction. ppt—providing vivid PowerPoint of this chapter

☞ http://myphlip1. pearsoncmg. com/phlip/mpchapter. cfm? vbcid = 2499—about objectives and exercises of segmentation, targeting and positioning

☞ http://www. pearsoned. co. uk/Bookshop/detail. asp? item = 100000000015696 —introducing some good books on marketing strategy and competitive positioning

Chapter Eight   Strategies for Entering International Markets

☞ http://cba. fiu. edu/mgmt/kotas/powerpoints/ — supplying some related power points

☞ http://www. orientpacific. com/ — concerning about Asian market strategy

☞ http://www. informit. com/articles/article. asp? p = 101588 — providing an article on Strategies for Entering and Developing International Markets

☞ http://fisher. osu. edu/mhr/courses/Autumn03/ba555/ch14. ppt — showing power points on

mode of entry and strategic alliance

☞ http://www. asiastrategy. biz/SG%20Mkt%20Entry-A%202004%20Primer. pdf—introducing a book on Singapore marketing entry

Chapter Nine   Competitve Analysis and Strategy

☞ http://www. marketwise. net/strategic-competitive. html—concerning about strategic marketing, competitive analysis

☞ http://cba. fiu. edu/mgmt/Kotas/Powerpoints/ — supplying some related Power Points

☞ http://www. scoreknox. org/library/marketing. htm—supplying marketing tips on competitive analysis

☞ http://www. parlay. org/docs/Moriana_NGTSE_Report_TOC_and_Overview. pdf—about a competitive analysis of next generation telecom service enablers

☞ http://www. entrepreneur. com/article/0,4621,270372,00. html — showing a related chapter

Chapter Ten   Cooperation Strategies

☞ http://www. coop. org — about the International Co-operative Alliance (ICA)

☞ http://www. ncb. com — about the National Cooperative Bank (NCB)

☞ http://www. ncba. org — about the National Cooperative Business Association (NCBA)

☞ http://www. ncfc. org — about the National Council of Farmer Cooperatives (NCFC)

☞ http://cooperatives. ucdavis. edu — about University of California Center for Cooperatives

☞ http://www. ag. ndsu. nodak. edu/qbcc — about Quentin Burdick Center for Cooperatives at North Dakota State University

Chapter Eleven   Product Decision

☞ http://www. careers-in-marketing. com/pm. htm — a website about product design and management. Many are practical papers.

☞ http://www. toolkit. cch. com/text/P03_0101. asp — a very simple description about the process of marketing especially product marketing

☞ http://www. hbcollege. com/marketing/students/product. htm — about product design and other information

☞ http://www. foodproductdesign. com/archive/1995/0795DE. html — a case about product design

☞ http://www. rqriley. com/pro-dev. html — briefing the process of designing new product

☞ http://sol. brunel. ac. uk/ ~ jarvis/bola/operations/prodesign/ — about product design, some hints and tips

☞ http://www. e-works. net. cn/ewkArticles/Category36/Article11722. htm — about the new product development

Chapter Twelve   Pricing

☞ http://www. facmarketing. com/pricing. html — about marketing and other practical information

☞ http://www. nationalanalysts. com/marketing/pricing-strategy-research. asp — about pricing strategy research

☞ http://www. themanagementor. com/EnlightenmentorAreas/mrkt/Bps/PricingTo. htm — about pricing and method

☞ http://www. farmdoc. uiuc. edu/marketing/pricing. html — about pricing and management

☞ http://law. indiainfo. com/company/monopolies. html — about the pricing control

☞ http://www. vakilno1. com/bareacts/mrtpact/mrtpact. htm — The Monopolies And Restrictive Trade Practices Act, 1969

Chapter Thirteen   Developing Distribution

☞ http://www. chin. gc. ca/English/Intellectual_Property/CDRom_Practices/index. html — about market and marketing in Canada

☞ http://www. marketinged. com/library/newsltr/1301mhe. txt — about hybrid marketing

☞ http://rcirec. hypermart. net/doc3. htm — case study

☞ http://www. autointell. com/news-2000/July-2000/July-25-00-p5. htm — marketing of automobiles

☞ http://www. ebnonline. com/story/OEG20010622S0083 — about marketing channel in China

☞ http://www. themanagementor. com/EnlightenmentorAreas/mrkt/Cm/Distribution. htm — about channel

☞ http://www. marketingteacher. com/links_pages/links_1. htm — links of marketing

Chapter Fourteen   Promotions

☞ http://www. bls. gov/oco/ocos020. htm — about promotion and sales managers practice Advertising

☞ http://www. knowthis. com/advertising/advert. htm — virtual library with many information and papers about marketing and this is specially for advertising

☞ http://www. uiowa. edu/ ~ commstud/resources/adtexts. html — resources about promotion offered by the university of Iowa

☞ http://www. meesels. com/pages/home/index. asp — advertising and communication

☞ http://www. secondarydata. com/marketing/media. htm — media information and planning

Chapter Fifteen Marketing Plan

☞ http://www. bizmove. com/marketing/m2h. htm — help small business to make marketing plan

☞ http://www. mplans. com/ — marketing plan software and sample plans

☞ http://webquestpro. com/ — online marketing plans

☞ http://www. entrepreneur. com/Your _ Business/YB _ Node/0, 4507, 451----, 00. html — another website about small business marketing plan, e. g. how to create a marketing plan

☞ http://www. 7stepmarketingplan. com/ — 7 steps to make marketing plans

☞ http://www. knowthis. com/general/marketplan. htm — a library about marketing, this webpage is especially for marketing plan

☞ http://www. nsf. gov/od/gpra/cases/stratpln. htm — a case about market planning

Chapter Sixteen Organizing and Controlling International Marketing

☞ http://www. xrefer. com/libraries/index. jsp — a glossary website

☞ http://www. wordplusdirect. com/wordplus_marketing_audit. html — about audit

☞ http://www. copernicusmarketing. com/univers/docs/audit. htm — top ten aspects of marketing audit

☞ http://www. marketingteacher. com/Lessons/lesson_control. htm — online course

☞ http://www. multimedia. calpoly. edu/development/busen/alpha/m/marketing _ control _ systems. html — online dictionary

☞ http://www. buseco. monash. edu. au/Depts/Mkt/MTPonline/impcont. html — online course about marketing control

☞ http://www. australianpubliclaw. com/marketing-audit. htm — a resource website about audit

Chapter Seventeen Basic Knowledge of E-commerce

☞ http://www. all-biz. com — All Business Network

☞ http://www. businessforum. com/ — The Business Forum Online

☞ http://www. chaseonline. com/ — Chase Online Marketing Strategies

☞ http://www. strom. com/ — a consulting firm specializing in Internet product testing

☞ http://www. successful. com — Successful Marketing Strategists, who count AT&T, Lotus, and Day-Timer among their clients, provide useful Internet marketing information on this site. The Cybermarketing Info Center houses articles, shorter tips articles, and more in-depth reports, all of them useful for planning and strategizing your Internet marketing

☞ http://www. tenagra. com — Tenagra is a well respected Internet consulting and design firm that is home to the Tenagra Awards for Marketing Excellence and also provides a very thorough look at Net-acceptable and Net-presence Internet marketing practices

☞ http://www. covisint. com/ — about Covisint, which is the technology services company whose business-to-business applications and communication services connect the global automotive industry

Chapter Eighteen   E-commerce Marketing

☞ http://www. E-commercetimes. com/ — e-commerce online magazine

☞ http://www. internetnews. com/ec-news/ — e-commerce magazine for IT manager

☞ http://www. ftc. gov/bcp/menu-internet. htm — many papers about e-commerce

☞ http://www. cio. com/research/ec/ — e-commerce research center, the executive's resource for doing business online

☞ http://ecommerce. ncsu. edu/seminar/index. html — some lectures about e-commerce; use Realplayer to listen to the audio document

References

参 考 文 献

［1］ANDREW G. Advanced business studies through diagrams. 上海：上海外语教育出版社，2000.

［2］BELL E D, WATER J S. Introduction to retailing. 大连：东北财经大学出版社，1998.

［3］WIND Y, DOUGLAS P S, HOWARD V P. Guidelines for developing international marketing strategy. Journal of Marketing, 1973；April：14 ~ 23.

［4］CHURCHILL A G, Jr. Marketing：creating value for customers. 北京：机械工业出版社，1998.

［5］CURRY E J. A short course in international marketing. 上海：上海外语教育出版社，2000.

［6］STANLEY J P. International marketing. 北京：中国人民大学出版社，1998.

［7］PHILIP K, GARY A, JOHN S, VERONICA W. Principles of marketing. 2nd European ed. Prentice-Hall Europe, 1999.

［8］PHILIP K. Marketing management. 9th ed. 北京：清华大学出版社，1997.

［9］WARREN J K. Global marketing management. 北京：清华大学出版社，1998.

［10］关翔，秦琼. 中国电子商务与实践. 北京：清华大学出版社，2000.

［11］洪瑞云，梁绍明，陈振忠. 市场营销管理. 北京：中国人民大学出版社，1998.

［12］黄京华. 电子商务教程. 北京：清华大学出版社，2001.

［13］王林生. 跨国经营理论与实务. 北京：对外贸易教育出版社，1994.

［14］JOEL R E. 市场营销教程. 张志勇译. 北京：华夏出版社，2001.

［15］张文贤. 简明英汉市场营销词汇. 上海：上海辞书出版社，2001.

［16］王国志. 国际市场营销. 沈阳：辽宁教育出版社，2001.